I0033213

Privatization in South Asia

Minimizing Negative Social Effects through Restructuring

Edited by
GOPAL JOSHI

South Asia Multidiscipilnary Advisory Team (SAAT)
International Labour Organization (ILO)
New Delhi, India

Copyright © International Labour Organization 2000

Publication of the International Labour Office enjoy copyright under Protocol 2 of the Universal Copyright Convention. Nevertheless, short excerpts from them may be reproduced without authorisation on condition that the source is indicated. For rights of reproduction or translation, application should be made to the Publications Branch (Rights and Permissions), International Labour Office, CH-1211 Geneva 22, Switzerland. The International Labour Office welcomes such applications.

First Published 2000
ISBN: 92-2-111901-7

The designations employed in ILO publications, which are in conformity with United Nations practice, and the presentation of material therein do not imply the expression of any opinion whatsoever on the part of the International Labour Office concerning the legal status of any country, area or territory or of its authorities, or concerning the delimitation of its frontiers.

The responsibility for opinions expressed in signed articles, studies and other contributions rests solely with their authors, and publication does not constitute an endorsement by the International Labour Office of the opinions expressed in them.

Reference to names of firms and commercial products and processes does not imply their endorsement by International Labour Office, and any failure to mention a particular firm, commercial product or process is not a sign of disapproval.

ILO publications can be obtained through major booksellers or ILO local offices in many countries, or direct from ILO Publications, International Labour Office, CH-1211 Geneva 22, Switzerland. A catalogue or list of new publications will be sent free of charge from the above address.

Printed in India

Preface

In the wake of increasing globalization and liberalization of world trade and investments, governments around the world have embarked on privatization of public enterprises to be better able to withstand competitive pressures and also to have more resources available for the social programmes. Privatization has opened up the possibility of economic democracy with the widest possible participation of the public in the economic activities thus resulting in higher levels of economic return, employment and efficiency. However, the privatization efforts have not been without adverse social consequences, particularly when they are rushed through without providing adequate measures for workers' protection.

South Asian countries also have been engaged in privatization and restructuring of various public enterprises. But such efforts have often attracted criticisms even though potential future economic benefits may be understood. Although the mechanisms for voluntary or involuntary retrenchment have been in place whenever the workforce is reduced, only in a few cases open discussions have taken place that have included retrenched workers. Public discussions leading towards the greater understanding of the rationale for privatizations have been thus lacking.

The question is not only whether or not to privatize but also when and how the privatization should take place providing adequate safeguard of the interests of all parties - workers, employers and the general public. Interests of the public and the workers would be safeguarded only when there is a periodic examination of the methods of privatization and when there is a greater degree of discussion on the ways in which adverse social consequences are to be dealt with. Public consensus as far as possible on the methods of privatization would ensure not only the success in privatization but also equitable distribution of the fruits of such success. Such equitable distribution can take place only when the restructuring of the public enterprises before or after privatization takes into consideration the negative social effects and proceeds by evolving social consensus.

Similarly, regulatory mechanisms to be created to safeguard public interests against monopolies have to be examined in a larger economic perspective, in terms of overall growth of the private sector and particularly of small enterprises generating new jobs. Any regulatory mechanism must also address the issue of treatment of the workers in privatized enterprises. Thus, restructuring and development of regulatory mechanisms require informed discussions among the workers as well as among employers during the process of privatization.

To examine such issues, five country case studies were commissioned in South Asia - Bangladesh, India, Nepal, Pakistan and Sri Lanka. The work related to the preparation of these studies was coordinated by Mr. Gopal Joshi, Senior Specialist on Small Enterprise and Management Development at ILO-SAAT. The results of the Country case studies were discussed at a Tripartite Meeting organised in Kathmandu in November 1999. The individual case studies and the report of the meeting are included in this volume. It also includes an overview chapter prepared by Mr. Joshi which provides broad information on trends and consequences of privatization in the sub-region. The volume should therefore be of interest to policy makers, development specialists, academics, privatization commissions, industry groups, workers' and employers' organisations. Assistance received from Ms. Kavita Sherchan in preparing this volume is gratefully acknowledged.

A.S. Oberai
Director
South Asia Multidisciplinary Advisory Team (SAAT)
International Labour Organization (ILO)
New Delhi

Contents

Page

1. Overview of privatization in South Asia

1. Reasons for privatization   1
2. Social effects of privatization   3
3. Compensation and safety net   4
4. Regulatory reform   6
5. Social dialogue for privatization   7
6. Summary   7

2. Privatization in Bangladesh

1. Background and rationale   9
2. Privatization policies in Bangladesh   13
3. Current status of privatization of SOEs in Bangladesh   20
4. Post-privatization measures adopted to minimize adverse social consequences   30
5. Conclusions and recommendations   37
Annex 1   40
Annex 2   41
Annex 3   42
Bibliography   43

3. Privatization in India

1. The concept   45
2. Context of privatization   51
3. Consequences of privatization   64
4. Regulatory bodies   68
5. Overstaffing   69
6. Compensation   71
7. Social safety net   74
8. Summing up   80
9. Recommendations   84
Annex - A   88
Bibliography   93
Press Reports   104

4. Privatization in Nepal

1. Brief background of privatization   105
2. Preparations for privatization   110
3. Approaches to privatization   114
4. Economic and social effects of privatization   117
5. Privatization: Future programmes and strategies   129
6. Recommendations for minimizing social effects   131

Annex 1: Information on capital market situation of Privatized units   136
Annex 2: Nature of job losses in Privatized units   136
Annex 3   Privatization: Employees' perceptions and responses   137
Table 3.1 Workers' perception of post privatization changes   139
Annex 4   List of Persons Visited for Interviews   141
Bibliography   142

5.   Privatization in Pakistan

1. Introduction   143
2. Rationale for privitization   144
3. Modes of privitization in Pakistan   146
4. Privatization and fiscal deficit   148
5. Privatization and levels of efficiency   149
6. The Impact of privatization on employment   156
7. Wage rates and social protection of the workers   160
8. The environment for private sector and medium term projections of
    investment and employment   161
9. Regulatory reform   163
10. Summary and conclusion   164
Annex I   168
Table A-1   168
Table A-2   168
Table A-3   169
Annex II   170
Bibliography   172

6.   Privatization in Sri Lanka

1. Introduction   175
2. Brief Background on Privatization   176
3. Preparations for Privatization   177
4. Approaches to Privatization   181
5. Economic and social effects of privatization   184
6. Post privatization actions   198
7. Future privatizations planned   199
8. Recommendations for minimising the social effects   199
Bibliography   204
Annex 1   206
Annex 2   208
Box 1: Privatising Bus Transport   181
Box 2: Privatisation in the Plantation Sector   183
Box 3: Recommendations made for Handling Labour Issues during Privatization   189
Box 4: Handling Worker Issues during the Sri Lanka Telecom (SLT) Privatization   197

7.   Report of the Sub-Regional Workshop on Privatization in South Asia

List of Table

		Page
1.1	Butgetary deficit and privatization	2
1.2	Redunancy resulting from privatization in South Asia	4
2.1	Labour restructuring after divestiture of the currently running enterprises	28
2.2	Change in employment status of the currently operating enterprises after privatization during 1991-96	29
2.3	Retrenchment of manpower from state owned enterprises in manufacturing sectors since privatization started	29
2.4	Estimated number of workers who might lose jobs as a result of privatization in the near future	31
2.5	Recommended benefits for retrenched workers by Mustafiz Committee and Mannan Committee	31
2.6	Compensation paid to the retrenched jute mill workers	32
3.1	Changes in reservation policy towards public sector	50
3.2	Group-Wise employment of scheduled castes and scheduled tribes persons in CPSEs (as on 1.1.1998)	54
3.3	Employment of women in CPSEs (as on 1.1.1998)	54
3.4	Distribution of central public sector companies according to the extent of disinvestment	59
3.5	Select asset utilisation and profitability ratios for government and private sectors	67
3.6	Trends in industrial disputes	71
3.7	Extent of variation in average compensation in CPSEs	72
3.8	Estimates of cash payments* under voluntary retirement scheme in select Madhya Pradesh state PSEs	73
3.9	Age profiles of workers covered by VRS in CPSEs	73
3.10	Number of employees availing VRS covered by NRF and expenditure on VRS and NRF: 1992-93 to 1998-99	75
4.1	Stands taken by Nepali congress and UML	107
4.2	Investment in Privatized units	119
4.3	Before after profit/Loss situation of Privatized units	122
4.4	Total employment in Privatized units: before and after	123
4.5	Reported positive and negative changes in salaries and benefits	127
5.1	Results of Regression of post-privatization output against time, dummy and manufacturing output	154
5.2	Total factor productivity	154
5.3	The incidence of golden handshake	158
5.4	Bid value and golden handshake payments	159
6.1	Size and performance of the Government Sector	176
6.2	Redundancy rates in selected SOEs	187
6.3	Average compensation (excluding gratuity) from 1987-1997	190

List of Figures

Page

2.1   Decline in the size of the SOEs sector in the economy between
1993 and 1997/98   11
2.2   Decline in employment from 1993 and 1997-98   11
2.3   SOE Losses (after tax) Overtime   12
2.4   Progress in the pace of privatization from 1972/75 to 1991/96   21

3.1   Public sector employment   52
3.2   Targets and realisation of disinvestment proceeds   58
3.3   Net profit of CPSEs   65
3.4   Ratio of net profit to capital employed   66
3.5   Vacancies notified and placements by employment exchanges   76
3.6   Share of wages & salaries in net sales in the Indian corporate sector   80

4.1   Growth of employment in public enterprises   106
4.2   Flow of Funds   108
4.3   Average Rate of Return from public enterprises   109
4.4   Growth of capital employed in public enterprises   109
4.5   Productivity growth in Harishiddhi Bricks, Balaju Textile and Bhrikuti Paper   120
4.6   Productivity growth in Nepal Bitumen, Nepal Lube and NFL   121

5.1   Privatization and fiscal deficit   149
5.2   Average and compound growth rates of GDP, Investment and Employment   151
5.3   Fixed investment ratios   151
5.4   Average and compound growth rates of GDP, investment and employment   152
5.5   Investment in manufacturing   152
5.6   Nominal and real wages   153
5.7   Performance of the banking sector   155
5.8   Growth rate of employment   157
5.9   Growth rate of employment in large scale   157
5.10   Labour productivity and real wages   160
5.11   Projected level of investment GDP ratio   162

6.1   Compensation packages (excluding gratuity) offered: 1989 - 1996   189

1

Overview of Privatization in South Asia

GOPAL JOSHI*

1. Reasons for privatization

In an environment of increased globalization and liberalization, privatization of public sector enterprises has become an important agenda for the governments in South Asia. Although the process of privatization has taken varying paths in the subregion, and the pace has been different depending on the situation, there is an historical effort to alter the role of the state in economy and participation of the populations in the economic activities. The trend is towards reliance on private initiatives to spur economic growth and generate employment for rapidly growing populations. However, the reasons for privatization do not seem to be always clear in these countries. The reason why a state would wish to privatize has a great deal of bearing on the results of privatization, particularly in terms of social consequences.

While scanning through all the rationale advanced in planning documents in the subregion, it seems that there are three general reasons why privatization is being pursued.

- Greater economic democracy through increased private initiatives in economic activities.
- Achieving higher levels of economic growth and employment.
- Reducing budgetary deficits.

Expanding economic democracy through privatization needs to enhance the faith of the people in taking risks and investing in public enterprises being privatized. If the public sector enterprises being privatized happen to be the smaller ones, the goal of economic democracy may be better achieved. But transparency in the privatization process is most essential in pursuing such goal, particularly to avoid crony capitalism. Sale of profitable public sector undertakings would build the enthusiasm of the public in participating in the privatization process. India has divested shares of 39 public sector enterprises, many of which were profitable as well.[1] However, none of the equity issue to the public relinquished the majority ownership of the Government, thus making it more of an exercise to generate resources for bridging the budgetary deficit. Widely dispersed holding of the ownership through public sale of shares in the well-developed share markets could increase the number of people owning the newly privatized enterprises. Greater participation of the public through widened capital markets (as

---

* Senior Specialist on Small Enterprise and Management Development, ILO-SAAT New Delhi.
[1] Institute for Studies in Industrial Development, *Privatization in India: Social Effects and Restructuring*, a paper presented at Sub-regional Meeting on Privatization in South Asia, Kathmandu, 24-26 November 1999.

reported on the post privatization situations in Nepal and Sri Lanka)[1] also would have such effect. However, capital market has had negligible role in the overall economies in these two countries.

Achieving higher levels of economic growth and employment requires similar strategy as above. But the consideration for spreading economic ownership and increasing employment may be secondary to achieving economic efficiency, which can often be achieved through strategic sale or partnership. For instance, Indian Airlines is being sought to be privatized through strategic sale of 26 per cent of the equity to a strategic partner. However as a result of such strategic partnership, a few entrepreneurs or business houses may come to own privatized enterprises. In Nepal, a large majority of the shares of privatized units (51-72%) is being passed on to a small group of entrepreneurs while the public participation has been limited to 25 to 30 per cent.[2] The need for transparency and accountability becomes even greater in such a scenario.

Lastly, privatization is also undertaken under the economic compulsion of having to reduce budgetary deficit resulting from heavy losses of the public sector enterprises and subsidization by the government. The economic compulsion also is manifested by the conditionalities put forward by the Brettonwoods institutions. In such a scenario, loss-making organizations are first disposed off while retaining 'cash cow' enterprises with the government. By examining the pattern of privatization in South Asia (Table 1.1), it is quite evident that the governments are motivated to accelerate privatization largely due to fiscal deficits. Privatization of public sector enterprises accelerated in India and Pakistan initially as a result of the adverse balance

Table 1.1: Budgetary deficit and privatization

	Deficit (% of GDP)[a]	Privatization receipts	No. of units privatized
Bangladesh	5.4	$ 2.0 million[c]	1083
India	6.5	Rs. 126.38 billion	39
Nepal	6.4	Rs. 797 million	10
Pakistan	5.4[b]	Rs. 59.6 billion	106
Sri Lanka	7.7	$ 715 million	75

[a] for the year 1998. source: Asian Development Bank, *Asian Development Outlook 1999*, Oxford University Press, Hong Kong.
[b] with accumulated debt of Rs. 2,500 billion during 1990-97
[c] 3-4 small manufacturing plants over past three years
Sources: Country papers presented during the Sub-regional meeting on privatization in South Asia, Kathmandu, 24-26 November 1999.

---

[1] Narayan Manandhar and Pushkar Bajracharya, *Privatization in Nepal: Social Effects and Restructuring*, a paper presented at Sub-regional Meeting on Privatization in South Asia, Kathmandu, 24-26 November 1999 and Rozana Salih, *Privatization in Sri Lanka: Social Effects and Restructuring*, a paper presented at Sub-regional Meeting on Privatization in South Asia, Kathmandu, 24-26 November 1999.
[2] Narayan Manandhar and Pushkar Bajracharya, *Privatization in Nepal: Social Effects and Restructuring* Op. Cit.

of payments in the early nineties and as budgetary deficits have risen. Huge deficits in Nepal and Bangladesh also forced the governments to privatize the public sector enterprises (PSEs). However, proceeds from such privatization has been hardly adequate to bridge the deficit.

2. Social effects of privatization

When the public sector undertakings are privatized largely to reduce the fiscal deficit, there is bound to be a tendency to focus on off loading heavily loss making enterprises as quickly as possible without much regard to long term consequences to such privatized units. Studies[1] indicate that 40 to 50 per cent of the privatized units in Bangladesh closed down after privatization. Due to the closure of four units after privatization in Nepal, 3,200 jobs were lost.[2] Similarly, six public sector units closed subsequent to privatization in Sri Lanka.[3] When the employment in organized sector is limited and private initiatives are few in developing countries such as in South Asia, failure of such privatized units to continue to provide employment or even large scale worker redundancy can be catastrophic. Thus, the social effects of privatization have been presumably much greater than what would be the case, had the privatized public enterprises not been loss making. Therefore, the social effects of privatization in South Asia have been manifested by the following:

- Worker redundancy
- Retrenchment of workers
- Stagnation of employment in organized sector
- Growing casualization of labour

Often, loss-making public enterprises are presumed to be overstaffed regardless of the share of the wage bill. Therefore, both the government and the interested buyer of the public enterprise tend to focus on estimating worker redundancy and attempting to resolve such redundancy through worker retrenchment. From the standpoint of the buyer, quicker the redundancy is resolved, quicker would be the prospects of profitability. Plant upgradation and product innovation are expensive, time-consuming and uncertain for many buyers, who may not be very familiar with the subsector, which was previously protected. As a result of privatization, redundancies, whether in the form of retrenchment or voluntary retirement, have been evident in all South Asian countries (Table 1.2).

Since the employment in organized sector is stagnated or declining in the South Asian countries, growing trends of casualization and informalization of labour are evident. It has been estimated that 20,000 jobs have been contractualized in *Navratnas* (nine top performing enterprises) in India.[4] Even the retrenched workers are being recruited back in Nepal on

---

[1] World Bank, *Bangladesh – Implementing Structural Reform,* 1993, Dhaka and Binayak Sen, *Whither Privatization: results of an Exploratory Survey of the Disinvested Industries in Bangladesh,* mimeo, 1997, BIDS, Dhaka.
[2] Manandhar and Bajracharya, *Privatisation in Nepal: Social Effects and Restructuring* Op. Cit.
[3] Rozana Salih, *Privatisation in Sri Lanka: Social Effects and Restructuring* Op. Cit.
[4] Rozana Salih, Ibid.

contractual basis, thus denying them the normal benefits available in regular employment. On the other hand, governments are seeking to promote self-employment, mostly in the informal sector to combat the situation of growing unemployment.

Table 1.2: Redundancy resulting from privatization in South Asia

	PSE employment	*Redundancy*	*Retrenchment costs*
Bangladesh	240 thousand	25%	TK 7 billion
India	9.8 million	23%[a]	Rs. 48,092 billion
Nepal	46.7 thousand	60%	Rs. 9,914 million[b]
Pakistan	34.6 thousand	63%[a]	Rs. 3,559 million
Sri Lanka	120 thousand	53%[b]	Up to 53 month salary

[a] voluntary retirement
[b] ILO estimate in 1992 for a scenario of 50% redundancy
Sources: Country papers presented during the Sub-regional meeting on privatization in South Asia, Kathmandu, 24-26 November 1999.

3. Compensation and safety net

In dealing with the redundant workers, several options are available. Not all are equally attractive in solving the problem of unemployment. Some of these have been tried in South Asia. These options are given below:
- Voluntary Retirement Scheme
- Cash Compensation or golden handshake
- Retraining of the workers
- Redeployment
- Creation of unemployment benefit and social security

At huge costs to the public exchequer, retrenched workers are being compensated through golden handshakes and voluntary retirement schemes. Almost a quarter of the bid value for privatization was utilized for payment on golden handshake in Pakistan.[1] While workers are being compensated on the short-term basis, it does not provide any long-term solution in regard to their employability.

Having relatively large amount of money does not necessarily guarantee that the retrenched workers would be economic contributors to the society in the long run. India has launched Voluntary Retirement Scheme for compensating redundant workers and has established National Renewable Fund for their retraining. Although over 129,000 public sector employees received benefits from such funds, National Renewal Fund was largely used for retirement benefits rather than retraining or redeployment.[2] Only 36,889 workers were retrained, and

[1] A.R. Kemal, *Privatization in Pakistan: Social Effects and Restructuring*, a paper presented at Sub-regional Meeting on Privatization in South Asia, Kathmandu, 24-26 November 1999.
[2] Institute for Studies in Industrial Development, *Privatization in India: Social Effects and Restructuring* Op. Cit.

11,623 were redeployed. Similarly, a Special Workers' Fund was created in Bangladesh with Tk 150 million (equivalent to $3.0 million); however, there is yet no evidence that the fund has been used for retraining and redeployment.[1]

Thus, how workers are to be retrained and redeployed is less clear while workers continue to lose their jobs. On the other hand, the prospects of unemployment benefit and universal social security in populous countries of South Asia seem to be quite remote at the present time. References are made to establish and strengthen employment exchanges, which could make some impact if they prove more effective than other public service providing government agencies.

3.1 Restructuring of public enterprises

Rather than create large-scale redundancies and deal with the requirements of retrenched workers stretching the limit of the public resources, it would be more cost effective to restructure the public sector enterprises and attempt to turn them around before privatization. There may be restructuring before privatization, and additional restructuring may take place during and after privatization. Several approaches have been tried for restructuring public enterprises.

- Management Contract
- Performance Contract
- Unbundling of public sector undertaking
- Consolidation of activities

Professional managers from private sector could be contracted to turn around the public sector undertaking without divesting the equity. On the other hand, performance contract has been tried in many cases with the existing management of the public sector. Many times organizational restructuring in the form of either unbundling of the public sector undertaking or consolidation of activities may take place. Worker managed companies or outright buyout is another scenario.

However, the effectiveness of all these activities would ultimately rest on non-interference by the bureaucracy and politicians. Performance contracting and management contracting have not necessarily yielded intended desired results so far in South Asia, as attested by the experience in Nepal. The results of pre-privatization restructuring in Bangladesh were also at best mixed although some improvement in labour productivity in the enterprises placed under performance contract in the early nineties was reported.[2] Political instability has also added the complexity and difficulty in attempting to restructure the public enterprises.

Seemingly, the situation is hopeless. If the public enterprises are sold off in the loss-making state without turning them around, then the social consequences are high. If the attempt is first made to restructure them, then the bureaucratic and political interference derail such efforts. What is the solution available in such a seemingly no-win situation? There are certain

---

[1] International Labour Office, *Retraining and Redeployment of Workers Affected by Privatization in Bangladesh,* 1999.
[2] Ibid.

steps that can be taken to restructure with less interference and then privatize the enterprises that have been turned around.

- Creation of a transparent, accountable and representative system of regulating the enterprises.
- Involvement of employers and workers even before the turnaround and privatization begin.
- Development of a system of independent monitoring of the public enterprises by people other than the bureaucrats and politicians during the time bound period of turnaround.
- Privatization of profitable enterprises so that all the concerned parties would have faith in the process.

Effective regulatory reform and social dialogue are needed for implementing above strategy with desirable results. Although both have been weak in South Asian countries, improvements in these mechanisms are not difficult.

4. Regulatory reform

Privatizations have taken place without adequate reforms, which would have set the regulatory framework within which the private enterprises and public sector undertakings would participate. The reforms that have been half-hearted do not help either. Instead, such reforms create additional confusion since even after announcing them, governments continue to interfere. Such confusion has been evident in India in relation to the establishment of the Telecommunication Regulatory Authority of India (TRAI), wherein the reluctance to vest full powers to TRAI has not been helpful in carrying out full regulatory reform. Another sector suffering from such confusion has been air transport. However, the process of regulatory reform in the insurance sector in India seems to be so far well planned. Reforms should be transparent, accountable, complete and representative.

Regulatory reform should set the stage for the public sector to operate independently. When carried out properly, it would allow turning around of the public sector in a professional manner. Regulatory reform usually consists of three levels of actions:

(a) Formulation of a policy for the subsector
(b) Setting up of a Regulatory Body with its statutory mandate
(c) Representation in the Regulatory Body

Each subsector often requires a policy that clarifies what would be the role of the government. The South Asian experience in setting regulatory policies has not been helpful for establishing independent, transparent and accountable regulatory body. If such policy still reserves the right of interference for the government, it would be a non-starter. Once, the policy is formulated, an independent regulatory body needs to be formed. The regulatory body packed with former or present bureaucrats would be inviting again interference in its work. It should have representation of the stakeholders, employers and workers. The procedure and tenure of their appointments would determine the extent to which the body will enjoy independence. The regulatory body should have similar status as a court without possibilities of its decisions being overturned, except in very rare cases. Some of the issues that could be dealt by the body are the following:

- The terms and conditions of the private sector enterprises to enter and exit the subsector.
- Pricing mechanism, especially in view of the public investments already made.
- Dispute settling mechanism.
- Review of the policies.

Although the labour disputes are settled through separate mechanism of arbitration and mediation, there would be much more clarity of the issues if proper regulatory mechanism is established with clear policies.If a public sector undertaking does turn around as a result of the restructuring, the stake and ownership of the workers would enhance in such a situation.

On the other hand, the private sector and the employers would view favourably such clarity of policies and fair treatment as they participate in the privatization process. They would have less fear from the uncertain policy situation while taking risk of investing in public sector undertakings.

5. Social dialogue for privatization

The success of privatization would depend in the extent to which the mechanism for social dialogue effectively operates between workers and employers. The countries in South Asia need to promote and strengthen social dialogue so that the labour-management issues can be settled through negotiations. Many disputes arising from privatization would not have been as inflamed if the dispute settling machinery was in place even before the privatization process starts. In Pakistan, an agreement was reached between the workers' representatives and the Government for workers' protection against the loss of jobs. However, the agreement could not ameliorate the situation with a large percentage of employees opting for voluntary retirement.[1]

In many situations, labour unions have been weakened or abolished as a result of privatization. In Pakistan, the role of labour union has been greatly diminished as privatization of a public utility, WAPDA (Water and Power Development Authority) as well as some other public sector enterprises, has taken place. Some buyers may have preferred such situation for the short term reasons; however, in the long run, existence of a bargaining agent allows the labour disputes to be settled through negotiation.

6. Summary

This paper has attempted to emphasize that the rationale for privatization and preparations for the privatization are very important to minimize the social costs and dislocations causing from such initiative. Most South Asian countries have come to realize that privatization for the purpose of reducing fiscal deficit has caused them to off load those enterprises first, which

---

[1]   A.R. Kemal, *Privatisation in Pakistan: Social Effects and Restructuring,* Op. Cit.

are loss making. Such action has not inspired the private sector confidence and has resulted in large-scale worker retrenchment. On the other hand, the response to worker redundancy has not been very effective either.

Absence of a strategy whereby the enterprises are restructured and then privatized has also caused a great deal of loss in public investments when privatized. The restructuring experience has not been a very satisfactory one in South Asia due to the long-standing habit of interference of the government. Therefore, it is essential to first carry out the regulatory reform that would clarify the roles of government, workers and employers in the process of privatization. A transparent and accountable reform process would not only instill confidence among the private sector and the general public, it would also assure the workers about the fairness of the system. Additionally, effective social dialogue plays an important role in negotiating the disputes arising out of privatization. South Asian countries would need to further promote and strengthen the social dialogue mechanism in their respective countries.

2

Privatization in Bangladesh

DR. MOMTAZ UDDIN AHMED*

1.   Background and rationale

1.1   Switch from nationalization to privatization

Despite a significant degree of public ownership in health, education, communication, utilities and energy sectors in the pre-independence period, Bangladesh inherited basically a private sector dominated economy at the time of independence in 1971. However, the devastation caused by the War of Liberation left the economy in a paralysed state with much of the infrastructure destroyed and a large number of industrial enterprises and commercial establishments damaged and abandoned by their former non-local owners and managers. The government tried to get the economy moving by restarting abandoned enterprises and by providing entrepreneurial support in a period of chaos and uncertainity. The government took .over the management of all abandoned factories and commercial establishments. This was followed by large-scale nationalization schemes of the key large and medium industries banks and financial institutions. Private sector ownership in industries was allowed only to a limit of Tk. 1.5 million. In addition to the pressing need for restarting the idle industrial enterprises, the nationalization move was also prompted by the ruling party's election pledge to pursue a socialist path of development in independent Bangladesh.[1] The nationalization programme led not only to the transfer of ownership of the abandoned private enterprises of the Pakistani period, but to significant enlargement of government ownership in the industrial sector, which shot up from 34 per cent in 1969-70 to over 90 per cent in 1972. According to a World Bank study (1994), around 305 state-owned enterprises (SOEs) comprising industries, banks and financial institutions came under public ownership and control by 1974-75. Side by side, severe restrictions were imposed on both domestic and foreign private investments by officially disallowing large-scale industrial ownership and prohibiting foreign direct investments and international joint ventures within the private sector.

But soon the government realized that nationalization was hasty and without adequate preparation for efficient management of the nationalized industries. While some people would try to justify the take-over of abandoned enterprises as a situational necessity, the wholesale

---

*   Professor, Department of Economics, University of Dhaka, Bangladesh.
[1]   The genesis of a socialist transformation of the Bangladesh economy by pursuing the strategy of a state-sponsored industrial development is clearly reflected in the country's First Five Year Plan (1973-1978) document. (Cf. GOB, 1978).

nationalization of the Bengali-owned jute and cotton textile industries was an outcome of the ideological conviction of some members of the ruling party and of the handful of economists working at the Planning Commission during that time. The absence of a clear vision about the goals of the nationalization programme, lack of trained and efficient management to run the SOEs, excessive over-staffing of the SOEs, rigid wage structures and controlled pricing policies etc., turned the nationalized industries into loss-making concerns. These concerns thrived on huge state subsidies which proved to be exceedingly costly to the national exchequer and caused the national economy to stagnate and suffer from corruption and operational inefficiencies.

Much discussion has taken place about the public sector performance, particularly about the losses suffered by the SOEs. One of the recent studies, which was done by Satter (1997), reports that the persistent losses by the SOEs was costing the national exchequer nearly one per cent of GDP by 1991. This, among other things, provided the most emphatic argument for privatization in Bangladesh. A reversal of the policy of state ownership and control of industries began as early as 1974 and the size of the public sector declined significantly thereafter. What is ironical is that despite the gradual decline of the size of the public sector, losses suffered by the SOEs kept increasing every year, as noted below.

1.2 The current size and performance of the SOEs

The size of the SOEs sector has shrunk considerably after the shift in the Government's economic policy towards encouraging private sector participation in the economy, greater market orientation and liberalization, and successive divestments of the SOEs, Nevertheless, data presented in Appendix Table A-1 show that some 218 SOEs (grouped under 36 sector corporations) are still in operation. The largest number of SOEs (121) are in the manufacturing industries sector, which comprises jute and cotton textiles, chemicals, sugar and food, steel and forest industries in descending order of importance. While declining importance of the public enterprises is evident, (Figure 2.1 and 2.2 based on Appendix Table A-1), the losses incurred by these enterprises are reported to have been increasing (Figure 2.3). The Monitoring Cell of the Ministry of Finance (MOF), Government of Bangladesh, estimated the after-tax losses of the SOEs to have increased from Tk. 3.8 billion (or US $ 0.12 billion) in 1986 to Tk. 4.8 billion (or US $0.13 billion) in 1991,Tk. 7.5 billion (or US $0.19 billion) 1995 and Tk. 12.7 billion (or US $ 0.29 billion) in 1997. The comparable figure estimated by the World Bank (1999) for FY-97 stands at Tk. 14.1 billion (or US $0.33 billion).[1] Notwithstanding the variations affecting different estimates of the SOE losses, these have been rightly termed by Satter (1997) and Mondal (1997) as proverbial losses of SOEs which have significant economic implications. Needless to reiterate, a resource-poor country like Bangladesh can not afford to sustain losses of this magnitude year after year. While the Governments' resources are limited, there are more pressing demands for financing the social sectors such as health,

---

[1]   The latest MOF estimates put the SOEs losses at a much higher figure, around Tk. 45.5 billion (or US $1.03 billion) for the year 1997-98.

education and housing for the poor and for environmental protection. Besides waste of scarce resources, colossal losses incurred by them pose negative externalities to the entire industrial sector, i.e. in terms of poor operating efficiency and depressed performance. While an analysis of the SOE performance is beyond the purview of the present study,[1] it can perhaps be suggested that healthy development of a competitive and private enterprise system is essential for paving the way for privatization.

Figure 2.1

Decline in the size of the SOEs sector in the economy between 1993 and 1997/98

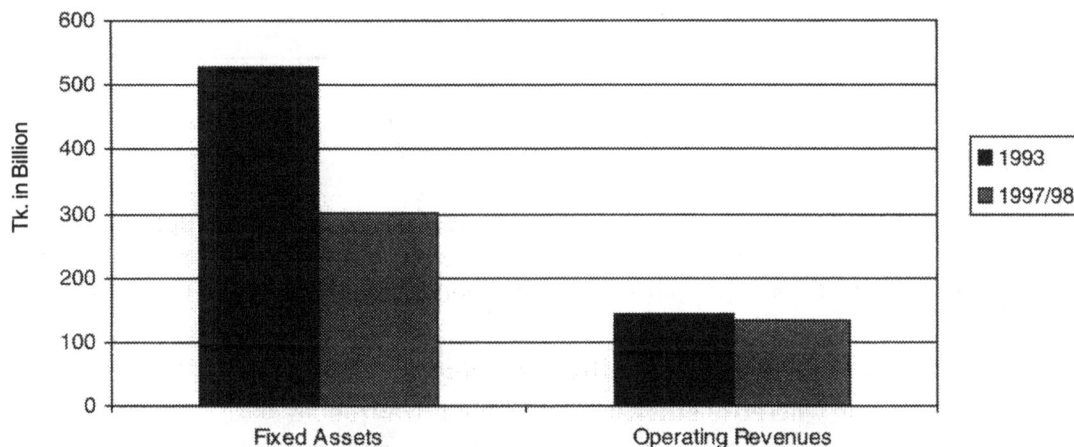

Figure 2.2

Decline in employment from 1993 and 1997-98

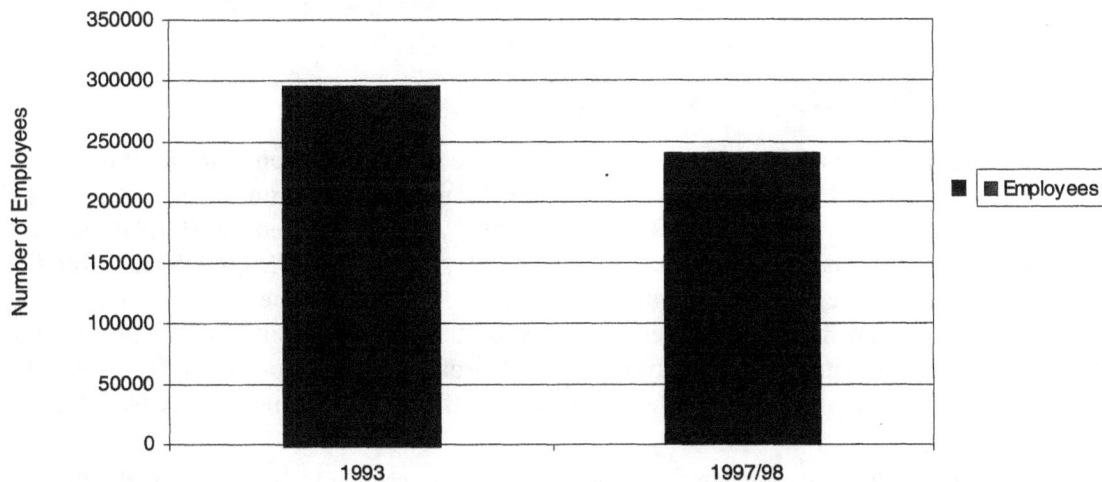

---

[1]   The interested reader is referred to World Bank (1994) and Satter (1997) for details on the SOEs' performances and their socio-economic implications for Bangladesh

Figure 2.3
SOE Losses (after tax) overtime

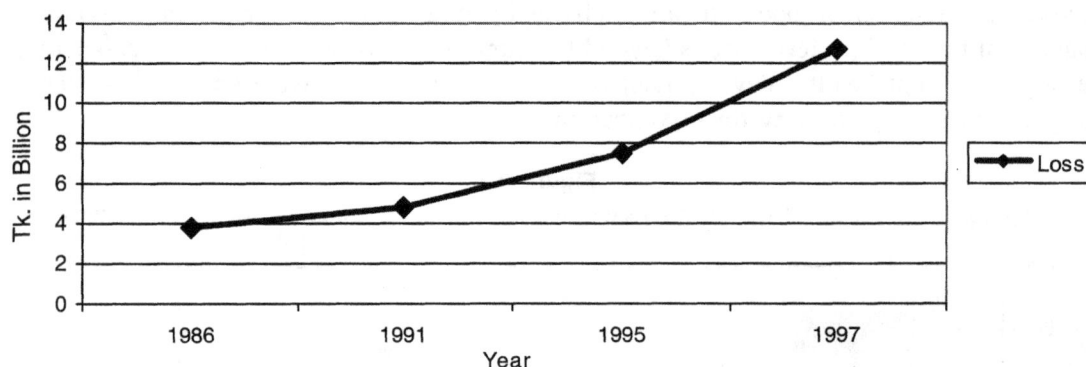

1.3 Privatization: A necessity in Bangladesh

Any rational assessment of the SOE sectors' predicaments would suggest that the pertinent question is not whether to privatize; it is rather how fast and how best to do it. A set of three inter-related reasons are put forward as rationale for privatization in Bangladesh.[1] These are:

- improvement of the governments' fiscal situation;
- improvement in enterprise efficiency following privatization; and
- mobilization of greater domestic as well as foreign investments for higher growth in the medium-term.

Privatization in Bangladesh has also formed part of the Government's overall market-oriented adjustment strategy under which privatization and market-based economic reform measures have tended to reinforce one another.

1.3.1 Reducing the Government's fiscal deficit

By privatizing the SOEs, it is not only possible to eliminate revenue losses, but also to create an expanding revenue base through the development of a vibrant private sector. The accommodation of the persistent losses of the SOEs by unmitigated NCB (Nationalized Commercial Banks) lendings endorsed by the Ministry of Finance (MOF) through regular infusion of bonds and cash into the NCBs, limit the scope for commercial bank lending to the private sector and makes the latter suffer from "the crowding out" effect. The NCBs, in turn, suffer from capital inadequacy because of providing 'lead loans' to SOEs and the government's strategy of fiscal prudence is undermined by the existence of the 'soft budget

---

[1] Summarizing myriades of privatization goals followed in different countries Lieberman (1993) classify them into three broad categories: (a) reduction of government's fiscal deficits and its external and internal debt, (b) generation of new sources of cash flow and financing for enterprises and (c) getting Government out of business.

constraints'. Improving the fiscal situation is thus one of the key arguments for privatization, as it promises to provide a lasting cure to financial malaise by eliminating indiscriminate financing of SOE losses.

1.3.2 Improving enterprise efficiency

Another overriding argument in favour of privatization is the improvement of enterprise efficiency under private ownership. Empirical evidence of better performance under private ownership across a wide range of efficiency indicators (i.e. profitability, productivity etc.) and industry groups are available internationally as well as in Bangladesh.[1] The limited evidence available from Bangladesh in this regard shows that a number of private sector jute and textile mills have been economically more efficient than their public sector counterparts (Satter, 1997). However, the results of other studies (discussed later) have been contradictory, leaving the overall post-privatization economic performance issue in Bangladesh rather inconclusive.

1.3.3 Generation of new sources of capital investments

One of the important achievements of privatization in the countries of Latin America, Asia and Eastern Europe have been the revitalization or development of capital markets, increase in domestic investment, return of flight capital and inflows of external resources. All these along with the availability of cash from the sales of the SOEs is expected to help mobilize greater resources for investments and enhance the prospects for higher medium-term economic growth. While these are potentially direct and immediate positive outcomes of privatization, other objectives, such as increasing allocative and productive efficiency; absorption of new technology and management skills; and creation of employment opportunities through higher growth etc., are long-term goals and depend on the extent which the private sector is capable of achieving them.

2. Privatization policies in Bangladesh
2.1 Evolution of privatization policies in Bangladesh

The privatization process in Bangladesh evolved gradually tbefore taking a concrete shape in 1993. The switch from state sponsored capitalist mode of industrial development to private sector-led industrial growth in Bangladesh began in the mid 1970s. With the famine in 1974, rising prices and a dwindling economy led to gradual shifts in the government's policies towards encouraging private sector participation in manufacturing and reducing the role of public sector through disinvestment (vide Investment Policy 1974). After the political change in August 1975, the new Government declared a revised industrial policy, through which the public sector led industrialization strategy was abandoned. Between 1975 and 1981, a number of important changes in the policies and institutions were introduced (i.e. declaration

---

[1] For a summary of evidence on the efficiency gains under private ownership at the international levels the reader may see, World Bank (1994) and Megginson (1998).

of Industrial Investment Schedule 1976, withdrawal of the private investment ceiling in 1978, etc.) to broaden the scope for private sector participation in the industrialization process. The major elements in the policy to bring about a decisive shift towards a private sector driven industrialization during this period included: (i) elimination of ceiling on private investment, (ii) reduction in the reserve list of industries under the public sector and creation of "free sectors", (iii) relaxation of investment sanctioning procedures, (iv) amendment of the Constitution to allow disinvestment and denationalization of both abandoned and taken-over industries, (v) establishment of a Disinvestment Board in 1975, (vi) reopening of the stock market, (vii) shift to a floating exchange rate, and (viii) introduction of various export promotion measures.[1]

The most significant move in the privatization process occurred in 1982 with the announcement of the New Industrial Policy (NIP). The Government introduced fundamental changes in the industrial policy environment and the adoption of various promotional measures, designed to accelerate the pace of private sector-led industrial growth. A number of large industries in the jute and cotton textiles sectors (33 jute mills and 27 textile mills) were returned to their owners under the auspices of the NIP.[2] In order to encourage foreign private investment, the Foreign Private Investment (Promotion and Protection) Act of 1980 was promulgated and a "One-Stop" service agency, i.e. Board of Investment (BOI), was set up, commencing its operations in January 1989.

The Government announced the Revised Industrial Policy (RIP) in 1986 with a view to further expanding, relaxing and strengthening the measures required to provide further impetus to the privatization process through a deliberate denationalization programme. The RIP provisions also encouraged foreign private investment, allowed liberalization of imports, export incentives, and liberalization of fiscal and monetary measures. The Government's strong commitment towards rapid expansion of the private sector through progressive deregulation, liberalization, trade policy reforms and encouraging foreign private investment was reiterated through the declaration of yet another industrial policy in 1991. Indeed, privatization of the loss-making SOEs was one of the major objectives of the 1991 policy in order to increase the efficiency and productivity of the industrial sector. Thus, the gradual but definite shift towards privatization policies continued throughout the 1990s. A brief discussion on the regulatory reforms to stimulate growth of the private sector and also privatization may be relevant here.

2.1.1 Regulatory reforms geared to encourage development of the private sector

In tandem with GOB's overall policy shifts to a private sector-led growth regime, Bangladesh introduced a variety of economic reform measures to stimulate private industrial

---

[1] Between 1973-1980, a total of 199 industrial units were disinvested by the government at a total sales value of Tk. 115.8 million. The privatization Board sources quote a figure of 225 SOEs, which have been privatized during 1976-1981.

[2] An elaborate treatment of the introduction of policy changes, domestic and foreign investment incentives and export promotion measures provided under the NIP is available in Bhuiyan et. al. (1993).

investment by domestic as well as foreign investors. Various economic reform measures introduced under the Structural Adjustment Programme led privatization of SOEs have included decentralization of industrial investments and loan sanctioning procedures; liberalization of import procedures; restructuring and relaxation of the tariff structure; reduction of quantitative restrictions, deregulation of exchange rates, various export promotion measures and an array of fiscal, monetary and other incentives aimed at attracting foreign private investment. It is outside the scope of this study to discuss these issues in details.[1] Decentralization and deregulation of the industrial investment approval and sanctioning procedures; introduction of the "one-stop-services" at the BOI, simplification of the industrial term loan sanctioning procedures; and simplification and standardization of import procedures have greatly liberalized the overall regulatory framework and have contributed significantly towards creating a conducive environment for growth and expansion of private investment.

Liberal policy measures and attractive incentive packages (i.e. tax exemptions, tax holidays, concessionary duty of imported machineries, facilities for repatriation of invested capital, profits and dividends etc.) have been designed to attract larger flow of foreign direct investment (FDI). FDI-related administration as well as sanctioning and registration procedures and regulations have been simplified and strengthened.

In order to implement the new liberalized policy measures, the reorganization and strengthening of the relevant institutions, such as, BOI, BEPZA, NBR, EPB, BTC etc. are on the agenda of the Government. Such revamping and reorganization are being examined, studied and recommended by the Public Administration Reorganization Commission (PARC). A National Law Commission is also working towards reforming and modernizing the legal procedures required to simplify and quicken the law-enforcement practice and dispute-settlement procedures.

In short, necessary administrative reforms, institutional restructuring, capacity building, and judicial reforms etc. are part of the process to ensure speedy and effective implementation of the changed policies and a prudent adoption of the liberalization measures.

2.1.2 Regulatory mechanism for controlling monopolies and ensuring competitive environment

Privatization programme to be successful requires a set of prudential economic policies and establishment of institutions and institutional practices that encourage enterprise formation and growth and support the smooth operation of markets and production processes. In general, privatization needs to be implemented as an integral component of an authentic liberal economic order that ensures enforcement of the rule of laws, stable fiscal and monetary discipline, fair competition, effective microeconomic regulations, sound exit policies and equality of opportunity.

However, the present policy framework in Bangladesh does not contain any effective mechanism for controlling monopolies and protecting consumer interests in the event of

---

[1] Details on the deregulation and liberalization measures are available in Ahmed M. U. et. al. (1999).

transfer of public monopolies through privatization of utilities, telecommunications and transportation activities. In order to ensure gains from privatization of the non-competitive sectors, prudential industry regulations must be put in place and be rigorously implemented to protect consumer interests and social welfare goals. Thus, privatization and entry of the private sector operators in the public utility sectors should be accompanied by a strong, credible and transparent regulatory framework that limits the scope for abusing market power and controls rent-seeking behaviour.

2.2 Privatization policy: New thrust and clear direction

In order to streamline the lagging privatization process, the Board of Disinvestment created earlier was replaced by an Inter-Ministerial Committee on Privatization (ICOP) set up by the Government in 1991. ICOP's responsibilities included development of privatization policy and approval and monitoring of specific privatization proposals for the various administrative ministries which have Privatization Cells to identify SOEs for privatization. ICOP worked as a coordinating body between the line Ministry and the Executive Committee of the National Economic Council (ECNEC) to implement privatization. However, although ICOP was created to expedite the privatization process, the lengthy process involving several layers of approval still remained; and ICOP lacked necessary technical capacity and autonomy leaving the privatization process to remain slow and cumbersome. To overcome these limitations, a Privatization Board (PB) was set up in March 1993 to formulate the modalities for transferring SOEs to the private sector. In order to further strengthen the role of the private sector by accelerating the privatization process, the Government has adopted a comprehensive privatization policy in June 1993 and laid down detailed procedures to facilitate the process of privatization. The policy has aimed at relieving the financial and administrative burden of the Government, improving efficiency and productivity, facilitating economic growth, reducing the size of the public sector in the economy and help meeting the national economic goals.[1]

2.3 Institutional arrangements, methods and procedures of privatization

The privatization policy statement has outlined the detailed methods, procedures, legal formalities as well as the institutional framework to carry out the process. Theoretically, PB has the sole responsibility of privatizing the SOEs and this provides a basis for transparency in the sale of the SOEs.

2.3.1 Institutional framework

In order to strengthen the PB structurally, improve its performance and also make its operations more transparent, the Government appointed a renowned private sector entrepreneur as the Chairman of the Board with the rank and status of a State Minister to the Government. The Board now consists of two full-time members, four full-time Directors and twelve part-

---

[1] Details on the salient features and procedures of the Privatization Policy are available with the Privatization Board (1996).

time members including six members of the Parliament both from the party-in-power and from the opposition. The Board also has the authority to engage consultants and specialists as and when necessary to execute its programmes. In contrast to the members of the civil servants only, the Board members now include representatives of the common public, private sector participants and professional groups. The Board, placed under the administrative jurisdiction of the Cabinet Division headed by the Prime Minister, reports directly to the Cabinet Sub-Committee for Finance and Committee on Economic Affairs chaired by the Finance Minister.

However, a few more steps need to be undertaken to put in place an effective institutional arrangement for privatization. For example, nothing has been mentioned in the privatization policy about the role and status of the sector corporations which manage the SOEs on behalf of their respective Ministries. While the sector corporations will lose their relevance after completion of the process of privatization of the SOEs, it may be useful to take a decision now as to when they will be abolished. Again, side by side with the PB, Bangladesh Railway, Biman Bangladesh Airlines etc. are known to have their own privatization process. Recently, the Ministry of Jute has floated a tender for sale of some of its own mills offering terms and conditions different from those of the PB. But expediency demands that there should be only one operational arm of the Government for executing its privatization programme.

2.3.2 Methods of privatization

There is no unique formula for privatization. The dominant prevailing methods include divestiture of government economic activities, private sale of shares, public offering of shares, lease and management contract, management/employee buy-out etc. of which divestment is the most widely used method in both developed and developing countries.[1] Divestment of a public enterprise takes place in many ways which include floatation of shares, sale of equity, sale of public enterprise assets etc. However, the appropriate method of privatization will vary from country to country, much depending on the state of the economy in general and of the private sector in particular.

According to the Privatization Policy Statement, one or both of the following methods are at present being followed for privatization in Bangladesh:

(i)   **Sale by International Tender:** Local and foreign buyers may participate in all such tenders. Association of workers, employees and officers of the tendered enterprise may also offer bids for purchasing the enterprise. The authorities have also declared that they would prefer to use Employee Stock Option Programme (ESOP) if the workers of the enterprise are willing to buy it.[2] Direct sale of SOEs has been the dominant method of privatization in Bangladesh. In fact, direct sales

---

[1]   A succinct description of the various privatization methods used in different countries is available in R. Mondal (1998).

[2]   The potentials of ESOP planned to be tried in the textiles sector is discussed at length by Akram (1998).

have been much more common than other methods (i.e. public share offerings) all over the world; there were 831 privatization cases involving US $ 176 billion through direct sales of SOEs compared to 630 cases of privatization through share issue during 1980-1997 (Megginson, W.L., 1998).

(ii) **Sale by Public Offer of Shares:** Under this method, government-owned shares in different companies and shares of the SOEs converted into public limited companies may be sold to the general public either directly or through the Stock Exchange. An SOE running as public limited company may sell whole or part of the block holding to the public at a pre-determined price or may issue new public shares (primary). With approval of the Prime Minister, shares of nine SOEs are currently being sold to the public through the Investment Corporation of Bangladesh (ICB).

However, the successful off-loading of the shares of an SOE by either of the two methods involves many complex and sensitive procedures, particularly in the developing countries like Bangladesh which need careful attention.

2.4 Tendering and payment procedures

According to the stipulations of the privatization policy, a chartered accountant or a consulting chartered accountant firm is appointed by the PB to make valuations of the assets and liabilities of the SOEs identified for sale.[1] After careful review and examination of the chartered accountant firm's report, PB may hire another chartered accountant firm for re-valuation if considered necessary. The valuation report is then sent to the Finance Division of the Ministry of Finance for comments and approval. Tender is invited after finalisation of the valuation report quoting the "reserved price" (i.e. minimum price below which the unit will not be sold) calculated by the consultant and agreed by the Ministry of Finance. The prospective buyers are allowed access to the valuation report and other relevant papers, such as three year's performance report of the enterprise prior to submission of the tender. The buyers submit quotations according to terms and conditions of the tender which are considered to be stringent by many experts as well as by the concerned shareholders. For example, the bidder has to accept all long-term loans against fixed assets, will be liable to pursue all pending court cases, and will not be allowed to sell the land under the enterprise.

The short-term liabilities, such as the claims of the workers and income taxes, shall be borne and written-off by the Government. However, if the value of the assets exceed bank loans, the buyer has to pay the excess amount either in cash in a single installment or within one year of purchase along with a simple interest of 10 per cent. It is thus important that the long-term and the short-term liabilities should be clearly defined, demarcated and the distinction established and upheld. There should be no scope for reinterpreting the terms and conditions of privatization after sale, because scope for reinterpretation provides opportunities

---

[1] While the chartered accountant firm follows the existing accounting principles and practices for valuation of the SOEs, it also follows the guidelines provided in estimating the values of various assets.

for rent-seeking and provides unequal advantages to the privatized units over other units in the same sector. To avoid such complications, it is also necessary to undertake restructuring of capital of the SOEs usually by writing-off loans, scrapping of obsolete assets, laying off surplus workers and improving overall operational efficiency etc. for preparing the SOEs for speedy and effective sale. The counter argument put forward by the leaders of the business community against these conditions is that the entrepreneur buying the unit should be left free to decide the courses of action after the hand over of the enterprise, because as he takes up the liabilities, there should be no strings in the hands of the Government to pull any more.

While the payment procedures are also considered equally stringent, there exists no window for financing (by the banks) of the privatization process.[1] The potential buyers need to submit 2.5 per cent of the negotiated sale price within one moth. The balance 75 per cent has to be paid within five years in half-yearly installments along with a compound interest rate of 9 per cent per annum. The buyer will be entitled to a rebate of 15 per cent if he can pay the entire amount within 30 days of signing the agreement. When payment is not made in cash, the buyer needs to provide a bank guarantee which involves various complications. On top of all these, the buyer is in a state of constant fear until the final hand over even after receiving the letter of intent (LOI) as the CBAs may prohibit such hand over process. Further, although all formalities relating to handing over is to be completed within 90 days of the issuance of LOT, the successful bidder often has to run from the pillar to the post to get the various formalities completed. As a result, between floating the tender and the issue of LOT to the party winning the bid, it takes on average 6-7 months as the final offer is also subject to approval of the Cabinet Sub-Committee and by the Prime Minister which often involves undue delays.

Thus, the PB in practice does not have the real autonomy and authority to take final decision regarding divestment of an SOE. The real power lies in the hands of the Cabinet Committee which takes the final decision regarding the sale of an SOE. It is thus suggested that in order to allow privatization effort to make significant headway, the autonomy of the PB needs to be significantly enhanced by giving it statutory status. A draft Privatization Law prepared with assistance of the Department of International Development (DFID), U.K. and the Adam Smith Institute (London) for privatization to provide PB with greater autonomy and authority for trying different privatization options is under consideration of the Cabinet Committee. The considered view is, however, that the proposed Privatization Bill will not go a very long way unless the Constitution of the country is changed to provide PB with enough legal authority. In this context, the existing Transfer of Properties Act and Negotiable Instruments Act also need to be modified and changed to facilitate quicker change of ownership of assets. In addition to the right to sell, PB should also be granted the right to liquidate the SOEs, so that it can sell the assets of an SOE part by part, i.e. land, machinery and other assets as demanded by the prospective buyers.

---

[1] The PB mentions however that the buyers are entitled to a rebate of 15 per cent if they can pay off the price in one single installment and may also obtain long-term loans from the banks.

Further, the PB officials must also change their attitude and start taking initiatives to expedite the privatization process. In particular, they must overcome the fear of public criticisms, harassment by anti-corruption officials, and most important of all, try to make their own decisions instead of depending upon the concerned Ministries in identifying and selling an SOEs. It is also suggested that like the BOI, the PB also should introduce "one-stop" service mechanism to make the privatization process more effective, transparent, well-coordinated and faster.

3.   Current status of privatization of SOEs in Bangladesh

3.1   Extent and pace of privatization

While Bangladesh is considered a fore-runner in carrying out privatization, there seems to be a common belief that the overall achievement has not been all that impressive. Lack of enough political commitment and determination, absence of sufficient legal framework, limited institutional capacity, mistrust among the workers and above all, political discord between the party-in-power and the opposition political parties are generally identified as important factors limiting the progress of privatization in Bangladesh. Moreover, opposition to the privatization of the SOEs is not limited only to the above factors, it is also orchestrated further by the country's left-leaning academics, political leaders and opinion moulders.

While privatization in Bangladesh began since mid-1970s and the process has evolved through many ups and downs till then, it is difficult to arrive at any conclusive judgement on the true magnitude of privatization of SOEs taking place because of lack of hard statistics on the one hand and the controversies sorrounding the mode and methods of privatization of the units involved on the other hand. For example, a study conducted by C.A.F. Dowlah (1997) for World Bank (referred to as World Bank Study, 1997, henceforth) points out that a total of 1089 enterprises consisting of industrial units, commercial businesses and banks etc. were privatized in Bangladesh between 1972 and 1996. The latest study conducted by ILO (1999) estimates a total 1083 SOEs being privatized during the same period of which 610 were industrial enterprises accounting for 56 per cent of the total denationalized units. The distribution of the 610 industrial enterprises by sectors of industry and over different periods of time between 1972 and 1996 are shown in Appendix Table A-2.

Of the total industrial enterprises privatized, cotton and jute textiles were the dominant sub-sectors, followed by metal works, engineering and steel enterprises and vegetable oils. What is, however, interesting that the overwhelming majority (over 70 per cent) of the units privatized between 1972 and 1981 were small-sale enterprises both in terms of investment and employment and were returned to their original owners.

Another feature emerged from the Table is the gradual tapering-off of the speed of privatization overtime as is evident from Figure 2.4. During 1975-81, a total of 255 enterprises (including the "abandoned" and the "vested" properties) were privatized, but the number declined to 222 during 1981-86 despite the fact that the 1982 Industrial Policy constituted historical landmark providing a significant policy shift towards privatization. More surprisingly, not a single SOE was privatized during the period 1986-1991 even though further greater impetus to privatization was provided through RIP-1986 by way of relaxing government controls and regulations and strengthening the denationalization programmes. Subsequently, a Privatization Board and a Privatization Policy Statement were put in place to streamline and expedite the lagging privatization process. The Government agreed with the donor agencies, i.e. ADB (under the Industrial Sector Programme Loan in 1992), and IDA (under the Jute Sector Adjustment Credit or JSAC) to a formidable programme of privatization of the SOEs. Accordingly the PB prepared a list of 105 SOEs for privatization during 1994-95, but the actual progress remained dismal with only 13 enterprises being privatized during 1992-1996.

The progress seems to have slowed down further as only four industrial enterprises have been privatized and transferred to private ownership between June 1996 and to-date. Additionally, LOI has been issued for eight enterprises after final approval of the Cabinet Sub-Committee for finance and economic affairs though their eventual transfer to the buyers is yet to take place. As noted before, the transfer process is often lengthy and subject to uncertainity due to legal complications, heavy loan liabilities, non-transparent bureaucratic procedures and opposition by the trade unions.[1]

Figure 2.4

Progress in the pace of privatization from 1972/75 to 1991/96

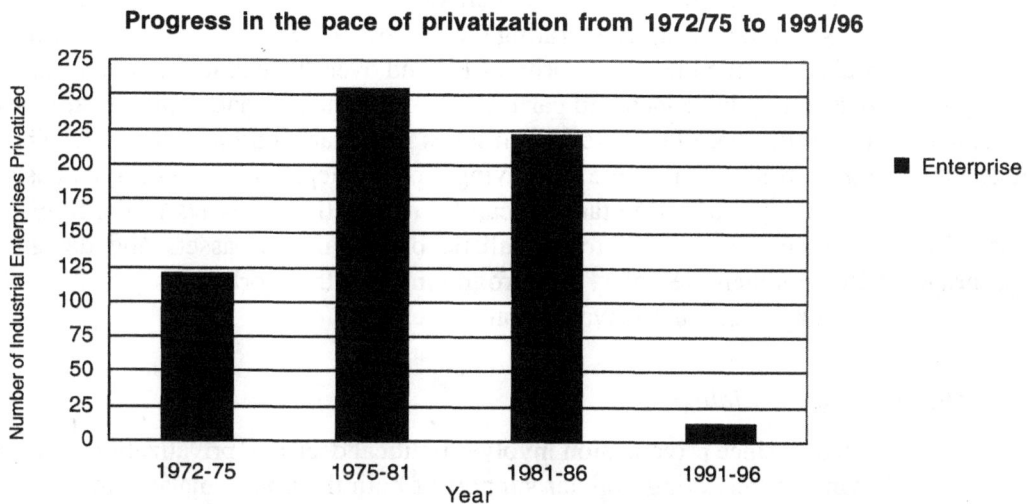

During 1998, PB identified 56 enterprises for sale, but could not sell any so far even after repeated tenders[2]. Lack of buyer interest arising from heavy debt liabilities, financial

---

[1] The problem seems intractable in view of the fact that the responsibility of the PB apparently ends with the issue of LOI. Final hand over of the unit and the execution of the sale deed remain the responsibility of the Ministry concerned causing inordinate delay and consequent frustration for the buyers.

[2] The financial and economic viabililty of many of the SOEs identified for privatization are so doubtful that selling such enterprises as 'properties' may be the only option left to minimize losses and draining away of the tax payers' money. Obsolete machinery, acute overmanning, low productivity, heavy loan liabilities, inefficient public sector management, loss of customers and market shares, frequent work stoppages etc., have made such units totally non-economic entities.

and commercial non-viability, and inadequate information about the stocks, spares etc. are indicated to be (i.e. Daily Star, July 30, 1999) important reasons. The contradictory signals about sincere implementation of the privatization policy by the Government, deterioration of the law and order situation and dramatic increase in rent-seeking by the musclemen are also regarded as other important factors underlying recent slow down in the pace of privatization.

While the Government is also trying to attract the foreign investors, the efforts so far have met with limited success. Political uncertainty, slow implementation of the policies and support measures, bureaucratic procedures, and lack of adequate legal protection have been the main deterrents to FDI inflows. Further, foreign investors will continue to remain hesitant in buying SOEs unless the domestic investors exhibit enough interest and dynamism and improves the image problem.

3.1.1 Donors' concern

While the donors are strongly supportive of the privatization programme in Bangladesh, they have expressed deep concern at the present slow pace of progress of the privatization process. The author's discussion with the concerned World Bank and ADB officials revealed that they are strongly in favour of accelerating the process which is at the moment considered to be virtually stalled. Limited legal authority of PB and overall weak institutional framework, feeling of mistrust among the concerned parties, sale of financially and economically unviable SOEs, and bureaucratic procedures are identified as important inhibiting factors.[1] Thus they suggest a more powerful and effective PB having a proper legal status, setting a phased time table for achieving the privatization targets, careful revaluation of assets of the SOEs on the basis of market prices as opposed to unrealistic book value of assets and design of an appropriate and comprehensive safety net programme for the workers as plausible counter measures towards expediting the privatization process.

3.1.2 The need for a dialogue

As noted already, since privatization involves political decision, privatization policy needs clear political mandate, reflecting popular support of both the policy makers and the general people. In particular, support for such a mandate needs to be obtained from the ruling party and the main opposition party so that there is no uncertainty and vacillations in the privatization process. An opportunity in this regard remains to be availed through putting the forthcoming Privatization Bill to the National Parliament for parliamentary debate and public dialogue. Unfortunately, no serious attempt seems to have been made so far by any Government in

---

[1] According to PB sources, 50 SOEs have been listed for sale during 1999 of which tenders have been floated for 11 enterprises after necessary valuation of assets and liabilities. Out of these 11, LOI has been issued for one, one has been earmarked for sale to the workers and one to the Bangladesh Rifles (BDR). For 12 others legal complications concerning transfer of ownership under preemptive rights is delaying the process of tendring.

Bangladesh to initiate such a dialogue, though it will provide an opportunity to clearly state the objectives of privatization and also set in motion a transparent institutional mechanism for transferring the SOEs from the public sector to the private sector.

However, the intended dialogue has to begin by putting the records right and providing the members of the public (and also the researchers and analysts) with all relevant facts and figures about the status and performance of the SOEs. In order to ensure transparency and credibility, the authorities must clearly define the goals of privatization, provide sound justification for valuation of assets of the SOEs to be sold and explain the mechanism for transfer of ownership. Other important issues, such as, criteria for selecting the SOEs for privatization, terms and conditions of sale, fate of the retrenched workers etc. may also be included in the agenda for public debates. In this way both Government and PB will be in a position to avoid criticisms, raise credibility and go ahead aggressively with the privatization programme. While this will pave the way for formulating a clear cut and strategic privatization policy, the authorities must also set a definite time frame for the completion of the privatization programme. An indicative time table for completion of the programme with the set goals and targets for different phases of privatization would send strong signals to the investors and create confidence in the authorities' commitment towards a goal-oriented privatization programme.

3.2 Effects of privatization

The most important aspect of the privatization programme which has been subject to very intense and recurrent public debates is the post-privatization performance of the privatized SOEs. Unfortunately, sometimes the debates are devoid of objectivity and thus lose much of its significance as the range of opinions swings like pendulum under the influence of push and pull by privatization's most ardent opponents and its proponents. Not surprisingly, therefore, each of these studies has its own policy biases.

Most frequent criticisms labelled at privatization in the recent periods are the following: (a) instead of augmenting new investments, higher industrial growth and generating additional employment opportunities, the privatized units are running at losses and/or are diverting resources into other use; (b) changing business or altogether closing down the operations; (c) the new owners are engaging in the speculative businesses and making commercial use of lands in the projects like housing and shopping complexes and (d) privatization is resulting retrenchment of surplus labour, causing unemployment and thereby contributing to the process of growing social unrest.

The research findings on these issues of economic performance of the privatized enterprises are at best mixed and hence inconclusive. This is primarily because of two reasons: one, privatization in Bangladesh has not proceeded under a coherent and consistent strategy and has not therefore been accompanied by desired improvements in the macro policy framework, institutional, legal and financial infrastructure and an overall conducive environment required for smooth functioning. Two, the process of privatization is not without some cost; on the contrary, it is fraught with political, social and economic problems which must be reckoned and the expectations must be kept within reasonable limits.

3.3 Current operational status and economic performance of the privatized units: An overview

One of the major objectives of privatization is to improve productive efficiency of the privatized firms. In Bangladesh context, this assumes crucial significance as the SOEs suffer from generally low levels of labour as well as capital productivity, huge revenue losses and hence lack of reinvestable surplus for further investments and long-term growth. However, it is by no means established that mere change of ownership from public to private sector will necessarily lead to improvements in productivity, especially when other policies and institutions remain unchanged.[1] Privatization to be gainful has to be accompanied by better management of the firm's capital and human resources under innovative entrepreneurs who are willing and able to transform the previously unprofitable enterprises into profitable ones by injecting additional investments, introducing new and improved technology and efficient corporate governance.

While sound management and improved corporate performance requires sound and disciplined financial institutions, favourable legal practices and standards etc., Bangladesh's overall production environment is characterized by volatile political situation, inadequate infrastructure, frequent power failures, labour unrest, rampant corruption, natural disasters etc. which seriously affect investors' confidence and industrial performance. This lack of a conducive investment and production environment does not guarantee improved economic performance of the privatized units, and this perhaps explains why privatization has not yet produced expected results in terms of higher investments and growth. Any assessment of the post-privatization performance has to be judged against this reality.

A World Bank (1993) Study of the performance of the privatized units divested during 1980s reports that nearly 50 per cent of the enterprises (e.g. 245 out of 497 small industrial enterprises excluding large jute and cotton textile mills) have been closed down. A depleted asset base, high debt liabilities and inefficient management are noted as important factors explaining poor performance of the divested units.

The privatized large-scale units within the jute and cotton textile mills have also been found (Sobhan 1985 and 1990) to exhibit mixed results in terms of investments, productivity, profitability and other measures of efficiency. The overall results were inconclusive as to the performance of the divested units, since the analysis carried out was somewhat premature in terms of time allowed to the divested units to assess full impacts of their transfer from the public to the private sector.

Analysing the current status of 205 industrial enterprises (divested between 1979 and 1994) in terms of either being in operation or being closed down after privatization, Sen (1997), on the basis of questionnaire-based information collected through Rapid Appraisal

---

[1] Akash and Sobhan's (1999) analysis of the post-privatization performance of the 35 Jute Mlls confirm this point when they conclude that in the Jute Sector the problem lies not in the ownership but in the managerial inefficiency and unfavourable policy environment.

(RA) technique reports a high incidence (40 per cent) of post-divestiture closures with five per cent of the units not being traceable at all. Lack of availability of capital for modernization, high debt burden and low capacity utilization were reported by the owners as the important reasons for closing down their businesses. While this prompted the author to interprete the situation as an instance of the "lost case" of privatization, the conclusion may seem unwarranted when judged against certain realities. First, over 70 per cent of the divested sample units were small enterprises which are characterized by a high rate (60 per cent) of business failures in the developing countries. Second, in roughly 30 per cent of the cases of closures, switching to alternative production/commercial activities after divestiture could be noted.

Similarly, the above study could notice capacity utilization to be below 75 per cent in 40 of (roughly 36 per cent) 112 enterprises and commented that capacity utilization was way below 75 per cent This statement could perhaps be reworded and put in a positive tone by saying that in 64 per cent of the cases capacity utilization was over 75 per cent. Indeed, capacity utilization being less than 50 per cent in only 11 per cent of the cases, the divested enterprises exhibit a much better situation than the general situation prevailing in the overall industrial sector of Bangladesh in this regard. Further, given the changed context after divestiture and the constraints of capital, technology, marketing and so on, a rate of capacity utilization of 50 per cent may be regarded as rather commendable.

Turning to the issues of economic performance, at least two features of the divested enterprises should have convinced Sen (1997) to conclude the study with a positive note on the impacts of privatization. For example, out of the 112 enterprises currently in operation, 44 (nearly 40 per cent) diversified their businesses by introducing new products. Needless to emphasize, product diversification is a reflection of dynamic entrepreneurial behaviour and market-sensitive enterprise restructuring which should have favourable effects on the overall enterprises efficiency. Not surprisingly, therefore, as against only 38 per cent of 195 enterprises yielding profits before privatization, the proportion jumped to nearly 60 per cent after divestiture suggesting that privatization has created the basis for higher long-term industrial growth. The convincing evidence of better financial performance of selected (eight of the sample enterprises studied by Sen) privatized enterprises has been provided by a recent study (Haque, 1999) conducted for the World Bank which found that gross profit margins more than doubled in all the eight enterprises. Further, an improved financial performance by the majority of these enterprises was also confirmed by increase in their working capital flows, net worth ratios, current ratios and assets turnover ratios which attested to their improved efficiency in resource use.

Finally, a much publicised study on privatization experience in Bangladesh undertaken by Dowlah (1997) for the World Bank also identified mixed results relating to the performance of a sample of 10 divested enterprises. In four enterprises, there was an increase in capacity utilization after privatization, though five enterprises experienced slight fall in this regard. Similarly, five enterprises experienced decline in production by 23 per cent after privatization, while three could raise production by 91 per cent. Again, while four enterprises were able to raise their gross sales by over 100 per cent after privatization, another four suffered decline in their gross sales revenues by 41 per cent A similar mixed performance of the sample privatized enterprises judged by their operational efficiency measured in terms of sales per employee and ratio of sales to fixed assets was also noted by the same study.

The results of the studies reviewed here do not permit any conclusive generalization on the performance of the privatized enterprises across the board after divestiture. Moreover, the findings of the studies also need to be interpreted with caution in view of the fact that they have used different methodologies, conducted their investigations at different time periods and also perhaps had different objectives to be pursued. An important point to be noted in this connection is that the estimation of macro effects of privatization, though important are outside the purview of this study

3.3.1 The case for restructuring and reform

The absence of any robust evidence about a generally improved enterprise performance of the privatized units seems to indicate the need for restructuring and reform of the SOEs both during pre and post- privatization stages.

In so far as the pre-privatization reform of the SOEs is concerned, there may be a variety of options to improve their performance. As an important part of such reform policy agenda implemented during early 1990s, 22 SOEs were put under "performance contract" (PC) of which 12 belonged to the manufacturing sector. Of the 12 SOEs 10 were able to raise their labour productivity, and five improved their financial performance compared to the levels at the beginning.[1] However, for better performance, the SOEs need to be provided with greater autonomy, flexibility in operation, transparency, and accountability in order to enable them to be managed like profit-making commercial enterprises as opposed to state-controlled entities without commercial autonomy.

In fact, to expedite the privatization of the potential SOEs, necessary restructuring measures need to be undertaken to improve their current financial conditions and write-off their future liabilities to attract the potential buyers. It may also be necessary to adjust their price structures, redefine their activities and revise their employment policies along with injection of new equity and other rationalization measures. To expedite the privatization process, donors and some of the stakeholders are however in favour of privatizing first and then going for necessary restructuring and reform.

As for the post-privatized enterprises, there should be constant surveillance and monitoring by the relevant Government organizations to review and examine economic performance of the enterprises. Regrettably, GOB is reported (Akash et.al., 1999) to have made no serious effort in this regard to monitor and assess the performance of the privatized units except undertaking a snapshot survey in 1991 to see if the privatized units were in operation.

---

[1]   Besides contrary opinions, the overall results of the pre-privatization restructuring in the early 1990s have been mixed. In addition, it is reported to have created an unfavourable impression as regards Government's motivation and determination to implement the privatization policy.

Reviewing the impact of privatization on a global scale, including both developed and developing countries, Megginson (1998) concluded that total earnings of the privatized companies increased on an average by 25 per cent, profitability (rate of return on sales) more than doubled and efficiency (increase in sales per worker) increased by 16 per cent and 11 per cent respectively in the developing and the developed countries within three years following divestiture.

However, the experience in privatization of public enterprises is diverse at the international level as well. Enterprise performance, productivity and profitability may not improve everywhere after privatization. The experience in former Soviet Union and in some other East European countries shows little evidence of higher growth even after several years of liberalization, privatization and macroeconomic stabilization.

The Bangladesh Cycle Industries (BCI) Ltd. represents a remarkable exception among the 13 SOEs privatized during 1991-1996 which experienced robust growth in production capacity (three times larger from pre-privatization period), a 600 per cent increase in employment and turned into an export-oriented industry as a result of efficient management. These evidence, while speak of economic success of the privatization programmes, do not by themselves guarantee that the process of privatization has always been an unmixed blessing. The most difficult challenges are encountered by the privatization process when it comes to labour restructuring, retrenchment and redeployment, especially in the developing countries like Bangladesh where problems of unemployment and underemployment reign supreme. The problem becomes especially difficult when privatizations are carried out in the SOEs which are excessively over-staffed and involve large-scale lay-offs. We turn to discuss these issues next.

3.4 Labour concerns

The most delicate issue in privatization in Bangladesh relates to labour restructuring and retrenchment with minimum social costs. The labour issues are generally sensitive for several reasons. The SOEs privatized in Bangladesh are excessively over-staffed and may involve retrenchment. The problem is further aggravated by the fact that the track record of many privatized units relating to redundancy payments has been poor. This tends to deteriorate the already poor labour-management relations in Bangladesh. However, discussions with various stakeholder groups, i.e. the trade union leaders, government officials, employers and researchers tend to suggest that the majority of the union leaders and workers are not in principle, opposed to privatization provided their interests are adequately safeguarded. Nevertheless, the gradual softening of the labour resistance does not suggest that they are less concerned about the outcomes of the privatization process. Large-scale job losses resulting from lay-offs and retrenchment (designed to raise enterprise productivity and efficiency) and closure of the privatized units after divestiture, and uncertainty about payment of adequate compensations etc. are the major concerns of the workers. All these remain very real concerns in Bangladesh and tend to be aggravated by a relationship of mistrust persisting among labour, government and the private sector employers.

3.5 Loss of employment and retrenchment of workers due to privatization in Bantgladesh

In the earlier quoted Sen (1997) study, the aggregate downsizing of labour in 112 SOEs (out of a sample of 205) which were in operation after divestiture was found to be roughly 25 per cent (Table 2.1). This perhaps represented, as the author noted, a measure of cutting the "fat" away from the public sector enterprises which are often used as 'employment centres' rather than market-sensitive firms. Such restructuring would entail significant gains in labour productivity in the privatized enterprises. More importantly, it was noted that 60 per cent of the currently employed workers in the SOEs under operation after divestiture were also working during the pre-divestiture period. This is expected against a relative paucity of skilled labour in Bangladesh and also essential in an open economy to gain productivity increases and remain competitive under a dynamic private sector-led economic system.

Table 2.1: Labour restructuring after divestiture of the currently running enterprises

(Figures in parenthesis represent column percentages)

	Before divestiture	After divestiture	Per cent difference
No. of production workers	97048	73711	-24.0
	(89.3)	(89.5)	
No. of non-production employees	11597	8643	-25.5
	(10.7)	(10.5)	
Total number of workers and employees	108645	82354	-24.2
	(100.0)	(100.0)	

Note: The estimates are based on 112 privatized enterprises which are currently running out of the total sample of 205 studied by Sen (1997).

Source: Adapted from Sen (1997).

However, the impact of closure of the privatized enterprises was found to have serious consequences as the aggregate loss of jobs due to closure alone was estimated to be 39007 by the same study. The most recently conducted ILO (1999) study in this respect estimates a 25 per cent decrease in employment (Table 2.2) after divestiture in 11 of the currently operating SOEs out of a total of 13 privatized during 1991-1996. While there were variations across industries in the proportion of decline between 10 per cent to 48 per cent in the privatized units, the important fact is that the employment loss after divestiture was quite significant. As noted before, Bangladesh Cycle Industries (BCI) Ltd. was the only remarkable case which experienced post-privatization growth in all departments, including employment. The BCI Ltd. recorded almost a seven-fold increase in employment after privatization, reflecting entrepreneurial performance of very high standards by its new owners.

The total retrenchment of workers, including both production and non-production workers, resulting from privatization of the six "loss making" public sector corporations as of end of June 1997 is estimated (ILO, 1997) to be 89,971 employees (Table 2.3).

Table 2.2: Change in employment status of the currently operating enterprises after privatization during 1991-96

Name of the enterprise	Employment		
	At the time of privatization	After privatization	Change (inper cent)
1. Dhaka Vegetable Oil Industries Ltd.	525	295	-43.8
2. Chittagong Cement Clinker and Grinding Co. Ltd.	318	252	-20.8
3. Kohinoor Chemicals Co.	889	798	-10.2
4. Kohinoor Spinning Mills Ltd.	1030	530	-48.5
5. Bangladesh Cycle Industries Ltd.	119	800	672.2
6. Barisal Textile Mills (New: Name 5R Ltd.)	1172	832	-29
7. Stile Fabrics & Embroidery Ltd. (Old Name: Zotime Fabrics)	61	50	-18
8. Kishoreganj Textile	1275	758	-40.5
9. Madaripur Textile Ltd.	1056	742	-29.7
10. Eagle Box & Carton Mfg. Ltd.	268	172	-35.8
11. Quontum Pharmaceutical Ltd.	283	n.a.	n.a.
12. Hamida Metal Industries Ltd.		Closed	
13. Sharmin Textile Mills	6996	5229	-25.3

Source: World Bank (WB): *Privatization Experience in Bangladesh*, 1991-96: A Study undertaken for the World Bank (Vol. 1); Sept. 1997.

Table 2.3: Retrenchment of manpower from state owned enterprises in manufacturing sectors since privatization started

Sector/Corporations	Retrenchment		
	Up to 30 June 1996 (Cumulative) %	1 July 1996 to 30 June 1997 %	Up to 30 June 1997 (Cumulative) %
Bangladesh Textile Mills Corporation (BJMC)	25.7	30.9	27.3
Bangladesh Steel & Engineering Corporation (BSEC)	4.0	0.7	3.0
Bangladesh Sugar and Food Industries Corporation (BSFIC)	4.2	2.0	3.5
Bangladesh Chemical Industries Corporation (BCIC)	1.9	-	1.3
Bangladesh Forest Industries Development Corporation (BFIDC)	1.6	-	1.1
Bangladesh Jute Mills Corporation (BJMC)	62.6	66.4	63.8
Total (%)	100	100	100
Total No.	61844	28127	89971

Source: ILO (1999).

Although privatization began since mid 1970s and 435 SOEs were divested between 1972-1986, there was no case of retrenchment as these were mostly abandoned and/or closed enterprises which were returned to their previous owners who took full responsibility to retain the previous employees. Thus actual retrenchment process began since 1991 (there being no instance of privatization between 1986-1990) and very large-scale retrenchment occurred during 1991 and June 1996 involving 61,844 workers or representing 68.7 per cent of the total. The rest 28,127 or 31.3 per cent of the employees were retrenched during July 1996 and June 1997. While reduction of previous over-staffing and closure of some of the units after divestiture might be the important reasons for employment loss, this has adverse impact on the welfare of the workers.

According to PB estimates based on future privatization of the SOEs in the next two to three years, the planned retrenchment of workers may reach a staggering figure of 88,612 employees (Table 2.4) from five sector corporations. While nearly 58 per cent of the workers are planned to be retrenched on an average from each sector corporation, more than 73 per cent of them will comprise production workers, 21 per cent non-production workers and about five per cent will be officers and managers. Needless to emphasize, the workers' interests and welfare need to be preserved and promoted both to minimize adverse social effects and ensure social justice.

4.   Post-privatization measures adopted to minimize adverse social consequences

4.1   Preserving workers' interests

The workers' interests can be safeguarded in two ways: (i) by offering a reasonable "golden handshake" and leaving it upto the employee to find a new job or take to a new profession, and (ii) by taking positive steps (i.e. retraining facilities) to find new job opportunities. In addition, various redeployment policies (i.e. proactive employment generation policies especially geared towards assisting the retrenched workers, micro-credit programmes supported by entrepreneurship training etc. and social safety net measures (i.e. creation of Special Workers' Fund or SWF as proposed by ILO) may also be designed to help the retrench workers. A brief account of the compensation and redeployment measures adopted in Bangladesh to assist the retrenched workers is provided below.

4.2   Compensation measures for the retrenched workers

The most important measure of assistance provided by the Government to the retrenched workers in Bangladesh consists of a compensation package called, "Additional Benefits on Top of the Gratuity Payments", which is popularly known as the "Golden Handshake". To determine the actual benefits offered to the retrenched workers within the framework of a total compensation package, a number of committees consisting of concerned high officials/ experts were formed of which Mustafiz Committee and Mannan Committee are important. These Committees recommended additional benefits ranging between 10 per cent to

27 per cent of the gratuity to be paid to the retrenched workers depending on their length of services (Table 2.5). The gratuity benefit itself amounts to two months of basic pay (last drawn by the incumbent) for each year of service.

Table 2.4 Estimated number of workers who might lose jobs as a result of privatization in the near future

Corporation	Planned retrenchment		
	Number of total workers	Retrenched workers as % of workers	% Distribution of retrenched workers by sector corporations
	(1)	(2)	(3)
BTMC	7152	50.46	8.1
BSEC	3653	54.68	4.1
BSFIC	13335	64.76	1.5
BCIC	3029	14.30	3.4
BFIDC	-	-	-
BJMC	61443	71.35	69.3
Total :	88612	57.92	

Source: ILO (1999).

Table 2.5: Recommended benefits for retrenched workers by Mustafiz Committee and Mannan Committee

Length of services	Additional benefits on top of gratuity payments	
	Mustafiz Committee (%)	Mannan Committee (%)
25 years and above	10	13
20-25 years	14	18
15 – 20 years	17	22
10 – 15 years	22	27

Source: Report of the Sub-Committee, headed by the Minister for Labour and Manpower, April 1997.

The financial compensation paid by a number of jute mills belonging to BJMC on the basis of the recommendations of the above Committees are sown in Table 2.6. It may be noted from the Table that during 1993-94 and 1994-95, 2648 employees of the age group 35-40 years and 3230 employees of the age group 50 years and above voluntarily retired from eight jute mills. The former group recevied an average severance compensation of Tk. 44,000 which was upto Tk.60,000 with arrears. The latter group received compensation package of upto Tk. 80,000 with arrears. Thus, so far financial compensation for voluntary retirement is concerned, a retrenched worker may get a one-time lump sum payment and no other benefits. This does neither compensate for the tens of thousands of Taka which a young worker might earn for the rest of his working career nor enable him to secure a lifetime income at a reasonable level even when he leaves the job at an age close to the normal retiring.[1]

Table 2.6: Compensation paid to the retrenched jute mill workers

Jute mills	No. of affected workers		Compensation (in Crore* Tk.)	
	1993-94 (35-40 yrs-age)	1994-95 (>50 yrs-age)	1993-94	1994-95
Adamjee	1211	1294	3.02	16.45
U M C	283	305	1.57	1.99
Latif Bawany	236	466	1.89	1.71
Nishat	168	174	1.89	1.71
Nabarun	146	100	n.a.	n.a.
Munawar	356	n.a.	1.82	n.a.
BD Jute	174	295	1.14	n.a.
Total	2574	2634	11.33	21.86
Average Compensation	44,000	80,000		

Source: Report of the Sub-Committee, Headed by the Minister for Labour and Manpower, April 1997.
  * 1 crore = 10 million.

Along with the 'golden handshake', another financial compensation scheme introduced initially in Railway, BJMC and BTMC was the "voluntary departure schemes" (VDS), under which the terms of payment appeared to be generous and workers' response was also favourable. According to the Jute Manufacturing Study (JMS,1989), the cash payment under the package would consist of two months salary for each year of service plus provident fund and accrued interest. On this basis, the workers would receive severance benefits varying between Tk. 100,000 to Tk. 500,000 per worker. An SOE employee, with 30 years of service would be entitled to five years' pay as gratuity alone and thus the workers' response to VDS has been quite positive during 1991-93, especially in the Railway, BJMC and BTMC. Thus the VDS was suggested by the World Bank Study (1994) to be continued along with other existing compensation packages.

The arrangement for a life time pension benefit might be thought of as another alternative, but the total benefits (estimated by ILO, 1999) actually available through an annuity-pension scheme from the approximate retirement age of 58 or 60 years at the rate of 40 per cent of the last basic pay, i.e. in the region of Tk. 5000 (which works out to be approximately Tk. 300,000) would be highly inadequate to support the workers surviving family members after his death.

---

[1] During earlier rounds of divestiture, the out-going workers did not receive such cash benefits. Besides non-payment of the entire accumulated gratuity money, the general provident fund money accumulated through joint contributions by the workers and the government prior to privatization was also not paid (World Bank, 1994).

In addition to the limited cash benefits, the reduntant workers also lose the health and medical service facilities provided by the employers. In such cases, the Government may consider making such medical services available to the retrenched workers through the Labour Welfare Centres even after retrenchment.

Introduction of the scheme of "unemployment insurance" could be another option. But for a resource poor, less developed country like Bangladesh, such a proposition seems unviable for at least another few years. The viability of this option for Bangladesh can be determined only by conducting a detailed study into the present and future prospects of economic growth and employment expansion in the economy.

Besides resource constraints, the introduction and implementation of various alternative compensation schemes are subject to serious administrative bottlenecks and other complications. For example, the financial and social safety net issues relate to the workings of a number of line ministries (i. e. Ministry of Labour, Ministry of Industry, Ministry of Finance) and departments, which makes the tasks of coordination exceedingly difficult. Despite these difficulties, however, the following options concerning social protection of the retrenched workers need to be seriously studied and investigated in order to facilitate future progress in privatization process at a faster pace:

- desirability of introducing a scheme of old age pension scheme after retirement and benefits payable in pension rather than as a lump sum cash compensation;
- feasibility of introducing an insured system of unemployment benefits; and
- ways and means of strengthening the health and medical facilities.

To ensure greater coverage of the workforce, a system of providing protection to the informal sector workers who constitute over 80 per cent of the total workforce of Bangladesh also needs to be borne in mind. More importantly, revision and modernization of the relevant legal framework applicable to the workers' social protection issues should also be incorporated in the scope of the suggested studies.

4.3 Retraining of the retrenched workers for redeployment

Under the Jute Sector Adjustment Credit (JSAC, the World Bank agreed to provide US $ 247 million over a period of four years between 1991 and 1997 to help reform the Jute Industry) a project, "Retraining of Affected Workers of Jute Mills" was taken up by the Government of Bangladesh as a part of the safety-net package. The purpose was to assist the retrenched workers, through training, to find jobs elsewhere after leaving the jute mills. Since the inception of the training programme in November 1995, a total of 8793 workers were retrained in 35 different trades (see Annexure II) in three zonal centres, (i.e. Dhaka, Chittagong and Khulna) of the country with assistance from selected NGOs. The training programme was conducted jointly by six foreign consultants and 37 local consultants under a Consultancy Contract. The NGOs were recruited later by the Consulting Firms primarily to locate and recruit the retrenched jute mill workers from different localities of the countryside where they had dispersed after retrenchment. The NGOs worked as subcontractors of the main contractors and provided training to some of the retrenched workers in their own localities in selective trades where they had specialized training expertise. Depending on the trade and the nature of the training programme, the training courses were of different duration varying between one week and three and a half weeks.

The training provided in 35 different courses were developed into four broad areas:

(a)   Agriculture;
(b)   Engineering;
(c)   Rural industry; and
(d)   Entrepreneurship development.

In the absence of any serious study on the impact and effectiveness of the retraining programme it is difficult to provide any conclusive judgement on its achievements. It is, however, commonly agreed that it marks the first organized effort of its kind in Bangladesh and reflects in principle the recognition of the fact especially by the government that the interests of the retrenched workers should be adequately safeguarded while implementing the privatization programme.

The most important reason for lack of enough interest among the target beneficiaries to avail the programme was the long time gap involved between job loss and inception of the training programme. While nearly an estimated 20,000 workers lost their jobs by 1993, the training programme started in 1996. By then, many of the workers left the mills, dispersed to their villages and perhaps also lost hope and self-confidence and were not keen to seek retraining for redeployment. This suggests that it is critically important to initiate the process of counselling and retraining of the retrenched workers soon after their retirement.

Discussions with selected officials of the Ministry of Labour gave the impression that effectiveness of any such programme is critically dependent upon the motivation of the workers about importance and relevance of training provided, the duration of training, selection of appropriate courses, and monetary incentives provided in the form of allowances throughout the training period. None of these factors was properly and adequately handled as part of necessary preparation for the training programme.[1] In particular, provision for adequate income support during the period of training has been found to be critically important determinant of the success of the programme also in other countries such as in Eastern Europe and China.

Based on a follow-up study of a sample of roughly 100 retrained workers from the Comilla region in Bangladesh, it was found that roughly 10-20 per cent of the retrained workers took to self-employment using their training skills. Among those who set up their own enterprises, 31 per cent were in poultry, 13 per cent in horticulture and nursery, 11 per cent in flower gardening, seven per cent in jute handicrafts and 3-4 per cent each engaged themselves in pisciculture, cane and bamboo handicrafts, candle making and various types of other small trades. The average monthly incomes earned from these enterprises were reported

---

[1]   Details on these and other issues relevant to designing and implementing a successful, retraining programme is available in ILO (1999).

to vary between Tk. 500 to Tk. 2000 ($ 10 to 40) which were much less than their earnings in the Jute Mills.

To ensure proper utilization of the entrepreneural skills imparted through the retraining programme provision of micro-credit support has been commonly identified as an essential ingredient by most observers. A logical suggestion in this context has been to establish linkages with the MFIs for successful implementation of the proposed special credit programmes. Thus, the implication is that an institutional framework may be designed to conduct such retraining programme on a regular and continuous basis not only to support the privatization programme but also to cater to the human development needs of a dynamic economy.

4.4 The current training infrastructure and existing training capacities in Bangladesh

The existing public vocational training system in Bangladesh is run by two Government agencies: (i) Bureau of Manpower Employment and Training (BMET) under the Ministry of Labour and Employment and (ii) Directorate of Technical Education under the Ministry of Education. BMET operates 11 Technical Training Centres (TTCs) which are widely dispersed across the country, including all the major industrial locations and offer training facilities in 12 different engineering trades.

There are 54 Vocational Training Institutes (VTIs) located primarily in the district and upazila headquarters which offer training courses in 8 different trades of different duration. The total annual training capacity of the TTCs and VTIs is estimated by ILO (1999) to be roughly over 10600 workers. It is also learnt that the TTCs are willing to organize training programmes for the retrenched workers in the trades in which they specialize. While the TTCs may be used to offer short-term training courses, they need financial assistance to upgrade their facilities, meet additional costs and provide income support to the retrenched workers.

Among other publicly owned training facilities, Directorate of Youth Development (DYD) under the Ministry of Youth and Sports has training centres located in all upazila headquarters throughout Bangladesh. They are currently offering training courses in various trades of different duration primarily to the unemployed youth. The DYD also administers donor funded micro-credit programmes for poverty alleviation.

The Bangladesh Small and Cottage Industries Corporation (BSCIC), the key public sector agency responsible for promotion and development of small and cottage industries in Bangladesh provides entrepreneurship and skill development training to managers, artisans and craftsmen, skilled and unskilled workers, bank officials and potential entrepreneurs through its design centres and the Small and Cottage Industries Training Institute (SCITI). The SCITT offers skill development training in 8 different trades from 14 different locations outside Dhaka. Like the TTCs, the BSCIC which has an annual training capacity of roughly 5000 workers is also willing to participate in the retrenched workers' training programmes at a modest training fee of only Tk. 400 per month per worker.

The Directorate of Women's Affairs under the Ministry of Women's Affairs, the Textile Directorate under the Ministry of Textiles and the Bangladesh Institute of Management (BIM) under the Ministry of Industries are the other major public sector training institutes which offer different types of training from various locations in and outside Dhaka.

In addition, the private sector organizations and NGOs also play important roles in offering vocational training facilities. According to ILO (1999) estimates, there are 126 private, 133 NGOs and 8 trust institutions which currently offer vocational training courses in both engineering and non-engineering trades of wide varieties and of different durations. Thus, depending on the different types of training needs (i.e. training for re-employment, conversion training, and training for self and wage employment etc.), the existing training facilities and training capacities of both public and private sector/NGO training institutes can be profitably used for retraining of the retrenched workers.

4.5 Future social safety net programmes for the retrenched workers

The Ministry of Labour, Government of Bangladesh, has set up a "Special Workers' Fund" (SWF) by allocating Tk., 150 million (or roughly US $ 3.0 million) for retraining and redeployment of the retrenched workers in Bangladesh. The amount has been earmarked in the national budget 1998/1999 and is currently under consideration by the Ministry of Finance for final approval.

Based on data on the current cost of training in both public and private sectors (for upto a period of six months) the cost of training per person has been estimated to be Tk. 10,000 (or US $ 200). In addition, a cost of Tk. 5000 (or US $ 100) per worker has been estimated for meeting the expenses of other support services (i.e. registration, career and vocational guidance, job placement, credit support, technical assistance etc.), the total retraining and redeployment cost has been worked out to be Tk. 15,000 (or US $ 300) per worker. Thus the government allocation of Tk. 150 million should be adequate to defray the training expenses of an average number of 15,000 workers per annum for several years. Further, if it is assumed that all retrenched workers will require training of much less shorter duration than 6 months and many will require simple counseling and no training, then it may be possible to serve the retaining and redeployment needs of between 10,000 to 20,000 workers. Given the rate of retrenchment of the past few years and also the future potential rates, an estimated yearly retraining provision of approximately 4000 workers per annum also seems reasonable. However, the provision of retraining may have to be expanded substantially if the pace of privatization increases substantially and hence the number of potential retrainees reaches an estimated 90,000 worker within the next two to three years. Even then, the total cost of retraining the dismissed workers would perhaps be much less and hence (cost-effective) compared to subsidies that need to be paid to the loss-making SOEs and also counter balance the adverse consequences of loss of jobs. This however remains to be verified through careful and systematic research in the area.

In order to avoid the rigid and bureaucratic public sector structure and ensure adequate operational flexibility the SWF is proposed to have a tripartite structure including representatives of the Government, trade unions and the employers' association. The involvement of a tripartite framework will also ensure linkage between the employers and the needs of the retrenched workers. While establishment of a separate organization may be desirable to undertake responsibility of implementation of the SWF, it may be expensive. Hence, given the limited availability of funds, a government department, i.e. the BMET, within the Ministry of Labour may be given the responsibility of administering it through a Board of Directors headed by the Minister (as Chairman) of the concerned line Ministry with members from other relevant government departments, trade unions, employers' associations, private sector and NGOs.

However, retraining and redeployment programme to be successful needs to be supported by pro-active labour market policies aimed at improving and facilitating employability of the retrenched workers and assisting them in finding new jobs. In this context, the ILO (1999) proposals for introduction of "Industrial Adjustment Services" (IAS) scheme and creation of a "Labour Pool" etc. appear quite interesting and useful as strategies for effective redeployment of the displaced workers.[1]

Finally, retraining is undoubtedly important but not sufficient as a social safety net measure to protect the interest of the displaced workers. At the same time, it is also important to look at the demand aspects of the labour market, e.g. its labour absorption capacity. Along with implementation of appropriate macroeconomic policies to achieve higher rate (at least in the range of 6 to 7 per cent per annum) of overall economic growth, the Government of Bangladesh has to encourage growth of certain dynamic and potentially dynamic industrial sectors in the export-led and domestic market-oriented small scale industries (i.e. ready-made garments, downstream production of jute articles, leather goods, food processing, software, electronics, light engineering goods, livestock rearing and dairy products, handicrafts etc.). Such initiative has to be taken by adopting appropriate policies and strategies on the basis of price and non-price incentive measures to ensure employment-augmenting as opposed to capital-deepening growth.[2]

5. Conclusions and recommendations

Under the current socio-economic, political and environmental realities, rapid privatization is an inescapable necessity for Bangladesh. Notwithstanding successive divestments, roughly

---

[1] The "IAS" provides financial incentives to businesses, organizations, committees and sector groups to help employers and workers jointly meet the challenges in adjustment to industrial change. Its focus is on the development of preventive measures through joint consultation between the management and the workers so that the situation may be dealt with before it becomes problematic. The concept of "Labour Pool"(LP) envisages the establishment of a separate institution which functions like an employment service office to help train and employ the redundant employees by providing essential services to the retrenched workers and arranging operational contract with the old companies to manage employment opportunities for all their retrenched workers.

[2] For details on the relevant promotional policies and strategies required to encourage growth and expansion of the dynamic labour industries, see ILO (1999).

220 SOEs continue to exist and operate in the public sector causing excessive fiscal burden to the tune of US $ 500 million worth of revenue losses annually in a resource poor country and also posing negative externalities to the entire industrial sector in terms of a depressed economic performance.The predicament of the economy and society is well understood by all quarters and in recognition, the political support for privatization in Bangladesh is at present much stronger than any time before. To expedite the privatization process the Government, at least in principle, seems to have put all its weight behind the privatization programme by establishing the Privatization Board (PB) and also declaring a Privatization Policy. But despite being a front-runner in carrying out the privatization process, the overall achievement in privatizing the SOEs has not been impressive. An inquiry into the current privatization experience reveals that the pace of privatization has not only slowed down it has remained practically stalled. Over the last three years only 3 to 4 small factories (i.e. ice, cold storage, pulse mills) were privatized involving a sales revenue worth US $ 2.0 million, although the World Bank gave a target for divesting 18 SOEs. To expedite the privatization process, most experts opine that there should be grading of the identified SOEs into at least three categories: (i) those with heavy long-term debt liabilities and being currently economically unviable should be straight away liquidated to avoid incurring further losses; (ii) those which are making profits and growing and expanding should be tendered for sale and (iii) those which can be made profitable and viable should be restructured through enhancing the operational and managerial efficiency and then put on sale.

A host of limitations and constraints, such as, absence of a clear cut and strategic privatization policy mandated by various social groups, lack of political determination, absence of an efficient institutional framework, adequate legal back-up, complicated bureaucratic procedures and interferences, inadequate transparency of the procedures, trade union and workers' opposition, deteriorating law and order situation and lack of potential buyers' interest etc., are identified as the important bottlenecks inhibiting the progress of privatization in Bangladesh. The implication is that to enable the privatization process to make serious headway important reforms and reorganizations at both policy and institutional levels have to be carried out including procedural simplification, strengthening of PB by giving it more power and autonomy and improvements in the legal framework.

More importantly, it must be recognized without pretension that privatization is a political exercise and not only an economic one. To make desired progress, what is needed in Bangladesh is "political courage and initiative" in addition to "political willingness and commitment". Some of the stakeholders interviewed suggested that to dispel the disbelief and mistrust among the potential buyers, the right step would be to privatize first and think of restructuring of the SOEs later. Yet another suggestion made was that the 1972 Presidential Order of Nationalization of Industries should be immediately amended to increase private sector buyers' confidence.

Available evidence on the effects of privatization suggest that the economic performance of the privatized units after divestiture has at best been mixed, there being cases of both good and bad performances. However, privatization itself does not guarantee overnight improvements in the economic efficiency of the divested units, especially if they are loss-making enterprises and do not have an overal macroeconomic environment conducive to private enterprise growth. Further, the process of privatization is not without some cost, and hence the expectation must be kept within reasonable limits.

As to the labour issue, there has been an average rate of 20-25 per cent retrenchment of labour after divestiture primarily aimed at downsizing the pre-divestiture burden of overmanning to improve labour productivity. While closure of many privatized units after divestiture has added to the problem of employment loss with adverse effects on labour welfare, the Government of Bangladesh has attempted to safeguard workers' interests by offering "golden handshake" and arranging for retraining of the displaced workers. Reflecting the willingness to protect the interests of the workers, the Government of Bangladesh has also set up SWF to implement successful retrenchment and redeployment initiatives. The SWF is a step in the right direction and if implemented effectively, it will go a long way in safeguarding workers' interests and welfare and provide required support to the desired progress of the privatization process.

In addition to the safety net measures, the Government needs to launch a vigorous public awareness campaign before going for large-scale privatization. The key objective of such a campaign will be to get popular mandate from the opposition political parties and representatives of the workers, employers and civil society, and motivate the workers about the long-term beneficial effects of privatization and thereby dispel their basic concerns. They should be told that some job cuts and wage cuts would be necessary for saving and generating a large number of jobs in future. To gain support and confidence of the labourers, the gains to be expected and the safety net measures to be instituted should be clearly spelt out.

Annex 1

Table A-1: Size and importance of the SOEs in Bangladesh, end-1997/98 (Tk. in million)

Corporations	No. of enterprises	Fixed assets	Sales	No. of employees
Manufacturing / Industry	121	87114	19940	149724
Electricity, Gas and Water	13	145425	37665	39158
Transport and communication	8	25434	18580	26234
Trade / Commercial	10	3773	50394	3996
Agriculture and Fisheries	18	998	472	2705
Construction Sector	4	8220	277	1294
Services /Others	44	31871	7836	16720
Grand Total	218	302835	135164	239831

Source: Monitoring Cell, Ministry of Finance, GOB.

Table A-2: Types of industrial enterprises privatized during 1972-96

Type of enterprise	No. of privatized industries in different periods				
	1972-75	1975-81	1981-86	1991-96	Total
Rice and Flour Mills	20	21	8	-	49
Vegetable Oil	5	21	12	-	38
Food Products	-	5	3	-	8
Ice and Cold Storage	-	7	5	-	12
Sugar and Food	-	-	-	1	1
Textile	11	21	27	6	65
Jute Products	-	9	35	-	44
Wood Products	3	9	-	-	12
Rubber Products	-	16	1	-	17
Tanneries and Bones	-	25	5	-	30
Chemicals	4	-	-	4	8
Soaps and Chemicals	-	7	12	-	19
Glass and Optical	-	3	1	-	4
Paper and Printing	8	7	2	-	17
Engineering and Steel	12	8	10	2	32
Metal Works	7	25	5	-	37
Film	-	3	1	-	4
Hotels	-	2	1	-	3
Trading	-	3	6	-	9
Others	50	63	88	-	201
Total	120 (19.6)	255 (41.8)	222 (36.3)	13 (2.1)	610

Source: Adapted from ILO (1999).

Annex 2

List of stakeholders interviewed

Ahmed, Dr. Chowdhury Saleh
Director General
Monitoring Cell (Finance Division)
Ministry of Finance
Government of Bangladesh

Alam, Dr. Khurshid
World Bank, Dhaka

Ferdousi, Mr. Shawkat Ali
Associate Professor
IBA, Dhaka University

Haque, Dr. Shamsul
Professor
Institute of Business Administration IBA,
Dhaka University

Hossain, Mr. Md. Shawkat
Deputy Secretary, Ministry of Labour
Government of Bangladesh

Jafar, Mr. Shah Md. Abu
President, National Workers Federation

Khan, Mr. Md. Nazrul Islam
General Secretaqry, Jatioytabadi Sramik Dal

Rahman, Mr. M. KH.
President,
Dhaka Chamber of Commerceand Industry (DCCI)

Rahman, Mr. Gazi Mahbubur
In-Charge
Jute Sector Adjustment Credit
Ministry of Jute
Government of Bangladesh
Adamjee Court

Rabnbi, Mr. Reza-e
Joint Secretary
Ministry of Labour
Government of Bangladesh

Rao, Dr. Narahari
Senior Economist
Asian Development Bank

Quashem, A
President,
Bangladesh Employees Association (BEA),
Dhaka

Zafarullah, Kazi
Chairman (State Minister) Privatization Board
Government of Bangladesh

Zakaria, S. M.
Member, Privatization Board
Government of Bangladesh

Annex 3

List of trades in which retraining has been arranged

Sl. No.   Name of Courses designed and offered

1.   Integrated Horticulture Development
2.   Bamboo and Cane Handicrafts
3.   Integrated Pest Management
4.   Rickshaw Van Repair
5.   Dahi & Cheese
6.   Tailoring
7.   Village Mechanic
8.   Radio / TV Mechanic
9.   Carpentry
10.   Plumbing
11.   Basic Welding
12.   Integrated Seed Production
13.   Block Printing
14.   Screen Printing
15.   Masonry / Boat Making
16.   House Wiring
17.   Auto Mechanic
18.   Apiculture & Candle Making
19.   ED & Business Management
20.   Jute Handicrafts
21.   Ornamental Plant and Flower Gardening
22.   Pisciculture
23.   Poultry
24.   Horticulture & Nursery Development
25.   Farm Machine Operator
26.   GeneralMechanic
27.   Rural Masonry
28.   Irrigation &Pump Operator
29.   Rod Binding
30.   Cultivation of Mushroom
31.   Bamboo and Cane Cultivation
32.   Fish-cum Duc Farming
33.   Dairy Cattle
34.   Fattening of Cattle / Goat and Sheep Farming
35.   Driving

Bibliograply

Ahmed Momtaz Uddin et.al. (1999): *Promotion of Private Investment for Industrial Development in Bangladesh: Implications for Public Administration Reform*, Report prepared for PARC, Dhaka.

Akram, T. (1999): "Public Enterprise Inefficiency and the Road to Privatization in Bangladesh", mimeo, CPD, Dhaka.

Akash, M.M. et.al. (1999): *Outcomes of Privatization: The Search for A Policy*, mimeo, CPD, Dhaka.

Asian Development Bank (ADB), (1985): *Privatization – Policies, Methods and Procedures*, Manila, Philippines.

Bhuyan, A. R. et. al. (1993): *Trade Regimes and Industrial Growth – A Case of Bangladesh*, ICED and Bureau of Economic Research, Dhaka University

Dowlah, C. F. (1998): *Privatization Experience in Bangladesh, 1991-1996,* A study undertaken for the World Bank, Dhaka.

Government of Bangladesh, Ministry of Planning, Planning Division (1978) First Five Year Plan (1973-1978), Dhaka.

Haque, S. (1999)*: Privatization of SOEs in Bangladesh: A study on Recent Experiences,* Draft prepared for World Bank, Dhaka.

International Labour Organization (ILO), (1999): *Retraining and Redeployment of Workers Affected by Privatization in Bangladesh,* ILO, Geneva.

Liberman, W. I. (1993): "Privatization: The Theme of the 1990s" *Columbia Journal of World Business,* Vol. 28, No.1.

Megginson W.L. (1998): "The Impact of Privatization" *Economic Report To-day, No.1.*

Mondal, R. (1998): "Privatization – A Global Perspective" paper presented at RAPPORT Seminar on Privatization in Bangladesh, during 19-20 March.

Mondal, W.I. (1997): "Privatization and the Growth of Entrepreneurship in Bangladesh", paper presented at the Seminar organized by the Centrte for Development Research Bangladesh (CDRB), December, Dhaka.

Privatization Board, (1998): *Privatization in Bangladesh,* April 12, Dhaka.

——, (1996): *Privatization Policy,* September, Dhaka.

Satter, Z. (1997): *Macroeconomic Impacts of Privatization Programme in Bangladesh,* an unpublished paper presented at the ADB Workshop in Dhaka, 9 July.

Sen Binayak (1997): *Whither Privatization : Results of an Exploratory Survey of the Disinvested Industries in Bangladesh, mimeo,* BIDS, Dhaka.

Sobhan, R. (1985): "Disinvestment and Denationalization Profiled Performance", The Bangladesh Journal of Political Economy, Vol. 6, No. 2.

Tanweer, A., (1998): *Problems of Privatization and Policy Options,* Working Paper, CPD, Dhaka, June.

World Bank, (1993): *Bangladesh – Implementing Structural Reform,* Dhaka.

——, (1994): *Bangladesh –Privatization and Adjustment,* Dhaka.

3

Privatization in India*

Privatization of public enterprises has generated much debate in developing economies, which had previously opted for planning as a strategy and system for national socio-economic development. Under the Five Year Plans, the Indian state took upon herself the responsibility to undertake investments in basic and strategic economic activities and to control and direct private sector through a network of regulatory institutions. After pursuance of planned development for nearly half a century, a stage was reached when questions were raised about the relevance and the need to continue the planned development strategy. There is an ideological position that asserts to 'end all direct and indirect state interventions in the economy'. The state should, according to this viewpoint, roll back and occupy the minimum possible space. The market forces instead of the arbitrary decisions undertaken by bureaucrats and politicians should decide all economic decisions. The contrary viewpoint is that since the Indian economy is ridden with extreme disparities in incomes, wealth and consumption, macroeconomic decisions cannot be left to the operation of the free market system. Third World economies suffer from so many socio-economic limitations that it is obligatory on part of the state to operate from the 'commanding heights' and aim at the highest level of socio-economic good for the largest numbers.

1. The concept

Privatization, in its broader sense, stands for policies to reduce the role of the state, assign larger role for the private sector pursuing the logic of the market in all economic decisions. Viewed in this perspective departure from the policy of reservations of certain economic activities for exclusive development by the public sector (dereservation) implies a reduction in the relative position of the state sector and larger role for the private sector. The entry of new private sector enterprises could introduce competition where public sector enjoyed monopoly. The existing public enterprises (PSEs) would be forced to go commercial and respond to the market discipline. The dereservation process has sometimes been described as 'Parallelization' in the privatization framework. Privatization is also witnessed when governments take a decision to reduce their obligations to regulate and direct the behaviour of private actors in the economy. Pursuance of deregulation policies is aimed to make the

---

* The paper was presented by Prof. S.K. Goyal on behalf of Institute for Studies in Industrial Development, New Delhi.

restrictive regulatory system less important. In India, deregulation would imply loosening such statutes like the Industries (Development & Regulation) Act, 1951 (IDRA), Monopolies & Restrictive Trade Practices Act, 1969, (MRTPA), Foreign Exchange regulation Act, 1973 (FERA), Capital Issues Control and technical scrutiny by the Directorate General of Technical Development (DGTD).

Privatization, however, is most often associated with transfer of public sector enterprises and services to private ownership, management and control. The privatization process for public enterprises can involve steps ranging from dilution of state-held equity, to adoption of practices like franchising, award of lease and management contracts, sub-contracting of select activities and tasks, down-sizing of workforce, and changes in the process of decision-making even without change in ownership, so that business decisions are guided by market and commercial principles of profit maximisation than vague societal concerns.

Privatization in Inida has been carried out in several stages; such as, deregulation, dereservation, privatisation and disinvestment. These are discussed in the subsequent sections.

1.1 Deregulation

Under the Indian planning system public sector investments are financed through financial allocations by the government. While there were no administrative restrictions on cottage, village and small scale industries most large investment proposals by the private sector have had to pass through the scrutiny by a multiple of regulatory agencies. The most important scrutiny being at the stage of the grant of the industrial license. Under the Industries (Development and Regulation) Act, 1951 (IDRA) new investment proposals have to be processed from the viewpoint of national priority, location, expected demands on scarce national resources and from the viewpoint of concentration of economic power by way of product and financial monopoly. The Mahalanobis Committee was the first official body to point out that contrary to the Directive Principles of State Policy of the Constitution of India, the Indian economic system in general had helped only a few and there were indications of growing concentration in the economy.[1] The Monopolies Inquiry Commission (MIC) and the Industrial Licensing Policy Inquiry Committee (ILPIC) provided an extensive empirical base to understand the trends. The two reports brought out the built-in weaknesses of the Indian regulatory mechanism because of which a few powerful business interests could flourish rapidly.[2] The operation of the regulatory system was periodically reviewed and it was on the advise of expert committees that the late sixties and early seventies witnessed efforts at tightening of the regulatory system. The Monopolies and Restrictive Trade Practices Act, (MRTPA) was enacted in 1969. Substantial changes were introduced in the industrial policy in 1970 to restrict areas open to large monopoly houses and foreign subsidiaries. The Foreign

---

[1] India, Planning Commission, *Committee on Distribution of Income and Levels of Living: Report*, 1964. (Chairman P.C. Mahalanobis).

[2] See: India, *Report of the Monopolies Inquiry Commission,* 1965 (Chairman: K.C. Dasgupta) and India, *Report of the Industrial Licensing Policy Inquiry Committee,* 1969 (Chairman: S. Dutt).

Exchange Regulation Act, 1973 (FERA) sought to limit the level of foreign equity in Indian companies at 40 per cent.[1]

Operation of the MRTPA also suffered from major weaknesses. Inadequate criteria for determining composition of large business houses had the consequence that many of the close business associates were left outside the Act's ambit. The government also denied the Commission an effective role by retaining to itself the power of reference and by progressively expanding the scope of industrial activity open to large houses.[2] The FERA had a similar fate. The Act placed the upper limit on foreign equity in a company at 40 per cent. The FERA proved to be a misplaced legislation on two counts: one, dividend outgo formed only a small portion of total foreign exchange remittances of foreign controlled companies; and two, in the process of equity dilution, the quantum of foreign equity instead of declining, increased substantially and foreign controlled companies expanded faster by availing the liberal licensing provisions offered to non-FERA companies. The objective of 'indianisation', also failed because foreign companies could retain control over their Indian associates through non-equity forms.[3]

Due to conceptual and structural weaknesses of law combined with poor administrative support and absence of political will, the Indian regulatory system failed to achieve the desired objectives. The private sector continued to enjoy freedom that was very different from what the existence of the plethora of regulations suggests. For instance, the large private sector did not strictly adhere to the restrictions placed on production capacities under the IDRA. The installed capacities and actual production had little relationship to the licensed capacities.[4] Most policies with regard to the small-scale sector were violated without any fear of penalty as large companies directly owned small-scale units, produced in excess of their licensed capacities in the case of small scale reserved items and circumvented the small scale reservation policy in a variety of ways.[5] How weak was the regulatory mechanism is reflected in the fact that there was not even a single case of conviction for violation of the system during nearly four decades of its existence.

---

[1]   Relaxations were, however, allowed for high technology and export oriented companies and certain activities like, shipping, banking and airlines.

[2]   See: S.K. Goyal, *Monopoly Capital and Public Policy*, Allied Publishers, Delhi, 1979.

[3]   See: S.K. Goyal, *Impact of Foreign Subsidiaries on India's Balance of Payments*, Indian Institute of Public Administration, Delhi (mimeo), 1979. The study was prepared for the UNCTC-ESCAP Joint Unit, Bangkok. This issue was also examined empirically in Sudip Chaudhuri, "FERA: Appearance and Reality", *Economic and Political Weekly*, April 21, 1979, pp. 734-744 and Sudip Chaudhuri, "Financing of Growth of Transnational Corporations in India: 1956-75", *Economic and Political Weekly*, August 18, 1979, pp. 1431-35. For a detailed presentation of the non-equity forms of control employed by foreign companies see: S.K. Goyal, "The New International Economic Order and Transnational Corporations", in ICSSR and Institute for Social Science Research in Developing Countries, *New International Economic Order: Problems and Perspectives*, 1983.

[4]   See: S.K. Goyal, et. al., *Functioning of Industrial Licensing System*, Indian Institute of Public Administration, Delhi, (mimeo) 1983.

[5]   See: S.K. Goyal, et. al., *Small Scale Sector and Big Business*, Indian Institute of Public Administration, Delhi, (mimeo) 1984.

The process of deregulation was initiated in the mid-seventies as a follow up of the recommendations of a series of committees which examined India's trade and industrialisation policies in the context of the country's poor export performance.[1] Further, the Industrial Policy Statement of 1980 allowed automatic enhancement in licensed capacities and regularisation of the excess capacities established in contravention of the then existing laws.[2] The eighties witnessed another series of Committees which provided a justification for further deregulation of the industrial sector.[3] In 1985 and 1986 major relaxations were allowed through broad banding, partial delicensing, re-endorsement of capacities, enlargement of the list of industries open for MRTPA/FERA companies, exempting MRTPA companies from the obligation of seeking approval under the MRTP Act in case of 27 high technology and heavy investment industries, etc. Exemption limits under the Capital Issues Control Act, 1947 were also enhanced to free a large number of companies from seeking approval under the Act.

The Statement on Industrial Policy, 1991 (IPS 1991) and other measures announced during the year marked acceleration of the trends towards deregulation and an enlarged scope for large private Indian and foreign capital. IPS 1991 virtually abandoned the industrial licensing system under the IDRA, removed restrictions on large industrial houses under the MRTP Act and dispensed with the general ceiling of 40 per cent on foreign equity under FERA. The policy mix included increasing external competition through lowering of customs duties and relaxations in the quantitative restrictions. This was followed by dismantling of the Directorate General of Trade and Development (DGTD) and the repeal of Capital Issues Control Act, 1947. Thus, the process of freeing the private sector from regulations and enabling it to respond to market forces was nearly complete. Government's response to the

---

[1]   The prominent ones are: India, Ministry of Commerce, *Report of the Committee on Engineering Exports*, 1974 (Chairman: Mantosh Sondhi); India, Ministry of Commerce, *Report of the Committee on Import-Export Policies and* Procedures, 1978 (Chairman: P.C. Alexander); India, Ministry of Industry, *Report of the Study Group on Industrial Regulations & Procedures*, 1978 (Chairman: G.V. Ramakrishna); and India, Ministry of Commerce, *Report of the Committee on Export Strategy: 1980s,* Final Report, 1980 (Chairman: P.L. Tandon). Relaxations to the industrial licensing policy included diversification into related areas of production, re-endorsement of capacities on the basis of maximum utilisation of plant and machinery, recognizing capacity increases arising out of modernisation and replacement of equipment, automatic increases in licensed capacities and exemption from industrial licensing for medium level entrepreneurs.

[2]   For a description and empirical assessment of the changes in the industrial licensing policy in the early 'eighties, see: S.K. Goyal, "A Preliminary Survey of Excess Industrial Capacities with the Indian Corporate Sector (Some Implications of Industrial Policy Statement of July 23, 1980", 1980 and S.K. Goyal, "New Industrial Licensing Policy – An Empirical Assessment", 1982. Both are working papers of the Corporate Studies Group, Indian Institute of Public Administration, Delhi.

[3]   Mention can be made in this regard of: India, Ministry of Commerce, *Committee on Free Trade Zones and 100 per cent Export Oriented Units,* Final Report, 1982 (Chairman: P.L. Tandon); India, Ministry of Commerce, *Report of the Committee on Trade Policies,* 1984 (Chairman: Abid Hussain); India, Ministry of Commerce, *Report of the Committee on Perspective Plan and Strategy for Export of Engineering and Capital Goods,* 1984 (Chairman: D.V. Kapur); and India, Ministry of Finance, *Report of the Committee to Examine Principles of a Possible Shift from Physical to Financial Controls,* 1985 (Chairman: M. Narasimham).

shortcomings of the regulatory system was in winding it up. The alternative policy choice could be in affecting administrative reforms and system's genuine restructuring. This remains unattended.

1.2 Dereservation

IPS 1991 announced a number of important steps with regard to the public sector. The areas reserved for the public sector under Schedule A to the Industrial Policy Resolution, 1956 were reduced, initially from seventeen to eight, and later to four. The remaining four areas related to defence equipment, atomic energy and associated minerals, and railway transport (Table 3.1). Schedule B in which public sector was to play the lead role was entirely dispensed with to enable greater private sector participation and to provide competition to the PSEs.[1] Following the dereservation of public sector reserved areas, a number of local and foreign companies received approvals for entry into the energy and telecommunication sectors. A few well-known foreign entrants are: Enron Corp., Cogentrix, AES Transpower, Rolls Royce, Powergen, Bell, British Telecom, AT&T, US West, Deutsche Telekom, Nippon Telegraph, etc.[2] Similarly, in the financial sector changes have been made to permit entry of new private banks and private mutual funds. The private sector entrants in the financial sector include Global Trust Bank, Indusind Bank, Times Bank and Bank of Punjab. The new policy has also come handy for the public sector financial institutions to set up commercial banks like IDBI Bank, ICICI Bank and UTI Bank. The mutual funds segment which was once the preserve of public sector has been opened to the private sector and it has already attracted well known foreign fund operators like Morgan Stanley, Jardine Fleming, Templeton and Merril Lynch. The efforts at private sector entry into the insurance sector are under way.

The entry of private sector into the erstwhile public sector reserved areas is bound to introduce a certain degree of competition. This could help, in the first phase, meet shortages due to which the consumers and the society at large suffered. For instance, privatization of bus routes in Delhi did help commuters in a significant manner. The same is true of the aviation industry. In the aviation sector an improvement has been noticed in the quality of

---

[1] Dereservation has been accompanied by promotion of joint ventures by Central PSEs. For instance, the joint ventures between Indian Oil Corpn. (IOC) and Mobil, and IBP and Caltex are significant. IOC is pursuing a refinery joint venture with Kuwait Petroleum. Similarly, Hindustan Petroleum and Bharat Petroleum have planned a joint venture with Oman Oil Co.

[2] A question, however, arises whether the 'Indian' private sector has come of age and is ready to take up the responsibilities from the public sector. If the 'Indian' private sector is not in a position, then an alternative to public sector could be in the large foreign private corporations. It has been noticed that the opening up of public sector reserved areas has already attracted a good number of transnational corporations (TNCs) to enter into critical economic sectors. TNCs are not known to bring much of investible resources in the long-term framework. TNCs operating in the Third World continue to remain dependent upon their parent companies for technology and guidance on the one hand and are susceptible to home government influences. Acquiring control over crucial sectors as a result of privatization could, therefore, have long term implications. See: S.K. Goyal, *Impact of Foreign Subsidiaries on India's Balance of Payments*, *op. cit.*

Table 3.1: Changes in reservation policy towards public sector

Under the Industrial Policy Resolution, 1956	Under the Statement on Industrial Policy, 1991
1. Arms and ammunition and allied items of defence equipments.	1. Arms and ammunition and allied items of equipment, defence aircraft and warships.
2. Atomic energy.	2. Atomic energy.
3. Iron and steel.	
4. Heavy castings and forgings of iron and steel.	
5. Heavy plant and machinery required for iron and steel production, for mining, for machine tool manufacture and for such other basic industries as may be specified by the Central Government.	
6. Heavy electrical plant including large hydraulic and steam turbines.	
7. Coal and lignite	3. Coal and lignite.
8. Mineral oils.	4. Mineral oils.
9. Mining of iron ore, manganese ore, chrome ore, gypsum, sulphur, gold and diamond.	5. Mining of iron ore, manganese ore, chrome ore, gypsum, sulpher, gold and diamond.
10. Mining and processing of copper, lead, zinc, tin, molybdenum and wolfram.	6. Mining of copper, lead, zinc, tin, molybdenum and wolfram.
11. Minerals specified in the Schedule to the Atomic Energy (Control of Production and Use) Order, 1953.	7. Minerals specified in the Schedule to the the Atomic Energy (Control of Production and Use) Order, 1953#
12. Aircraft.	
13. Air Transport.	
14. Railway Transport.	8. Railway Transport.
15. Shipbuilding.	
16. Telephones and telephone cables, telegraphs and wireless apparatus (excluding radio receiving sets).	
17. Generation and distribution of electricity.	

Note: Items struck off in Col. (2) are no longer reserved for the public sector.

\#   The nomenclature changed to: "Substances specified in the schedule to the Deparment of Atomic Energy notification No. S.O.212(E) dated 15-03-1995".

ground and cabin services. The entry of global players in the banking sector may bring in a number of new and more consumer friendly banking services. There is reason to believe that privatization of power distribution could cut down on electricity leakages and the new power projects may help bridge the gap in demand and supply. The tariff implications of privatization, however, have yet to be seen. To the extent privatization in the power sector helps meet the demands of the Indian industry it may help improve industrial production and other economic activities which need stable and regular power supply. The same holds true of other public sector reserved areas wherein demand was far in excess of the supply or the areas in which there have been marked developments in technology and the earlier argument of 'natural monopoly' is no more relevant. One such area is communications.

2. Context of Privatization

Soon after the initiation of development planning in India it became evident that the public sector was an economic necessity for the economy and the private sector.[1] Public sector was envisaged as a major instrument for pursuance of plan targets. It was universally accepted that the Indian private sector was neither capable of making the necessary large investments nor was it expected to take up projects with long gestation periods and carrying low rates of return. Industrial Policy Resolution, 1956 reserved a large sector both for exclusive (Schedule A) and priority (Schedule B) development by the public sector. The government took upon herself the task of providing essential infrastructure and utilities as also heavy industries. This process was aided by nationalisation of certain sectors and selected undertakings. By mid-seventies public sector accounted for a little less than one-fifth of the GDP and nearly half of the Gross Capital Formation (GCF). In the organized industrial sector, it accounted for about two-thirds of the fixed capital invested.[2] In certain industries public sector acquired a dominating position, often accounting for ownership and production to the extent of near 100 per cent.

Public sector in India has two main forms. One, the departmentally owned and managed establishments like railways, posts, telecommunication, irrigation, and power projects; and two, enterprises established under the Companies Act, 1956 and under special statutes. At the end of 1992, there were 1,180 undertakings in which government owned majority equity capital and which were categorised as government companies. Of these, the Central government undertakings numbered 239. While in numbers the Central PSEs accounted for only a fifth of the total, these accounted for nearly 85 per cent of the overall risk capital and assets of the PSEs organised as joint stock companies. The State-owned PSEs were 941.[3] The central government manufacturing companies accounted for 41.12 per cent, and those engaged in mining and quarrying for 28.62 per cent of the total PUC. Combined with

[1] See: S.K. Goyal, "Spectrum of Public Sector in India", in Shastri Indo-Canadian Institute, *Issues in Public Sector Analysis*, 1987.

[2] Share of public sector was 18.82 per cent and 51.34 per cent of GDP and GCF in 1976-77. While the share in GDP continued to increase, the share in GCF fluctuated but continued to remain high. In mid-'eighties its share in GCF was more than half of the total while that in GDP reached one-fourth. See: Centre for Monitoring Indian Economy, *India's National Income Statistics*, October 1996. The share in fixed capital was based on the *Annual Survey of Industries, Factory Sector* for 1978-79.

[3] Based on the data provided in India, Department of Company Affairs, *Registrations and Liquidations of Joint Stock Companies in India, 1993-94*. Included under the State total were three companies promoted jointly by the state and Central governments. The publication was suspended after the 1994-95 issue.

electricity and water the three sectors accounted for nearly 90 per cent of the risk capital of Central public sector companies. The State sector had a different pattern of activities. In their case, manufacturing accounted for nearly one-third, agriculture and forestry a little more than one-quarter, and finance and business nearly 20 per cent. In the present study we are not attempting to review the State enterprises for reason of time available with us as also due to the lesser significance of State PSEs in the national set up.

Public sector has been an important employer, especially in the organised labour market. The sector accounted for 56.84 per cent of the total number of 14.3 million workers in the organised sector[1] in 1980-81. From about 8.1 million in 1980-81, those employed in public sector manufacturing increased to 9.8 million by 1990-91. In spite of the efforts at downsizing workforce by public sector during the nineties, the number of workers remained at 9.8 million at the end of 1996-97. During the nineties, its share in total hovered around 60 per cent. (Figure 3.1)

Figure 3.1
Public sector employment[#]

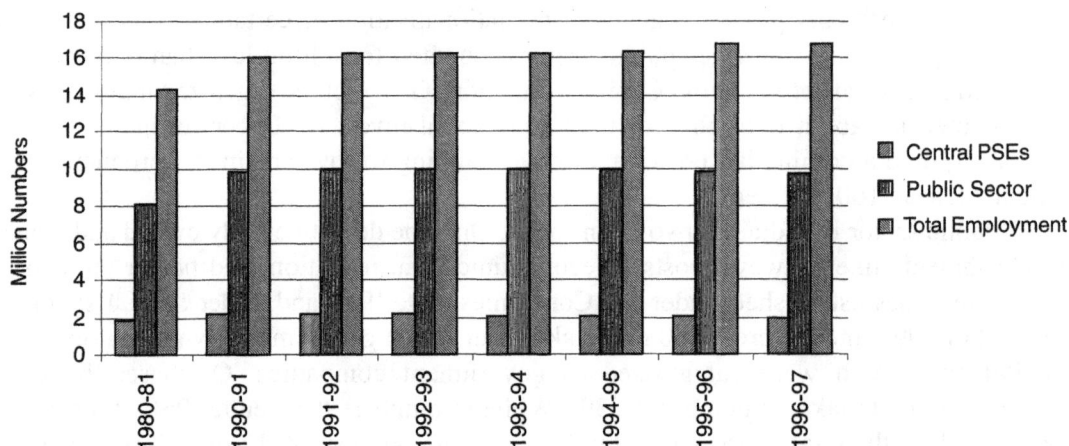

Excluding Community, Social and Personal Services.
Source: Cols. (2) & (3) India, Ministry of Finance, Economic Survey, 1998-99. Col. (6) Department of Public Enterprises, Public Enterprises Survey, various years.

Central PSEs employed about 2.0 million persons during the nineties. Most of the central PEs are large-sized and multi-plant undertakings with nation-wide spread of activities. As a national policy public sector has helped emergence of a strong trade union base in the country. Exercise of personal discretion in matters of labour is extremely low in PSEs

[1] This is after excluding community, social and personal services from the total employment in the organised sector. The sectors covered are: Mining & Quarrying; Manufacturing; Electricity, Gas & Water Supply; Wholesale & Retail Trade; Transport, Storage & Communications; Finance, Insurance, Real Estate, etc.; and Agriculture & Hunting.

especially when compared to the private sector. Public sector establishments invariably provide housing, health, and education facilities to families of their workers. Conditions of employment are more stable and just. One does not need to spell out the merit of being an employee with well-protected rights in a PSE. In the background of the extent and variety of worker protection in public sector, there may be apprehensions among public sector workers regarding the benefits they may receive once public sector enterprises are privatized.

Public sector in India follows the same policy of preferences in employment for women and the underprivileged sections of the society as the government. The underprivileged categories are based on socio-economic considerations like membership of Scheduled Castes and Tribes, backward classes, weaker sections, women and the handicapped.[1] As on 1 January, 1998 workers belonging to the Scheduled Castes and Tribes constituted 26.83 per cent of the total employment in the Central PSEs (CPSEs) (Table 3.2). An overwhelming numbers (90.89 per cent) of the Scheduled Castes and Tribes fell in Groups C and D, the lowest income levels. Among the PSE workers, more than a quarter are supposed to be belonging to Other Backward Classes (OBCs) which are known to have remained economically and socially backward and had suffered social and economic deprivation for long.

Public sector, in general, provides a larger share of employment to women workers.[2] Central PSEs employed 110,134 women who accounted for 5.72 per cent of the total workers in 1997-98. (Table 3.3) Women workers are more prominent in clerical and unskilled categories. Coal & Lignite group employs 64.2 per cent of the unskilled women workers. Telecommunication Services and Coal & Lignite account for 38 per cent and 21.26 per cent respectively of the clerical category workers.

There seems to be a good deal of truth in the view that public enterprises are over-staffed. If the Indian public sector with so many facilities and employment security remained understaffed it would have been a surprise. Better emoluments and service conditions of public sector attract workers, and all possible political lobbies and pressures are employed to get a place in public sector. Under, the present pattern of employment in PSEs, while there is excess manpower at lower levels with little skills, there is invariably a shortage of specialised and skilled personnel. Skilled professionals and experienced senior workers of PSEs find an easy alternative in the private sector. This is not so for the lower wage groups and those who secured employment in the public sector on considerations of ST or SC or reservations for backward classes.

---

[1]   There is 15 per cent reservation for Scheduled castes, 7.5 per cent for Scheduled Tribes, 27 per cent for Other Backward Classes, and three per cent for Physically Handicapped persons, making a total of 52.5 per cent. These percentages are applicable to all categories of employment. In addition, in Groups C and D, there is a provision for reserving 14.5 per cent and 24.5 per cent respectively for Ex-servicemen and dependents of those killed in action. See: India, Department of Public Enterprises, *Public Enterprises Survey: 1997-98*, Volume 1, p. 175.

[2]   Public sector had 2.347 million women employees in 1990-91. By 1996-97, while the absolute number of women employees increased to 2.728 million the share of women employees in the total declined. See: India, Ministry of Finance, *Economic Survey: 1998-99*, p. S-53.

Table 3.2: Group-Wise employment of scheduled castes and scheduled tribes persons in CPSEs (as on 1.1.1998)

S.No.	Group	Total no. of workers	Representation of SCs/STs	
			Scheduled castes(SCs) %	Scheduled tribes (STs) %
1.	Group 'A'	199,682	9.56	2.62
2.	Group 'B'	164,351	10.53	3.88
3.	Group 'C'	1,122,741	18.97	8.47
4.	Group 'D' (Excl. Safai* Karamcharies)	451,320	22.57	10.86
5.	Total	1,938,094	18.12	8.04
6.	Group 'D' (Safai* Karamcharies)	26,316	73.99	2.58
7.	Grand Total	1,964,410	18.87	7.96

Source: India, Department of Public Enterprises, Public Enterprises Survey: 1997-98, Volume -1 and is based on information provided by 238 PSEs.

   * Safai Karamchari means staff for cleaning/sweeping.

Table 3.3: Employment of women in CPSEs (as on 1.1.1998)

S.No.	Category	Total number of workers	Women workers (Percentage)
1.	Managerial & Supervisory	362,902	6.50
2.	Clerical	252,085	10.05
3.	Skilled	592,854	2.26
4.	Semi-skilled	423,099	4.97
5.	Unskilled	295,987	9.05
6.	Total	1,926,927	5.72

Source: India, Department of Public Enterprises, *Public Enterprises Survey*: 1997-98,Vol-1.
Note: Excludes casual and daily rated workers.

Indian public sector has been studied extensively.The last two decades have seen frequent and loud criticism of the working and the financial performance of the sector. Criticism of the sector, in the main, has not originated from any ideological stance; it has been moulded by the observed shortcomings. In spite of the continuing monitoring and supervision by elected representatives and their bodies and periodic reports by other investigating agencies, a variety of distortions have crept into the public sector as a whole.The most frequent criticism of the public sector has been with regard to its financial losses which, it is argued, impose heavy burden on the exchequer. The inefficiencies of the PSEs, it is further argued, get passed on to the private sector which depends heavily on the public sector for supply of raw materials and infrastructure support. Factors which have been identified for the poor financial performance include: lack of managerial autonomy, excessive interference and failure of the government in meeting its obligations in time, long delays in project implementation, overstaffing, lack of motivation, indiscipline and undue demands of workers, taking onto itself losses of the private sector sick companies, burdening the sector with a variety of labour welfare schemes and social obligations[1], diversification into non-priority areas, and non-materialisation of assured developments in related industries.

The cumulative effect of the growing literature on the non-performance of the public sector has been to question the very need to continue government support to the public sector. A question asked by many scholars has been: whose interests does the Indian public sector promote? Is not it that the sector's control has passed over to a small group of politicians and bureaucrats who cannot operate the sector strictly according to the business principles. There is also a view that the public sector operations being large in size and value, expose many a responsible person to indulgence in corrupt practices and manipulations for personal profit. It is widely believed that public sector's financial performance, both in terms of return on capital invested and net profits, has been disappointing.

The government appointed a Committee in 1984 to review and suggest a policy framework for public enterprise management.[2] The Committee suggested creation of holding companies to minimise the direct interface between the government and PSEs and signing of MOUs by the two. A World Bank study of 1989 also reiterated the recommendations of the Committee and further recommended removal of purchase and price preferences and access to capital and credit on concessional terms; limiting the social obligations in terms of employment and location and compensating the PSEs for assuming them and winding up of terminally sick public sector units. These measures were to be implemented in a phased manner, with appropriate transitional measures to assist affected workers.[3] Further, the Eighth Plan Working Group on PSEs stated that:

> ... public enterprises will have to learn to adapt themselves to a much more open economy than before.... Public enterprises can no longer count on captive markets and produce without regard to cost or quality or the pattern of market demand.[4]

This was the backdrop in which the privatization of public enterprises was initiated in 1991.

---

[1] For instance, reduction of inter-regional disparities being one of the objectives set for PSEs, public sector projects were set up in under-developed areas which, besides causing other limitations, entailed setting up employee townships which increased the start up expenses.

[2] See: India, Ministry of Finance, *Report of the Committee to Review Policy for Public Enterprises*, December 1984. (Chairman: Arjun Sengupta).

[3] See: World Bank, *India: An Industrialising Economy in Transition*, A World Bank Country Study, 1989, pp. 117-118.

[4] See: India, Planning Commission, R*eport of the Eighth Plan Working Group on the Management of PSEs*, 1989, (mimeo) p. 39. (Chairman: V. Krishnamurthy).

2.1 Disinvestment as a form of privatization

The process of privatization in terms of removal of administrative controls and regulations was discussed in the preceding paras. The process is, however, more frequently associated with transfer of public enterprises to the private sector. Privatization of public enterprises could take any one of the following forms:

(i)   Divestment of government-held equity to:

(a) strategic/joint venture partners through open bidding or negotiated settlement;

(b) financial institutions (foreign, public sector and mutual funds); or

(c) general public;

(ii) Promotion of joint ventures for further expansion or through transfer of certain existing units/operations;

(iii) Entering into management contracts with private professional groups or entre preneurs;

(iv) Nomination of private individuals on Board of Directors of PSEs even when their equity is insignificant; and/or

(v)   Contractualisation of operations.

IPS 1991 proposed to review public sector investments in order to limit their coverage to strategic, high tech and essential infrastructure. The objectives of unloading government-held equity were outlined as: (a) to further market discipline, (b) raise resources, and (c) encourage wider public participation in management of PSEs.[1] Chronically sick public enterprises were proposed to be referred to the Board for Industrial and Financial Reconstruction (BIFR) for revival or reconstruction. The IPS 1991 also proposed to provide for more professionals on Management Boards of PSEs. Social safety measures were proposed to protect the interests of workers who may be affected by other steps proposed under IPS 1991.

The process of disinvestment in CPSEs was initiated soon after announcement of the IPS 91. An expert body to advise on disinvestments was constituted, though much later. Between December 1991 and February 1992, disinvestment, ranging between 5 and 20 per cent, was affected in 31 PSEs of the Department of Public Enterprises.[2] The government itself categorised the companies, whose shares were selected for disinvestment, as very good (eight), good (twelve) and not so good (eleven). The shares of these enterprises were offered

---

[1]   See: "Statement on Industrial Policy", July 24, 1991, in India, Ministry of Industry, *Handbook of Industrial Policy and Statistics: 1996.*

[2]   India, Ministry of Finance, *Economic Survey: 1992-93* explained the process. The shares were offered to selected financial institutions and mutual funds. (p.149). See also R.K. Mishra, et. al., *op. cit.*

mainly to the Indian public sector Financial Institutions at a notional reserve price. Rs. 30.38 billion were realised as sale proceeds. This disinvestment created a national controversy.[1]

Appointment of the Committee on Disinvestment of Shares in Public Sector Enterprises was the first step at streamlining of the process of disinvestment.[2] The Committee recommended the setting up of a statutory Standing Committee on Public Enterprise Disinvestment with members drawn from the government, public enterprises, financial sector, professionals and academicians. The need to give statutory status to the proposed Committee was emphasised in view of the "financial magnitudes involved, multiple Ministries concerned, impact on economic reform and the need to monitor use of the proceeds of such disinvestment".[3] The Disinvestment Commission was constituted in August 1996. Its envisaged role was to advise the government on the extent, strategy, methodology and timing of disinvestment in individual PSEs.

Till April 1999, the Disinvestment Commission submitted nine reports containing recommendations on 45 Central PSEs. The Commission favoured strategic sale.[4] 'Strategic sale' implies selling a substantial stake in a PSE along with transfer of management control to a bidder who would complement the existing strengths of a PSE to impart long-term viability. For 21 PSEs the commission recommended bringing in of private strategic partner. Trade sale was recommended in case of six companies; offer for sale through GDR and domestic route was recommended for four companies. Closure was recommended in respect of four companies and no disinvestment was to take place in case of one PSE.

---

[1] In his response to the controversy the then Finance Minister, Dr. Manmohan Singh, admitted that while there was no intentional wrongdoing, the controversy arose due lack of experience in disinvestment. In this context, the Disinvestment Commission recommended that::

Disinvestment in PSUs by Government over the last five years has attracted considerable public attention, especially after reports of audit of such transactions were completed by the C&AG and submitted to the Parliament. ... *In order that disinvestment is implemented ultimately in the best interests of the public, while at the same time establishing a proper environment for decision making, it is essential that audit of each disinvestment by the C&AG is conducted thoroughly, expeditiously and with the involvement of professionals familiar with the working of the industry and the capital markets.* (emphasis as in original). See: Disinvestment Commission, *Report V*, p. 16.

An analysis of the early disinvestments observed that the government realised about Rs. 33 billion less than the amount that could have been realised if the best value method was followed. See: R.K. Mishra, R. Nandagopal and A Lateef Syed Mohammad, "Sale of Public Enterprise Shares: Frittering Away Nation's Wealth", *Economic and Political Weekly*, Vol. XXVIII, No. 48, November 27, 1993, pp. M-163 —M-168.

[2] The Committee, which was originally set up in February 1992, was reconstituted in November 1992 under the Chairmanship of Dr. C. Rangarajan.

[3] See: Rangarajan Committee, *op. cit.*, p. 20.

[4] See: Disinvestment Commission, *Report V*, November 1997.

In the case of the Indian Petrochemicals Corp. Ltd, (IPCL) the government has notified its intention of sale of 25 per cent of its shareholding to a long term strategic investor, and to transfer control to manage the affairs of IPCL to the strategic investor (*Economic Times*, May 18, 1999). Strategic sale is envisaged in the case of four other PSEs, namely, Bharat Aluminium, Modern Food Industries India Ltd., Kudremukh Iron Ore Co. Ltd. and India Tourism Development Corpn. The process for selection of global financial advisors for the strategic sale of BALCO and KIOCL has been initiated.

Recommendations were deferred in eight cases. Strategic sale could prove helpful for bringing in new management and adoption of professional and business like approach unlike the case when the government continues to hold majority equity. In strategic sales there has to be a highly transparent mechanism accompanied by competitive bidding for selection of the strategic partners. The strategic sale would avoid direct involvement of the capital market. The limited capacity of the Indian capital market and the trends observed due to the crises in the East Asian Markets would have little relevance in deciding on strategic partners. During negotiations with the new partner, a system could be evolved to safeguard public interest and protect consumers and workers of the enterprise.[1]

Recommedations of the commission include reation of a Disinvestment Fund by placing the proceeds of the disinvestment and merging the National Renewal Fund to it. The Commission suggested that the Fund be deployed to further the disinvestment process by (a) liquidating losses of the PSEs before disinvestment, (b) strengthening enterprises with marginal losses; (c) providing support to surplus labour; and (d) conducting publicity campaigns for disinvestment. The Commission was not in favour of using the resources mobilised through disinvestment to bridge the budgetary deficit.

A large part of the disinvestments was indeed affected before 1997 i.e., prior to when the Disinvestment Commission started offering its recommendations. (Figure 3.2) Disinvestment receipts in 1997-98 and 1998-99 were Rs. 21.02 billion out of the total receipts of Rs. 126.38 billion. The Disinvestment Commission's role appears to have been only a marginal one. The Commission was confined to advise on only the referred cases. The Commission could not take investigation on its own nor deal with general policy issues.

Figure 3.2

Targets and realisation of disinvestment proceeds

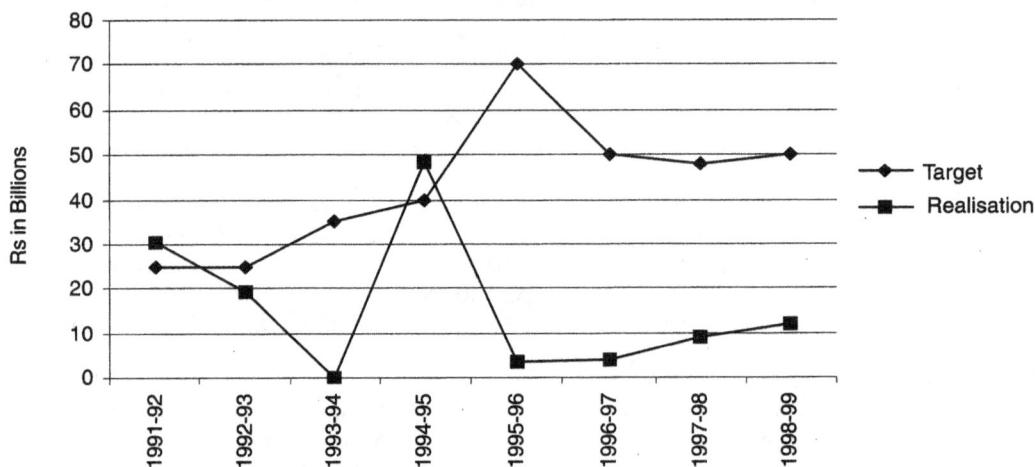

Source: Rajya Sabha question number 1,462 dated March 9, 1999.

---

[1]   Disinvestment Commission, *Report IX*, March 1999, p. 7.

Of the 240 CPSEs under the purview of the Department of Public Enterprises, the equity dilution strategy pursued by the Central Government affected 39 PSEs. There is, however, not a single case of reduction of government-held equity to less than 51 per cent.[1] Some of the PSUs are, however, now listed on the Indian stock exchanges.[2] The maximum number of undertakings fall below 10 per cent dilution range. Table 3.4 shows the distribution of PSEs according to the extent of disinvestment. The shareholding pattern of CPSEs shows that out of the 39 enterprises companies whose shares were partially divested, the government, together with financial institutions, holds over 76 per cent of the equity shares in 35 undertakings.[3] In only seven cases, including three, which made GDR issues, foreign institutions and collaborators together hold more than 10 per cent of the equity. In four companies shareholding of individuals and others is 10 per cent or more.[4]

Table 3.4: Distribution of central public sector companies according to the extent of disinvestment

S.No.	Range of equity dilution (%)	No. of undertakings	No. of workers in %	Equity in % (Rs. Million)
1	Below 10	20	32.0	47.5
2	10-15	3	29.2	34.0
3	15-20	3	2.1	2.8
4	20-25	4	8.1	4.0
5	26-30	1	0.3	1.2
6	30-40	4	14.3	3.3
7	40-50	4	14.0	7.2
8	50 and above	—	—	—
	Percent		100	100
	All Divested Companies	39	651,089	161,666.3
	All CPSEs	236	1,960,991	707,021.6

Note: Excluding four enterprises under construction.
Based on India, Department of Public Enterprises, *Public Enterprises Survey:* 1997-98, Vol. 1.

Workers do not figure as prominent shareholders after disinvestments. While in none of the companies workers hold more than 10 per cent, in two cases (IOC and Bharat Earth Movers) shares exceeding five per cent are held by workers. In only three other companies

[1] This analysis excludes issue of shares by public sector banks and the financial institutions like IFCI.
[2] Listing of government company shares, however, is not a new phenomenon. A few companies were listed because either at the time of takeover they were listed entities or the joint venture agreements provided for issue of shares to the public. Mention can be made in this regard of Andrew Yule, Balmer Lawrie, IBP, Cochin Refineries, Madras Fertilisers and Fertilisers & Chemicals Travancore.
[3] This is based on the shareholding distribution provided in Public Enterprises Survey: 1997-98. The categories under which the information has been provided are: (i) Central Government; (ii) State Government; (iii) Holding Company; (iv) Foreign Parties; (v) Financial Institutions; (vi) Employees; and (vii) Others (Indian).
[4] These are: Cochin Refineries, Hindustan Organic Chemicals, Indian Petrochemicals (IPCL) and India Tourism Devt Corp. (ITDC).

worker shares are higher than one per cent. Disinvestment affected so far is not very substantial when seen in terms of the number of CPSEs (39 out of 236), number of workers (Rs. 651,089 out of Rs.1,960,991) or the equity capital (Rs. 161,666.3 million out of Rs. 707,021.6 million). The number of enterprises in which disinvestment has been more than 25 per cent are only nine and their share in total number of workers was a little less than 10 per cent. In terms of equity capital involved in CPSEs, the share of the nine was a little more than 2.5 per cent. The extent of disinvestment of PSEs would appear to be very limited if one takes note of the shares taken over by public sector financial institutions and mutual funds. This would not be privatization in the true sense. In this manner, government does, however, raise resources which could help reduce the budgetary deficit. Besides holdings by the financial institutions there are reported cases of cross-holdings by major oil PSEs.[1]

An important feature of the present disinvestment is that two profit making sectors namely, oil and gas and communications (involving eight PSEs), contributed three-fourths of the Rs. 82.05 billion realised from the disinvestment during the period 1992-93 to 1997-98. Three major PSEs contributing to the revenue are Mahanagar Telephone Nigam Ltd (Rs. 23.6 billion), Oil & Natural Gas Corp. (Rs. 10.57 billion) and Indian Oil Corp (Rs. 10.34 billion). These in combination accounted for 54 per cent of the total amount realised during this period.[2]

In the Indian private corporate sector, most often, managements hold only a minority equity. Majority equity is not a prerequisite for sustaining management control. There has already been an intensive and long debate on this.[3] Ownership of equity offers two rights to a shareholder. One, the right to share profits, and two, to participate in determining the management control. Small shareholders, institutional investors and trusts are essentially concerned with the dividends and appreciation of their capital stock. There are only one or two groups of shareholders who have interest in gaining and sustaining management control over the enterprise. The existing managements, naturally, seek to ensure that their hold on

---

[1] See: Disinvestment Commission, *Report IX*, March 1999, p. 8. The Commission was reportedly not consulted in these cases and the GDR issue of VSNL.

[2] Lok Sabha Question No. 1666 answered on March 5, 1999.

[3] The Industrial Licensing Policy Inquiry Committee (ILPIC) classified companies under a large industrial house in which the industrial house held not less than one-third of the 'effective equity'. For arriving at the effective equity the Committee took out the shares held by passive shareholders such as government and government-owned and sponsored financial institutions, and foreign collaborators from the total equity. Under the MRTP Act, ownership of one-fourth of the equity (initially one-third) was chosen as the cut-off point for establishing inter-connection between the investing company and the investee undertaking. In practice, business houses were found to be controlling companies with far less share in equity. For instance, Tata Sons and its subsidiary held a little less than 3 per cent of equity in Tata Iron & Steel Co Ltd. (TISCO). See: S.K. Goyal, "Nature and Growth of the Indian Corporate Sector", Brij Narain Memorial Lecture delivered at Panjab University, Chandigarh, January, 12-14, 1987. The share of Shrirams in DCM Ltd. was about 15 per cent while public financial institutions owned as much as 42 per cent of the equity. In the case of Escorts Ltd the government was in fact in a majority but the control was with the Nandas. See: S.K. Goyal, "Private Managements and Takeovers of Public-owned Companies", in Ayub Syed (ed.), *Swaraj Paul Factor*, Palakmati Printing, Bombay, n.d.

the corporation is not threatened at the meeting of shareholders' general body. The necessary majority at the annual meetings of the corporations is often ensured with commitment and support of the institutional investors like LIC, ICICI, IFCI, IDBI, banks and non-voting trusts. While there is a provision for proxy voting, in practice smaller shareholders do not exercise their voting rights as it is neither convenient nor of much significance for them. Also, since shareholders are widely spread geographically, the percentage of shareholders' present at annual meetings is always low. The government domination in PSEs, in spite of the disinvestment, would, therefore, continue. The dilution strategy followed so far serves three objectives: help raise financial resources, ensure government domination and effective control of the enterprises, and also satisfy international lobbies which have been asking for adoption of privatisation of public enterprises.[1]

The IPS, 1991 visualised greater autonomy to profit making PSEs. It was, however, only during 1997-98 that the government gave powers to nine PSEs, the Navratnas, to take their own decisions regarding capital expenditure.[2] Implementation of the scheme of MOU has attracted severe criticism. In case of ITI Ltd, for instance, MOUs were being signed towards the end of the financial year. The agreement for 1995-96 was signed on 30th November 1995. This was in spite of the assurance of the Department of Telecommunications (DoT). The subsequent MOU was signed only in November 1996. The stated reasons for non-implementation of MOUs include the inadequate budget outlays, delays in settlement of outstanding dues and clearance of project proposals and inadequate reimbursement of VRS payments.[3] Appointment of chief executives are very often delayed for long periods.[4] The post of CMD of ITI Ltd. remained vacant for more than fifteen months "at a time when the profitability of the company was sharply eroding".[5] "The present MOU system has, in reality, failed to distance the Government from the PSUs".[6]

It is a widely shared view that privatization continues to be vigorously canvassed by multilateral agencies. The pace of implementation, however, has been determined by lack of political consensus, subtle resistance from civil services to surrender their control on PSEs,

---

[1] The Rangarajan Committee recommended that less than 40 per cent of the equity should be disinvested in industries reserved for the public sector and it should be over 74 per cent in other industries. Since even at that time the reservation was restricted to six areas (including coal & lignite and mineral oils which were dereserved afterwards) the recommendation amounts to government retaining 25 per cent or less in PSEs. (p. 6).

[2] *Navratnas* means nine jewels. The initial ones are: BHEL, BPCL, GAIL, HPCL, IOC, IPCL, NTPC, ONGC, and VSNL. Later two more enterprises were given similar status. During the same year it was reported that about 97 profit making companies were given the *Mini-Ratna* status with enhanced financial, managerial and operational autonomy. See: India, Ministry of Industry, *Annual Report: 1997-98*, p. 7.

[3] Lok Sabha Secretariat, Committee on Public Undertakings (Eleventh Lok Sabha), *Tenth Report*, p. 58.

[4] The Government informed COPU that as on April 30, 1998, 29 posts of chief executives were vacant in Central PSEs. See: COPU (1998-99), *First Report, op. cit.*, p. 17. COPU expressed its concern that in a number of sick PSEs there was no full-time chief executive and also there had been frequent changes of the incumbent. (p. 15).

[5] See: COP(Eleventh Lok Sabha), *Tenth Report*, p. 59.

[6] Disinvestment Commission, *Report I*, February 1997, p. 28.

the sheer magnitude of the task and the opposition from labour. In spite of a good deal of public posture, the private sector in India knows it well that if PSEs were to operate on business principles (take power supply for instance) the worst affected would be the private sector. The private sector should demand efficient functioning of PSEs as with this the price of their inputs obtained from PSEs could get reduced. On the other hand, apprehensions may exist as regards to whether there are many Indian private sector enterprises willing to invest large resources for takeover of public enterprises. The hands of the country's large industrial houses are full. Competence of private managements to manage massive enterprises of the size of central PSEs in its present form may also be doubtful. Besides this, it does not seem easy for any democratically elected government to handover large public enterprises to any private Indian or foreign industrial house. It is an extremely difficult political decision. An alternative, not seriously explored, happens to be the identification of professional management groups who could take up management responsibility. Formation of such professional groups could also be in close cooperation of workers, employers and consumers who have stake in these enterprises. So far, there have been many instances where workers have been fully supportive of privatisation efforts of the state. Thus, there has to be a solution to the problems faced by the sector.[1]

2.2 Contractualization

Some of the public sector enterprises have closed down certain of their activities by subcontracting them to private parties. Contractualisation of specific tasks has been assisted by the general ban imposed by government on new recruitments. The activities privatized and brought under subcontracting include catering; message and courier service; and security, cleaning and maintenance of office buildings and office transport (staff cars). Railways appear to have taken to sub-contracting of services in a big manner.[2] Sale of beverages and

---

[1] The case of Madras Fertilizers Ltd. (MFL) may be cited here to show how difficult is the process of converting a public enterprise into a non-government one. The Government had decided to bring down its equity to 26 per cent in this PSE.   Officers and workers of the company formed a Joint Action Council (JAC) and decided to take the issue to the public.   They intended to prevent the proposed global adviser from visiting the plant.   The JAC questioned the need to privatize the unit after spending Rs. 6.00 billion on modernisation and fears that privatization of fertiliser industry would endanger food security as private units may stop production if it turns out to be non-profitable.   They were also concerned about "job security, reservation for the weaker sections and welfare schemes carried out by MFL for poor farmers and tribals in the southern states".   They are hoping to succeed in their attempts. See: "MFL workers up in arms against privatization", *Financial Express*, August 23, 1999.   Resistance is also reported to be building up in case of converting BHEL into a non-government company and involving strategic partners in Modern Food Industries and IPCL. See for instance, "BHEL may face resistance from employees", *Hindu Business Line*, August 22, 1999 and "IPCL staff to boycott LS polls over disinvestment", *Hindu Business Line*, August 30, 1999.

[2] It is no surprise if employment in Indian Railways declined gradually since 1991-92. From 1.657 million employees in 1991-92 it has been reduced to 1.586 million in 1996-97.   See: India, Central Statistical Organisation, *Statistical Abstract: 1998*, Table 24.2, p. 272.

snacks on platforms by private vendors is an old practice but now the departmental catering on main routes has been privatized. Experiment has been undertaken in privatizing platform management and maintenance. Additionally, the railways are contemplating commercial exploitation of space over railway land and tracks in metropolitan towns with private sector participation.[1] Award of security contracts to private security agencies is gaining acceptance both in public and private sectors. There are no available estimates of the number of regular workers who have been affected by the introduction of the practice of contract labour or privatization of certain services. It is reported that the nine PSEs (termed as Navratnas) employ about 20,000 contract workers.[2] Another estimate has placed the number of contract labour at 16,000 in SAIL and 12,000 in NTPC.[3] The Chairman of Standing Conference of public Enterprises (SCOPE) is reported to have reacted to the Supreme Court's directive[4] to Air India for absorption of contract labour by saying that such a move will have major implications for most PSEs including NTPC, ONGC and SAIL. The Navratnas were reported to have requested the government to approach the Supreme Court to review its decision.[5] PSEs defend the use of contract labour on the ground of seeking to remain competitive. The Director, Personnel, NTPC said:

> *Outsourcing is an international business norm. If we are to handle our security, catering and health services departmentally, the cost will be enormous and we will be in no position to compete with private companies who are outsourcing a large part of their requirements.*[6]

The very fact that PSEs and their representative organisation reacted so strongly about contract labour is an indication of the importance already attained by contract labour services in PSEs.

Implications of the privatization of services by replacing regular workers with contract labour need an objective discussion. One likely consequence of this shift is the re-emergence of the 'Jobber' phenomenon in the labour market. The labour contractors, who often take up such responsibilities, offer no formal or assured employment; nor do the wage payments adhere to statutory minimum wage norms. Each labourer is only a casual worker having employment at the personal whims and discretion of the contractor/Jobber. The social aspects

---

[1] During 1995, the Indian Railways also decided to franchise the handling of major freight and parcel terminals. Privatization of maintenance and beautification of railway stations was introduced earlier in August 1992. See: Centre for Monitoring Indian Economy, *Infrastructure in India*, August 1995, pp. 19-20. Railways have also formed a joint venture for the tourist service 'The Royal Orient' with the Tourist Corporation of Gujarat Ltd. See the website www.indianrailway.com.

[2] "Standing Committee of Public Enterprises seeks review of Contact Labour Act following Supreme Court directive to Air India for absorption of contract labour", *Business Standard*, Internet Edition, February 11, 1998.

[3] "State-owned units want the government to contest the Supreme Court ruling on contract labour", *Business Standard*, Internet Edition, January 14, 1998.

[4] The *Contract Labour (Regulation and Abolition) Act, 1970* provides for abolition of contract labour in any sector on the recommendations of an advisory committee.

[5] Supra note 48.

[6] *Ibid.*

of the institution of 'Jobber' have been widely studied and commented upon.[1] Contract labour remains deprived of well accepted facilities offered by the organised sector. This includes a provision for provident fund, gratuity, health and educational allowance and housing.[2] The labour on contract never stays long enough to have legal claims to benefits that are available to regular workers. The worst of all is the absence of any possibility for trade union activity that has always been a lever to assert rights of labour. In a contractual system of employment one would not hear of any strikes or collective bargaining. Contractualization of services creates two distinct groups of labour – one well paid, protected and organized and the other wholly unprotected and unorganized.[3] With pursuance of policies towards privatization the relative share of the protected labour is bound to decline.

3. Consequences of privatization

Each form of privatization has differing implications for the labour, consumers and the economy. Dereservation, for instance, is likely to have little immediate adverse impact on employment. Dereservation, because of the removal of entry barriers, may motivate additional investments and offer enlarged employment opportunities. It is, however, possible that new private sector entrants may indulge in 'poaching' of senior and experienced workers of the public sector by offering attractive emoluments. The outgoing public sector workers would carry the advantage and access to business networks and knowledge of the market with them. This phenomenon has already been seen in the aviation sector and communications industry. Privatization could lead to a reduction in the workforce if the new managements were to opt for modernization and automation. This, in all probability, is unavoidable. Downsizing of labour is often considered a pre-condition to privatization of PSEs. Privatization in the form of sub-contracting could result in replacement of permanent and better-paid jobs with low wage unorganized casual labour. Dilution of government held equity by itself did not have any

---

[1] See: Jan Breman, *Footloose Labour: Working in India's Informal Economy*, Cambridge University Press, 1996.

[2] We made an attempt to see the nature of difference in costs under contract labour by informally discussing with employees of a security agency. A Security Guard under the Fifth Pay Commission recommendations would be eligible for a basic pay of Rs. 2,550 per month. The gross pay for him works out to Rs. 5,448 per month inclusive of all allowances, employer's contribution towards provident fund, etc. The private Security Agency charges the organisations studied by us Rs. 3,425 per month. The contract Guard receives only Rs. 1,937 per month. The Guard would get an additional Rs. 240 or so per month for additional duty on Sundays. Rs. 1,425 would, however, be *deducted* from his wages towards uniform. Thus, a Guard would get only a little above one-third of the wages fixed by the Fifth Pay Commission. He would have no security of employment, nor would he have the medical, conveyance and other benefits. The Agency keeps about 45 per cent of the amount collected from the employing organisations. It is no surprise that there has been mushrooming of private security agencies in most metropolitan cities.

[3] 'Contract labour' is nothing new to India. In the early 'sixties a number of steps for eliminating contract labour were widely discussed. It was suggested that steps need to be taken to improve their working conditions and protect their interests wherever it was not possible to eliminate the practice. See: India, *Second Five Year Plan*, 1956, pp. 582-583.

significant direct implications on labour. The general thrust at downsizing of labour in PSEs, however, had an across the board effect on PSEs whether profit-making or chronically sick. The existing PSEs are likely to lose a part of their market shares due to competition from new private sector entrants and from imports under the new liberalised system. It would in all probability become necessary for these enterprises to opt for technological upgradation and seek higher productivity. Adoption of new technologies may result in lowering of the overall labour requirements and making certain types of jobs wholly redundant. At the same time, however, adoption of new technologies could enlarge demand for certain type of skilled workers as also reduce avenues for employment in certain sectors. There is bound to be a change in the employment structure.

The process of privatization in India has moved fast. Will privatisation help CPSEs to become more labour and cost efficient? Will the PSEs, instead of incurring losses, make profits and become assets to the public exchequer? Entry of new entrepreneurs in dereserved areas would bring in new investments to expand production capacities. The overall production in these areas could rise but this by itself may not create sufficient condition for more efficient functioning of PSEs. Undoubtedly, end of the monopoly status of the PSEs and competition from new entrants would demand changes in PSEs. The erosion of monopoly rent may force economy and curtailment of wasteful and unproductive expenditure. Public sector undertakings and monopolies would need to face challenges of competition from the new entrants, and there could be a variety of new situations and market environment. Probably due to such likely challenges, there is already a visible impact on the performance of CPSEs. There has been an almost continuous upward trend in the net profits of the CPSEs ever since 1982-83. (Figure 3.3 & 3.4) The net profit of CPSEs stood at Rs. 6.13 billion in 1982-83 and it rose to Rs. 137.25 billion in 1997-98. A similar trend is visible in the net profits to capital employed ratio.

Figure 3.3
Net profit of CPSEs

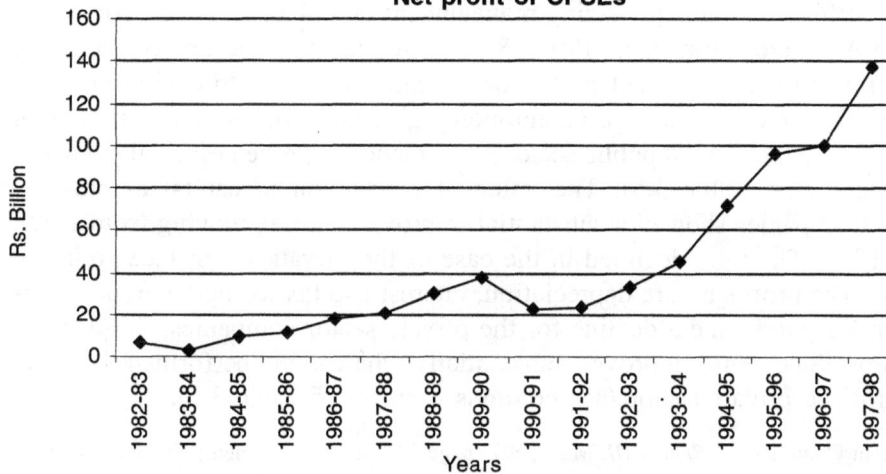

Source: India, Department of Public Enterprises, *Public Enterprises Survey,* volume 1 for the years 1991-92 and 1997-98.

Figure 3.4
Ratio of net profit to capital employed

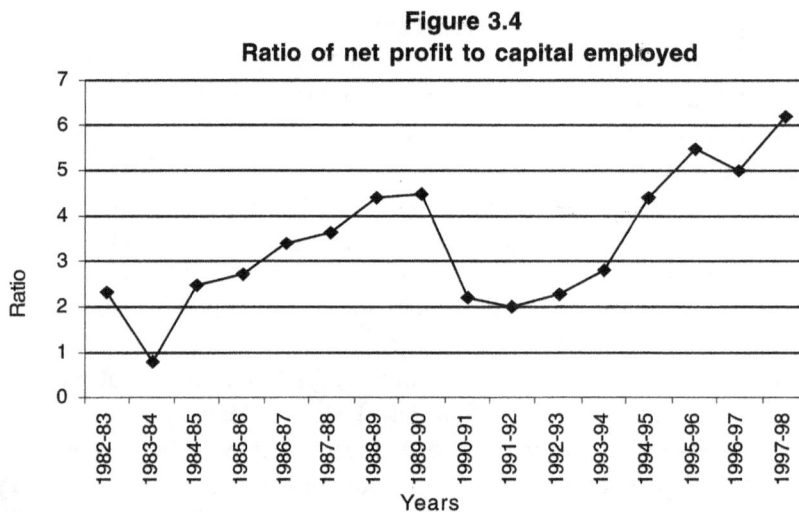

Source: India, Department of Public Enterprises, *Public Enterprises Survey,* volume 1 for the years 1991-92 and 1997-98.

In view of the perceived poor performance of public sector, privatisation would be justified if it results in improvements in the efficiency of these enterprises. For this, one necessary condition is that the enterprises under scrutiny should no longer be under government control and their managements should change hands. This was not the case even in one CPSE. Alternatively, one could examine the performance of PSEs where government affected privatization of management either through leasing/contracting out or through reorganization of PSE management boards with outside professionals. There has been no such clear case either. The fact is that "... even where disinvestment has already taken place, by and large, there has been no change in the composition of the Board of Directors to give representation to the non-government shareholders".[1] The functioning of the MOU system was also not satisfactory.[2] Efforts towards providing management and plant level autonomy as promised in the IPS 1991 were initiated in 1997-98 only. It may thus be not correct to relate the observed improvements in the net profits or the ratio of profits to capital employed to the process of disinvestment or managerial autonomy given to PSEs with adoption of MOUs. At the aggregate level, the Central public sector performance improved especially when compared to the private sector (Table 3.5). The value of production to capital employed ratio for Government Companies showed a substantial improvement i.e., moving from 1.622 in 1991 to 2.380 in 1997. The ratio declined in the case of the private sector (see columns 4 and 5 of Table 3.5). The profits before depreciation, interest and tax to capital employed witnessed enhancement for public and a decline for the private sector companies. Similarly, operating profits to Gross Sales ratio improved substantially whereas the performance improved only marginally for the private sector (see columns 8 and 9 of Table 3.5).

[1] Disinvestment Commission, *Report III*, May 1997 (page 148 of the combined publication covering Reports I to IV).
[2] Lok Sabha Secretariat, Committee on Public Undertakings (Eleventh Lok Sabha), *Tenth Report*, p. 58.

There is, however, a possibility that the very fact that many of the PSE shares have come to be listed on stock exchanges, it might have put pressure on the public sector managements to improve their performance.

Table 3.5: Select asset utilisation and profitability ratios for government and private sectors

(No. of times)

S.No	Year	No. of companies		Value of Production/Capital employed		Profit before depreciation, interest and tax/Capital employed		Operating profit/Gross sales (%)	
		Govern-ment	Private	Govern-ment	Private	Govern-ment	Private	Govern-ment	Private
1	1991	268	1,798	1.622	1.927	15.7	29.3	3.1	8.4
2	1992	276	2,156	1.677	1.921	17.2	29.7	3.3	8.3
3	1993	269	2,541	1.855	1.716	17.6	25.7	3.5	7.6
4	1994	283	3,376	1.913	1.533	18.1	24.0	4.3	8.8
5	1995	324	4,716	2.159	1.448	21.3	23.6	4.8	9.6
6	1996	343	5,958	2.336	1.399	23.0	23.0	4.9	9.7
7	1997	295	5,959	2.380	1.286	22.0	20.6	4.1	8.8

Source: Centre for Monitoring Indian Economy, Corporate Sector, April 1998.

This was necessary to ensure that the valuation of their stock does not suffer. While declaring the government's intention to disinvest its holding in PSEs, it was envisaged that this may provide 'market discipline to the performance of public enterprises'.[1] For perceptible changes to occur due to privatization a reasonable time should be allowed to lapse.[2] The initiation of the privatization process has not been long enough to permit statistical verification with regard to change in efficiency or otherwise. Nor should one expect dramatic improvements in performance as disinvestment has been confined to only the profitable enterprises. Last few years have been marked by drastic cut in new investments in the public sector. On the other hand, PSEs have been seeking to downsize their labour force, especially in the enterprises which do not fit in the changing environment and production basket/plans. These steps would have impact on productivity irrespective of the extent of disinvestment. In view of the multiple factors in operation, it would not be appropriate to compare the changes in performance of PSEs only whose shares have been divested.

---

[1] Statement on Industrial Policy, 1991.

[2] Privatization is often a long drawn process. UK is reported to have taken eight years to privatise 14 enterprises. *C.f.* Roger S. Leeds referred to in Javed Masud, "Privatization and Deregulation in Pakistan (Policy Framework and Strategy). It took seven years of restructuring before British Steel was privatized. See: Aaron Tornell, "Privatizing the Privatized", NBER Working Paper Series, Working Paper No. 7206, July 1999.

4. Regulatory bodies

Privatization of large public enterprises and entry of private sector in erstwhile reserved areas has the potential of giving rise to establishment of private monopolies. The interest of the consumers may therefore have to be protected from the normal instinct of private monopolies to exploit consumers in order to maximise their profits. One should not stretch the point too far as for the tendency of a public monopoly to be always better. Yet, there can be no denying of the fact that monopoly is a monopoly irrespective of it being in the private or public sector. Monopolies always need to be regulated to protect consumers and to control indulgence in wasteful and unproductive expenditure. It is only the regulations and obligations imposed on them that can ensure adequate attention being paid to R&D or participation in technological change.[1]

It is true that the government has appointed the Telecom Regulatory Authority of India Act, 1997, Electricity Regulatory Commission, and it is envisaged to have Insurance Regulatory Authority. The regulatory authorities are expected to oversee the operation of the sectors concerned. Given the experience of the functioning of the regulatory mechanisms in India it is only too early to assert the contribution of the newly appointed regulatory bodies. The example of SEBI has not been a very happy one.[2]

The jurisdiction of regulatory bodies and the government remains yet to be clearly defined in spite of many years having passed since enactment of SEBI legislation. For instance, when SEBI sought to penalise Hindustan Lever Ltd. and its officials for insider trading, the Ministry of Finance overruled SEBI. The Telecom Regulatory Authority of India (TRAI) is locked in a dispute with the government and has approached the Delhi High Court to define its role in a case of dispute between cellular operators and the government.[3] There were also disputes regarding fixation of tariff and permitting entry of MTNL into cellular

---

[1] VKRV Rao's foreword to S.K. Goyal, *Monopoly and Public Policy*, Allied, Delhi, 1979.

[2] For instance, pricing and timing of capital issues in the pre-liberalisation period were being approved on a case by case basis by the Controller of Capital Issues under the *Capital Issues Control Act, 1947*. The government, in May 1992, in spite of a massive securities scam which was exposed in the previous month, repealed the Act and handed over the responsibility of overseeing the stock market operations to the Securities and Exchange Board of India (SEBI) which was given statutory powers only a few months earlier (January 1992). While SEBI was learning the art of stock market regulation, companies flooded the market, at times repeatedly, with a large number of issues and raised hundreds of billions of rupees. A good number of the issues were found to be of dubious nature. The post-liberalisation period was indeed witness to a number of stock market related scams. As a result, Indian small investors lost confidence in the capital market. This disenchantment, coupled with the over cautious approach of SEBI consequent to the bitter experience of liberalising issue norms led to the 'drying up' of the primary issue market. SEBI is still grappling with the problem of 'vanishing companies'. This state of the stock market has in turn affected the PSE disinvestment plans of the government.

[3] "Trai moves HC to define role & reach", *Economic Times*, July 28, 1999. In a recent interview Chairman of TRAI said that "... the whole thing is in a mess. The Delhi High Court has reduced the role of the regulator to that of a tariff setter". See: "TRAI reduced to playing role of tariff setter: Sodhi", *Financial Express*, August 23, 1999.

service.[1] In the case of power and telecommunication sectors dereservation and approval for individual company entry preceded a number of important policy decisions leading to inordinate delays, controversies and scams.

The Indian experience tends to suggest that it is possible to create regulatory agencies but these do not perform their designated functions in a free and objective manner. The successful functioning of regulatory bodies pre-supposes a political will to perform. The cost of learning to administer regulations is high. This is especially so when the policies do not originate from within the political party in power or the government, and the timing and nature of regulations have to accommodate pressures from within and outside the country. If political leaders and the bureaucrats were in the main responsible for the problems facing the public sector, the same nexus could scuttle the functioning of regulatory institutions. The experience of Disinvestment Commission is a pointer to this possibility. The Monopolies and Restrictive Trade Practices Commission met with a similar fate earlier.[2] But the system takes a long time to change. Initial preparation may delay swift implementation of certain policies; but this still appears to be better than administering 'shock therapy' as indeed it was sought to be done for SAP. The period of transition could probably be reduced substantially.[3]

5.   Overstaffing

The last two decades have seen widespread criticism of the performance of the Indian public sector and this too on many counts. One cannot brush aside the criticism as if it was always a motivated one. The criticism of the public sector in Parliament, by expert committees and by independent observers has to be taken seriously. Of the many aspects criticized, a prominent one has been with regard to overstaffing in the public enterprises. Government's response has been to put a ban on new recruitments. The general ban has its own implications. With a certain number of workers retiring each year, the overall number of workers with the enterprises is bound to witness a decline. The ban on new recruitments has also been accompanied by a sharp decline in new investments in public sector projects. There has also been a lowering of the demand for labour within the public sector due to upgradation of technologies and replacement of labour by switching over to capital intensive and modern production systems. This is besides the impact of contractualization of certain activities in public enterprises.

---

[1]   For a discussion on the handicaps of TRAI, see: ".TRAI as the govt might... Unless legislative lacunae is fixed, the regulator will remain a toothless wonder", *Economic Times*, June 27, 1999.

[2]   See: S.K. Goyal, *Monopoly Capital and Public Policy*, Allied, New Delhi, 1979.

[3]   The Committee on Public Undertakings noted that as a result of the economic reforms initiated in 1991, PSEs, which were already suffering from, outdated technology, financial crunch and low productivity could hardly withstand the stiff competition without financial support. The Committee felt that "Before throwing the floodgates open to the multinationals an environment should have been created for the public sector to face such a challenge or some breathing period should have been provided for the weaker PSEs to cope up with the new situation". See: Lok Sabha Secretariat, Committee on Public Undertakings (1998-99), *First Report*, December 1998, p. 1.

Production processes have three main partners, namely, the owner/manager, the worker and the consumer. There is undoubtedly a certain degree of conflict of interest between management and labour. It is true for public as well as the private sector. For a healthy and stable growth there must be better appreciation of each other's viewpoint and problems. There is a growing awareness among trade union leaders that opposition to adoption of new technologies can no more be continued without hurting their own long term interests. While discussing with a trade union leader of the State Bank of India (SBI), it was surprising to find that the leader[1] himself explained that if the SBI does not adopt new technologies (e.g. computerisation) it would soon be left behind. SBI workers, according to him, recognise that foreign banks have already entered the Indian market in an aggressive manner. They are reaching out to clients. The SBI workers can no more behave indifferently nor oppose changes within.[2] To help strengthen such tendencies it is essential that there is continuing dialogue, communication and frank exchange of views among the management, labour and users of the services provided by the enterprises. Discussions with trade union leaders have revealed that while government and PSUs have pursued privatization policies there has been an absence of efforts to take the labour into confidence. It is fortunate that but for the token expression of disagreement with the package of liberalization and privatization, there has not been any violent organised opposition. There could have been unrest in the form of long-drawn demonstrations or strikes. So far this has been within limits. Whatever may be the reasons, it is necessary to understand that non-involvement of labour in the ongoing changes may delay the implementation of substantive changes in the public sector.

Governments of today everywhere, and India is no exception, are no more as sympathetic to labour as they were during the fifties and the sixties. While the socialist societies have witnessed a retreat, market-oriented policy propositions have become increasingly more acceptable to governments. While the government in India has agreed to the 'exit policy' and the 'golden handshake' for the private sector, there have been serious efforts to persuade public sector workers to accept the voluntary retirement scheme. Labour in the organised sector of India, broadly speaking, has been of late less aggressive to the exit policy than a few years back. It is for this reason that the number of mandays lost due to labour strikes has been lower than the mandays lost due to closures and lockouts declared by the employers. (Table 3.6) The number of disputes resulting in strikes fell from 2501 in 1980 to 681 in 1997. Similarly, the number of workers involved and the mandays lost nearly halved in the last few

---

[1]   These comments are of Mr. Ashok Kumar, an important official of the Trade Union of the State Bank of India (Punjab and Haryana region).

[2]   That this view is widely accepted is reflected from the fact that the All India Bank Employees Association (AIBEA) has assured that it would not oppose redeployment of staff, multi-shift banking, increase in business hours and computerisation of even semi-urban branches and would not place any fresh economic demands. The General Secretary of AIBEA, the largest bank union, said, "The public sector bank employees need to adapt themselves to the competitive climate. We will never say no to computerisation or, for that matter, anything that improves the health of the industry". See: "Largest bank union signals new flexibility", *Financial Express*, September 6, 1999.

years. On the other hand, the number of employer initiated lockouts and the number of workers affected has grown since 1990. The large number of public sector workers opting for voluntary retirement could be seen as the combined result of the environment and weakening of the trade unions' capacity to assert.

Table 3.6: Trends in industrial disputes

	No. of disputes			No. of workers involved ('000)			No. of mandays lost (Million)		
	Strikes	Lockouts	Total	Strikes	Lockouts	Total	Strikes	Lockouts	Total
1980	2,501	355	2,902	1,661	239	1,910	12.62	9.91	21.93
1990	1,549	366	1,825	1,162	146	1,308	10.64	13.45	24.09
1991	1,278	532	1,810	872	470	1,342	12.43	14.00	26.43
1992	1,011	703	1,714	767	485	1,252	15.13	16.13	31.26
1999	914	479	1,393	672	282	954	5.61	14.69	20.30
1994	808	393	1,201	626	220	846	6.65	14.33	20.98
1995*	732	334	1,066	683	307	990	5.72	10.57	16.29
1996*	763	403	1,166	609	331	939	7.82	12.47	20.28
1997*	681	453	1,134	564	316	880	5.02	9.90	14.93

Source: Ministry of Labour, *Annual Report: 1997-98.*
*   Provisional.

To facilitate voluntary retirement, the Government of India, like many other countries who have taken up similar schemes of privatization, accepted to support financially the Voluntary Retirement Scheme (VRS) in October 1988. While VRS has been in operation in India for more than a decade, empirical studies to assess the impact of the VRS on those who opted for it have not been many. From the responses of the trade union representatives and the few available studies,[1] it appears that the experience at VRS has not been very encouraging; and there continues to be confusion on certain aspects of the VRS.[2]

6.   Compensation

It is officially reported that the VRS has attracted nearly 0.23 million workers of the 169 central public sector enterprises. Of the total 169 CPSEs which implemented VRS, only 49 undertakings had more than one thousand workers under the VRS. There were corporations with a small number of workers opting for VRS. For instance, ONGC Videsh Ltd has shown only one employee seeking voluntary retirement. Similarly, Karnataka Antibiotics reported two workers opting for VRS. There are 13 corporations each having less than 10 workers opting for VRS. The average compensation per employee is estimated at Rs. 0.13 million.

---

[1]   See for instance, Maniben Kara Institute, *Voluntary Retirement Scheme and Workers' Response*, Friedrich Ebert Stiftung, New Delhi, 1994 and B.P. Guha, *Voluntary Retirement: Problems and Prospects of Rehabilitation*, Shri Ram Centre for Industrial Relations and Human Resources, Delhi, 1996.
[2]   See: Disinvestment Commission, *Report II*, April 1997.

The average compensation for workers differs widely from one undertaking to another. If there was one corporation with more than Rs. 0.5 million of average compensation, the average VRS compensation was less than Rs. 50,000 for 32 workers of the Visakhapatnam Steel plant. The reasons for this wide variation could be the category-mix of workers opting for VRS, the length of service, scale of emoluments, or adoption of differing formulae for calculations. Table 3.7 shows the extent of variation in the amount of average compensation.

Table 3.7: Extent of variation in average compensation in CPSEs

Avmerage compensation (Rs. Million)	No. of undertakings	No. of workers in %
Up to 0.05	6	1.7
0.05 - 0.10	19	32.0
0.10 - 0.15	51	24.2
0.15 - 0.20	37	19.0
0.20 - 0.25	20	9.5
0.25 - 0.30	8	3.2
0.30 - 0.40	6	.07
0.40 - 0.50	1	–
Above 0.50	1	.07
NA	21	9.0
Per cent		100
Total	169	227,103

Source: Based on the information provided by the Ministry of Industry, Department of Public Enterprises.

The enterprise-wise average compensation does not bring out the real nature of the disparities in the value of VRS. There is no official survey to suggest the number of workers who got compensation in different value ranges. We have made an attempt to arrive at the general pattern of distribution in an exercise undertaken by us for the Asian Development Bank for one state of India.[1] An analysis of the information on emoluments for nearly 18,683 workers of the State public sector enterprises has shown that an overwhelming proportion (94 per cent) of the workers may get Rs. 0.1 million or less with the general average being Rs. 62,000 only. (Table 3.8).

The average per employee compensation under the VRS for the CPSEs is estimated at Rs. 0.13 million. Given the differences in salaries and professional levels it does appear to us that an overwhelming number of the workers opting for VRS in the CPSEs would get an overall compensation in the range of Rs. 100,000 to Rs. 150,000. Will such compensation be adequate to support the retiring workers for life long? This is an aspect that needs scrutiny after an assessment of the average liabilities of different groups of retiring workers. Information on age-distribution of the 88,670 retiring workers is available for 62 CPSUs. (Table 3.9). Nearly half of those opting for VRS were over 50 years of age. The ones below 35 years of age were less than five per cent.

---

[1]   S.K. Goyal, *Madhya Pradesh: Implementation of Public Sector Restructuring Programme: A Poverty Impact Assessment Study*, prepared for the Asian Development Bank, June 1998.

Table 3.8: Estimates of cash payments* under voluntary retirement scheme in select Madhya Pradesh state PSEs

Compensation range (Rs. Million)	Number of workers Per cent in total	Compensation (Rs. Million) Per cent in total
Up to 0.05	51.64	33.79
0.05 - 0.1	42.36	50.79
0.1 - 0.2	5.08	12.31
0.2 - 0.3	0.81	2.60
0.3 - 0.4	0.11	0.51
Total Percent	100.00	100.00
Total Number/Amount	18,683	1,160.79

* The VRS compensation is calculated at 45 days salary for each completed year of service and the salary estimate for the remaining period of service. All those cases with less than 10 years of service have been excluded from the calculations.

Source: S.K. Goyal, *Madhya Pradesh: Implementation of Public Sector Restructuring Programme: A Poverty Impact Assessment Study,* prepared for the Asian Development Bank, June 1998.

Table 3.9: Age profiles of workers covered by VRS in CPSEs

Up to May 31, 1999

Type of enterprise	Total workers	Share in total workers in the category (%)		
		Below 35 years	35-50 years	Over 50 years
Sick Companies referred to BIFR	59,105	5.07	43.68	51.25
Other PSEs	29,565	3.66	46.30	49.84
Grand Total	88,670	4.64	44.55	50.81

Source: NRF Division, Ministry of Industry.

The 35-50 years age group was nearly 45 per cent. The nature of problems for 50+ age group workers could be substantially different from those in the less than 35 years age group. In all probability 50+ age group would consist of workers with children of marriageable age. Their view on retirement would be governed by their advancing age and a desire to help their children marry and settle in life. Given the Indian system one suspects that the workers in the 50+ age group would be willing to retire early and attempt settling their children. It could, however, be also possible that elderly ones would have limited personal demands and would invest their compensation amounts in assets which could give them regular income. The younger workers (below 35 years of age) may not have large compensation as most of them would not have long service to their credit. In any case their number is not very large. The main concern will have to be about those falling in the 35-50 age group. For well-qualified and skilled workers, alternative employment in private sector is not very difficult; in fact exit from public sector may mean an improvement both financially and socially. Private managements have the freedom to reward good performers unlike in the public sector where decisions have to be rule-based. Jumping of the line in matters of promotion is not easy in public enterprises. At times a single change in policy and procedures, to accommodate a deserving case may affect thousands of workers beyond the individual enterprise.

Probably, in response to the criticism of the VRS and the increasing lack of enthusiasm of workers for availing it, PSEs seem to be attempting to improve upon the initial compensation package. SAIL plans to pay quarterly (basic + DA) for the remaining part of the service of the workers who have put in 20 years or more of service with the company. The workers opting for VRS would also continue to receive medical facilities.[1] The workers with up to five years of service left before retirement were assured full basic pay plus dearness allowance, as on the date of separation for the remaining period of service. Those remaining with five to eight years of service would get 90 per cent and those with more than eight years left, 80 per cent of the salary with DA and medical support.[2] BHEL targeted senior workers and the average payout was placed at Rs. 0.6 million per employee. Like SAIL, the BHEL also decided to extend medical facilities to those who opted for VRS.[3] For lower level workers such packages appeared attractive. The Department of Telecommunications (DoT) planned to offer STD/ISD booths to non-officer category workers who were accepting VRS from ITI and HTL.

7. Social safety net

Adoption of privatisation policies would alter employee-employer relationship in a radical manner. A good number of workers are likely to lose service and stable source of income. To meet the problem of retiring workers, monetary compensation need to be accompanied by measures that would provide a safety net as a long-term solution to their present loss of employment. There would be many who would be physically and mentally healthy and have financial commitments of regular nature. Also, it does not appear a sound public policy to throw out able bodied and willing workers from the productive national stream. Measures could be devised to enable the retiring public sector workers to continue being productive. Workers may be retrained or imparted with new skills. The basic purpose would be to harness the potential capabilities of retiring workers as also to help their rehabilitation. Setting up a social safety mechanism has to be seen as a requisite to protect interests of the workers affected by PSE restructuring. The National Renewal Fund (NRF) was created by the GOI in October 1992.[4] The objectives of the NRF are to provide:

(i) assistance to cover the costs of retraining and redeployment of workers arising out of modernisation, technology upgradation and industrial restructuring;

---

[1]   See: "SAIL cites 7 plus points of VRS", *Economic Times*, September 2, 1998.

[2]   See: "6,000 opt for VRS at Sail", *Statesman,* September 6, 1998.

[3]   BHEL offered 45 days' pay (basic + DA) for each completed year in service or 30 days' pay for the number of remaining months till the age of 60 whichever is lower. See: "BHEL VRS achieves target before deadline", *Business Standard*, July 28, 1999.

[4]   A view was voiced in certain quarters that the government formulated the guidelines in view of the visit of a high-level IMF team to discuss a fresh loan under the Extended Fund Facility. This was done to assure the visiting team of the government's commitment to economic reforms. See: "CCEA approves guidelines for operating national renewal fund", *Economic Times*, October 29, 1992.

(ii) funds for compensation of workers affected by restructuring or closure of industrial
units in public and private sectors; and
(iii) funds for employment generation schemes both in organised and unorganized sectors
in order to provide social safety net for labour needs arising from restructuring.[1]

Till May 1999, 0.13 million CPSE workers opted for VRS under the NRF scheme. The
number of workers opting for VRS had started declining after 1994-95. This could indicate
possible loss of interest of the workers or the falling budgetary allocations to NRF, or both.
(Table 3.10) NRF allocations started looking up once again since 1997-98. In the initial years
the allocations were supported by contributions from the multilateral agencies. The allocations
remained low afterwards. The disinvestment of PSE equity did not proceed as expected. A
part of the financial resources raised through disinvestment were expected to be put aside
to support NRF. This did not happen.

**Table 3.10: Number of workers availing VRS covered by NRF and expenditure on
VRS and NRF: 1992-93 to 1998-99**

(Amount in Rs. billion)

Year	Budgetary allocation	Amount transferred to public account	Expenditure incurred on		No. of VRS availees covered by NRF
			NRF	*VRS*	
1992-93	*8.297	8.297	5.967	5.667	39.751
1993-94	# 10.200	7.000	4.782	4.781	34.232
1994-95	2.000	1.000	2.519	2.508	16.206
1995-96	1.400	1.400	2.170	2.096	12.583
1996-97	1.500	1.500	1.956	1.880	6.980
1997-98	3.069	3.069	3.304	3.267	14.815
1998-99	4.013	4.013	3.773	3.721	4.482
Total	30.478	26.278	24.172	23.920	129.049

Source: Government of India, Ministry of Industry.
* Includes Rs. 5 billion received from IBRD/IDA.
# Includes Rs. 5 billion received from IDA.

A widespread criticism of the NRF has been that while the main objective of NRF was
to help in retraining, counselling and redeployment of affected workers, and in employment
generation, an overwhelming portion of the total expenditure incurred on NRF was utilised
for compensation payments under VRS. The rate of redeployment of those workers who
benefited from VRS was quite low. Out of the 98,327 VRS beneficiaries under the NRF
surveyed, only 36,889 workers were retrained. The number of redeployed workers was still
lower at 11,623. Even considering the fact that some of the workers might not have opted
for retraining and redeployment these figures appear quite low; especially of those who got

---
[1]   India, Ministry of Industry, *Annual Report: 1992-93*, p. 16.

redeployed. Therefore, it is no surprise if the major Indian trade unions are extremely critical of the way VRS and NRF are being administered. A gist of their observations on privatization in general and VRS and NRF in particular is given in Annexure- A.

In the context of redeployment of workers a suggestion has been made that the services of employment exchanges could be made use of. It, however, appears that during the recent past the record of the employment exchanges in enabling job seekers to secure employment has not been encouraging. The number of vacancies announced through the exchanges and the number of placements made have been declining since the mid-eighties (Figure 3.5). Though the figures started looking up after 1994, the improvement does not appear to be of much significance. In this background, the potential of the employment exchanges for redeployment of workers benefiting from VRS appears very limited. This is probably because the employment exchanges in India are involved mainly with placements in the public sector and their records reflect only the employment opportunities available in the public sector. When new recruitment in government and public sector has been restricted it is only natural that employment exchanges would be seen as having fared badly.

Figure 3.5

Vacancies notified and placements by employment exchanges

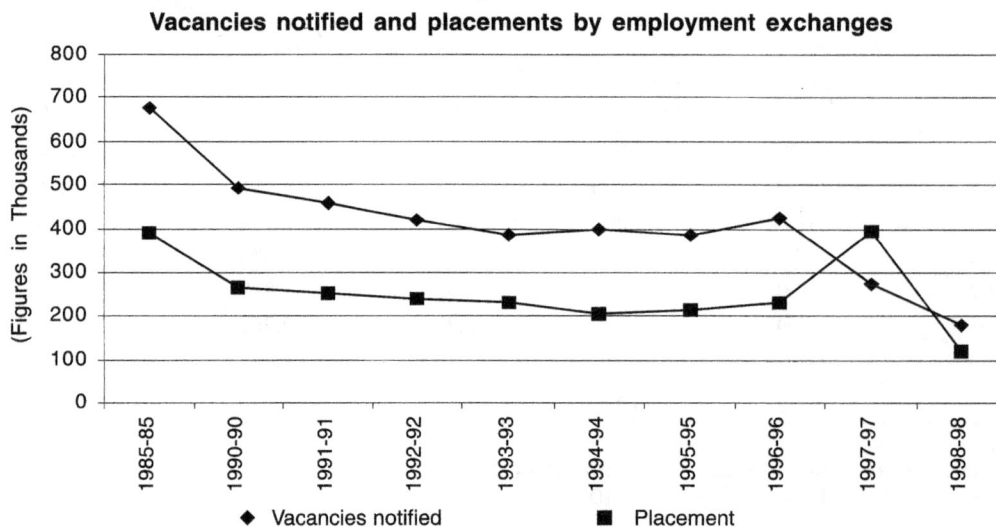

Figures for 1998 are extrapolated on the basis of registrations and placements during the first six months.

The weaknesses of VRS have come to be known widely. Individual enterprises are trying to improve the compensation packages. Whatever may be the size of cash compensation, the objective reality stays that no able bodied person wants to remain idle and sit at home. This is particularly true of persons who have remained employed in productive activity their entire lives. Retirement is a very depressing phenomenon if there is no alternative occupation available. Besides, the forced retirement offers no alternative for those who were keen to remain occupied, even on a part time basis, for additional income. This would be particularly true of lower income groups. Family conditions vary from one to another. The general cash compensation is not a full alternative to regular or part time employment. Some steps have to be taken to put the retiring workers into the productive stream. For this, public enterprises would need to undertake manpower planning and initiate advance action regarding the workers who would be expected to retire each year.[1]

Surplus manpower in each division of the PSEs needs to be identified. Once the exercise is completed and surplus manpower identified, the next step would be to classify these workers according to their basic characteristics: age; sex; hometown; family composition and dependents; academic and professional qualifications; experience and specialisation; economic status of the family; special attributes like Scheduled Castes and Scheduled Tribes; etc. A comprehensive socio-economic profile of the surplus labour is a pre-requisite to evolving a meaningful safety net and programme for rehabilitation and redeployment of the retiring workers.

There have been a variety of suggestions for training and counselling for those who take the option of VRS. The expectation that one can change the mindset of workers to become successful entrepreneurs overnight with financial support is not very realistic. Nor is it always possible to retrain each one of the retiring workers. A meaningful plan of rehabilitation needs to be worked out after assessing the potential, preferences and opportunities available in the immediate environment. Larger and growing townships would need a variety of skills which workers from engineering PSEs would have in plenty. We must emphasize here that there can be no generalised solution in the form of counselling or retraining. A detailed analysis of this was presented by Ashok Chandra.[2] Our own discussions support his conclusions. The major elements of the suggested strategy are as follows:

(1) Removal of the ten year limit on NRF and creating a stable mechanism for retraining;

(2) Retraining should be a continuing on-the-job process. Employers should be encouraged to plan for the development of their workers and create conditions for their continuing education and training;

(3) Retraining should be provided before retrenchment. It should be ensured that those threatened with redundancy should not be retrenched until they have been suitably prepared, through training and other measures, to enter the external labour market;

(4) Arrangements for operating a labour market information system and providing feedback to employment planners and retraining planners should be created;

---

[1] In the context of having an estimate of excess labour the case of ITI cited by COPU (1998-99) is quite relevant. COPU noted that while there was surplus manpower in the company and a VRS has been introduced, "no scientific study has been conducted to assess actual manpower requirement in each of the units of the company". See: Lok Sabha Secretariat, Committee on Public Undertakings (Eleventh Lok Sabha), *Tenth Report*, p. 65.

[2] See: Ashok Chandra, "Retraining and Redeployment: NRF Initiative and Challenge in Training", *The Indian Journal of Labour Economics*, Vol. 42, No. 1, Jan-Mar 1999, pp. 31-47.

(5) Employment promotion plans and area regeneration plans are important requirements particularly because of concentration of PSE workers in certain regions (e.g. textile workers in Ahmedabad). Retraining should focus on the analysis of projected investment into the area and the economic activities likely to be taken up;

(6) Enhanced financial provision for restructuring of labour in general and education and training in particular;

(7) Retraining should aim at enhancing core skills and help towards improving/creating work culture. Selection of institutions should be done carefully to avoid mismatch between requirements and capabilities;

(8) Special attention needs to be paid to vulnerable groups like older and women workers. This is because women have a greater tendency of going out of the labour market and with the disappearance of joint family system the support available to older displaced workers may disappear soon;

(9) Since the scope for employment in the organised sector is likely to be limited in the short run, it is desirable to transfer skills from the formal to the informal sectors especially with the help of NGOs;

(10) Provision of continuing education and further training should be an integral part of technical education and training; and

(11) Self-employment and entrepreneurship development should be a part of the larger strategy of enlarging employment opportunities.

We may also add that government departments are not very willing to take responsibility for operating the safety net. The plea is that they are already overworked and starved of competent and responsible staff at workers and supervisory levels. With regard to the role of voluntary agencies and non-government organisations there is conflicting evidence. This task has to be undertaken at each location by a group of experts who can identify employment opportunities in the area that exist or can be created. Expertise of this nature has to be built. It is not in ready availability.

Overstaffing in an enterprise causes low labour productivity, general inefficiency, high costs and low operational surpluses. While the reasons for overstaffing may differ from one enterprise to another, a few primary factors can be identified which make it obligatory on the part of PSEs to downsize their labour force. One, India had placed a premium on projects in public sector which offered larger employment opportunities. The size of new jobs created was an important aspect of project scrutiny for government approval. This is no more accepted as a national policy. Two, large PSEs were often located at new locations in backward and less developed areas having neither industrial nor urban infrastructure. It became obligatory for PSEs to build and maintain housing, transport and other social infrastructure (like schools and hospitals) as a part of the project. Employment of larger staff for supplementary services was the consequence. Three, PSEs were expected to expand in a long term national and developmental perspective. It could not be visualised that the role of public sector would be revised downwards in a short time. Four, as PSUs in non-strategic areas are now to be closed down in part or in full, emergence of labour surpluses is the unavoidable consequence. Five, with adoption of new technologies, economic and business logic would place more weightage to labour saving options than to administrative or political conveniences. Thus, many more enterprises are obliged to cut on new wage employment. Six, old enterprises while replacing equipment and machinery opt for more efficient alternatives which reduce the demand for labour. Seven, existence of surplus labour is also a problem carried over with nationalisation of sick private mills. And last, for some time new investments under economic plans have witnessed a downward trend. This has resulted in a reduction of new orders with public sector producers of heavy machinery and other inputs. The reduced capacity utilisation demands lesser labour and the result is in labour surpluses. Most of the public enterprises, especially the older ones, have been found with considerable excess staff. The precise level of the staff surplus in each PSE has not been identified in a systematic manner. The need for such exercises, however, has been repeatedly emphasised by parliamentary (COPU) and other committees. It was an expectation that data on surplus staff for each enterprise would be available with the Standing Conference on Public Enterprises (SCOPE). Which was, however, proved wrong.

A broad view on the question of excess labour could be had by comparing the size or value of labour per unit/value of production for comparable private and public undertakings. The extent of labour requirement is quite significantly dependent upon the technology, capital equipment and production processes. There are not many enterprises in any one sector of production to permit such a comparison. Indian public sector enterprises enjoy monopoly position in most cases and these are also multi-product units. It is often argued that the Indian public sector is highly labour inefficient. The labour costs are supposed to be high for it. If one compares SAIL and TISCO one does not, however, find on many counts, much of a difference between the two companies. The ratio of wages and salaries to net turnover stood at 16.95 per cent for SAIL and 16.33 per cent for TISCO in 1998. In 1995 and 1996 SAIL was in a more favourable position.[1] Facts appear quite contrary to what is generally believed. If one takes the ratio of wages and salaries to turnover as index of labour efficiency one finds that in 1997 labour efficiency with non-big business was the highest with the ratio being 4.0 per cent. This was followed by the CPSEs with 4.3 per cent. Foreign-controlled companies had the percentage at 5.2 and the top Indian Business Houses, 5.6. The private sector as a whole had this percentage as 4.9. Understandably, in the case of sick companies the ratio was substantially higher at 23.7. That this is not a one-time occurrence is reflected from the relative positions of different groups, which have remained broadly similar since 1991[2] (Figure 3.6).

---

[1] This observation is based on the data available in *Equity Research Station*, a corporate database developed by Asian CERC Information Services (India) Ltd., Bangalore.

[2] We are, however, aware that the ratio could be influenced by use of contract labour. The declining ratio of wages, etc. to operating income could indeed be indicative of the growing phenomenon of contractualisation of select operations. But since it has been happening in both the sectors and both are known to use such labour, it does appear that public sector is not worse off than the private sector.

Figure 3.6
Share of wages and salaries in net sales in the indian corporate sector

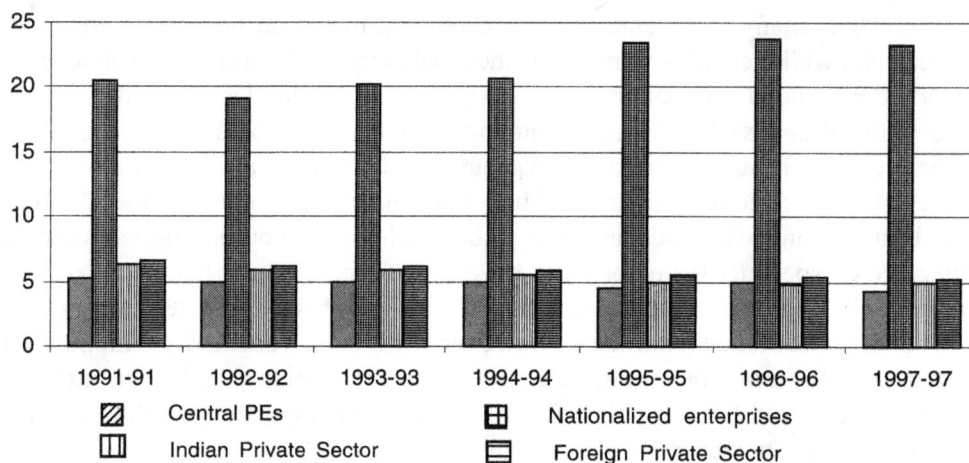

Source: Centre for Monitoring Indian Economy, Corporate Sector, April 1998.

We examined the share of wages and salaries in gross value added or conversely, gross value added per unit of wage input in value terms. The Indian private sector appears to be equally overstaffed in terms of the relative size of expenditure on workforce. The relative position of the two sectors suggests that for improving the efficiency of the public sector efforts may not be restricted to labour alone. There must be multi-pronged attack for improvements starting with managerial and technological aspects of the corporate life.

8. Summing up

End of the Second World War was succeeded by political liberation of third world countries. Most of the newly independent economies suffered from low GDP and per capita income, low agricultural and industrial productivity, absence of health and education facilities, existence of wide interpersonal, interregional and intersectoral disparities, domination of unproductive, wasteful and exploitative social and economic institutions and other symptoms that go with underdevelopment and backwardness. An assurance of the political leaderships in these countries was that after gaining political freedom the state would not remain a silent spectator to the problems of the country and the people. The need of the Third World countries was to drastically restructure their socio-economic and political systems and establish requisite infrastructure for a purposeful change. This, it was unanimously agreed, could only be undertaken with state initiative in a planned manner. Thus, the state was obliged to play the lead role. India was no exception to this pattern of thought and analyses.

Over nearly half a century of planned development, India has success stories on many counts. At the same time, there is a widespread consciousness of the distortions that have crept into the process of socio-economic development. The regulatory mechanisms were neither properly designed nor provided with built-in self-correcting system. The operation of regulatory machinery caused wide spread irritation as the administrative structures and bureaucratic procedures of work were neither transparent nor functional nor did these related to the purpose for which these were created. In any case, after half a century of administering regulations and controls in India it was time for having a fresh look at the entire gamut of economic regulations. There has not been adequate appreciation that a regulatory mechanism can provide appropriate mechanism to allow smooth functioning of the market forces. Besides the limitations caused by structural shortcomings it had not been fully recognised that the success and failure of a regulatory system depends on the clarity and understanding of those who are charged with the responsibility to administer regulations. Similarly, the working of public enterprises has not always brought credit either to the state or to the economy. The Indian public sector has been amenable to a variety of political and administrative pressures as it had to function under the heavy shadow of the respective administrative ministries.

The weaknesses of the present system of administration of public enterprises have been pointed out repeatedly and at differing fora. It is unfortunate that timely key decisions often get delayed or are never taken. Government responses have been poor in matters of ensuring efficient operation of public enterprises. The case for reform of the regulatory system and the Indian public sector is only too clear; and delays in initiating the corrective measures have already inflicted irreparable damage to the economy in general and the public sector in particular. There are two avenues before the policy makers: (a) to undertake comprehensive reforms and take corrective measures, or (b) to withdraw and leave the decision-making process to the private managements and forces of the market. State can roll back both in matters of regulations as well as her direct intervention in the form of public enterprises.

Privatization process in India has taken many forms. A dramatic change has been in opening up of the areas reserved for exclusive development in the public sector. But for the strategic and defence related areas, practically all economic activity has now been thrown open to private sector. Similarly, a host of the irritants in the form of industrial licensing, regulations to save foreign exchange and technical scrutiny to assess export potential and contribution to import substitution have been abolished. Government has taken a variety of initiatives to affect privatization of public sector in a phased manner. In spite of having undertaken so many important steps which have considerably altered the country's economic policy frame, there continues to be a widespread confusion in India about the primary objective of privatization. While resource mobilisation has been stated only as one of the many objectives of privatization of PSEs, the fact remains that this is the only objective that has so far materialised. The frequently stated objective of privatisation has been to manage exit from the situation under which huge public sector losses have to be met by the exchequer. This could help bridge the yawning budgetary gap which contributes to the fiscal deficit. In such a case loss-making public enterprises would be first targeted for privatisation or even liquidation. Instead, the present attempts do not singularly focus on loss-making enterprises alone. Little has been done to either close down or privatize the taken-over sick mills of the private sector. If the purpose of the take-over of private sick textile mills was to restore them to health there should have been efforts to modernise these mills or close these down in a phased manner. A decision has been pending on this for years.

The disinvestment of government equity in profitable PSEs has certainly helped the government mobilise one-time funds. The system of limited disinvestments, as pursued so far, can no way cause any change in the management of public enterprises. The initiative and approval for this has to be of the government only since majority equity in these enterprises continues to be with government. Additionally, the equity has been unloaded mainly to the public sector financial institutions. Should one consider these developments as privatization resulting in more professionally governed PSUs? It is debatable. While holding a little less of the full stake, say 90 per cent and not 100 per cent, the main responsibility for changing the nature of the management has to come from the government. If the government wished, it could have been done earlier without any fear of opposition from shareholders or workers.

Maybe the intention behind PSEs privatization was to deepen capital market and obtain larger public participation. Here, one suspects that the massive entry of public sector equity, in all probability would have had an adverse impact in the form of overall depressed stock prices. The profit making enterprises would have certainly attracted investors but then one does not gain much by public participation as a mechanism to improve further the working of these enterprises. Most small shareholders the world over remain dormant and do not take active interest in management. The primary concern of the equity shareholders is the return in the form of dividends and appreciation in the stock value. To expect widely spread small shareholders to bring in public involvement and perform the vigilance role is taking matters literally. Ultimately, it would be one or two large shareholders who could reach a position of influence even when they are in minority.

Two objectives, however, appear to have been pursued effectively by government initiatives at privatization. One, obtaining of funds by transfer of PSU equity to public sector financial institutions and mutual funds. And two, to honour the assurances that government had given during the negotiations with the Brettonwoods institutions that India would take effective steps to reduce the role of the state in internal management of the economy. India did take the measures agreed upon under the Structural Adjustment Programme and has succeeded to convince multilateral bodies that India was seriously pursuing the promised changes. As a result, two positive developments have resulted. One, the flow of foreign private capital has been quite substantial; and two international lending agencies have provided adequate support for India to maintain high credibility and business confidence in the international business community. India has been projected as a stable economy. This may not be the stated objective of privatization but the additional resources would help keep the fiscal deficit at a lower level than what would have been the case otherwise. This could be the strategy of the policy planners, though not spelt out openly.

If the present level of privatization is maintained and no PSE is allowed to change hands to the advantage of either the Indian big business or TNCs, the sting associated with privatization may not hurt public sentiments. The criticism that privatization amounts to sale of family silver would not hold true. In case of partial disinvestment, the management control continues to rest with the government not only because it would have a clear majority equity but also because government would retain controlling stake in CPSEs even after substantial disinvestment. If the debate remains confined to the privatisation processes, one would fear that the basic questions would not get addressed. What is needed in the PSEs is restructuring, not only in its shareholding structure but more so in management, pricing, autonomy from administrative and frequent political interventions. To start with, there has to be clarity on the business objectives of each PSE. Operationally, one needs to have a professional group as Board of Directors. The domination of bureaucrats needs to be replaced by those who have commitment and aptitude for corporate management. The role of nominee directors continues to be vague. Above all, it is not often that the Chairman and key Board members get appointed in time. Continuance of vacancies and too frequent changes at the top do not permit business stability of the enterprises. The top leadership of the PSEs needs to be assigned specific responsibilities and in doing so there has to be abundance of transparency in their work. What in essence is being suggested is the restructuring and stability of the Board of Directors with clearly defined objectives.

Privatization has been strongly opposed by labour. No one can dispute that from the individual and collective labour viewpoint, public sector would always be the preferred employer. It is not very correct to view that labour in PSUs is indifferent to the problems of the enterprises where they work. Labour knows that an unprofitable undertaking could only hurt their own interests. They have high stake in their place of work. However, what is essentially needed is the sharing of the basic problems by the managements of PSEs with labour. For instance, it would have been helpful if before taking measures to privatize, the government had shared the objectives of privatization and obtained their view. There is bound to be an expression of conflict between the managements and the trade unions if the two sides do not have regular lines of communication. One does need to recognise that today's labour is far more intelligent and able to appreciate problems and viewpoint of managements than what might have been true in the past. The remarks by SBI trade union leader are an important indicator.[1]

Privatization by itself cannot be considered as an ideology of development. At the same time it fits well in the overall scheme for reducing the rigour of directed economies and introducing market-oriented production and distribution structures. Quite different from the ideological stances, it is clear that there is growing awareness that over the past half a century, there have been a variety of important technological and other developments that warrant fine-tuning of the role of the state. It needs to be underlined that one cannot paint all public enterprises black, just as it would be wrong to consider all large private enterprises to be exploitative. There are areas in which private and decentralised sector have a built-in merit over large public sector establishments.

A live, sensitive and important issue as a fallout of privatization is the question of compensation and resettlement of surplus labour that have no option but to accept voluntary retirement. Cash compensation under the VRS, for a large majority, may not be adequate to help them obtain regular incomes. There are reasons to believe that if the entire compensation

[1] India, Department of Public Enterprises, *Public Enterprises Survey*, volume 1 for the years 1991-92 and 1997-98.

is handed over to VRS retirees it would get diverted to support un-productive expenditure. A better alternative, for an effective social safety net, may be in working out a pension scheme.

As a part of developing social safety net it has been suggested that the retiring workers should be given training for setting up their own enterprises. This may offer a good alternative and secure future. It is, however, not easy to change the mindset of persons who have for long pursued a certain way of life. A worker does not become an entrepreneur overnight as he has little knowledge to defend himself against business uncertainties and risks. It seems, therefore, doubtful if any generalised training to workers would help much to convert workers into entrepreneurs. Moreover, business opportunities and environments differ from place to place. Then, there are wide differences in the nature of experience of the retiring workers. Given these realities it appears that an effective method may be in preparation of local area employment plans for important public sector locations that could suggest opportunities for establishment of low investment service activities. For instance, most of the mechanics, drivers and conductors of public transport corporations may easily fill the fast growing demand of the automobile services for repair and maintenance as also privatized passenger transport service and individual taxi operations. Similarly, there can be new openings in the service sector especially in information technology. There is a need to prepare imaginative plans for employment in major locations. Public enterprises could also take advance action for the new opportunities and encourage discussions with other informed sections of the populations. Opportunities in the service sector may be more suitable to retiring public sector workers, especially those who had experience of secretariat and staff support.

One assertion that one may make is that unless political leadership recognises the need for adoption of appropriate corrective measures for improving the working of public enterprises with the utmost promptness, no production system can survive without difficulties for long. Secondly, there can never be any substitute for regular exchange of views and mutual consultations on common problems. There is a need to strengthen the consultative mechanisms. And lastly, many of the problems which are sought to be settled through measures like privatization could be better attended to in the spirit of mutual understanding with labour.

May be this is the time to restructure our approach and systems of management in the true sense. Public sector needs restructuring in terms of its goals, system of decision-making, adoption of reward and penalty mechanism and in determining the pricing policy. There will have to be a change including organizational restructuring. Mere transfer of ownership to private sector may not help achieve higher productivity without high social costs.

9.   Recommendations

Privatisation in its various forms attempts to reduce ownership, direction and regulation of the economic activity by government and expand the area of decision-making processes by the market forces. These attempts need to be viewed against the background of bureaucratic rigidities, misconceived regulations and controls and high cost of direct government interventions by way of public sector and other policies, which inhibit optimal allocation of the factors of production. The process need not necessarily aim at elimination of the state in the economy. Pursuit of privatisation policies, there is no denying, will cause a shift from the public to a private system of ownership and adoption of commercial values in its operations.

It has to be accepted by government, workers and public that privatisation needs to be accompanied by restructuring of the existing regulatory mechanism. The new system must have well defined objectives and should allow full transparency and adequate powers to effectively administer the regulatory provisions of law and least possible discretion. Privatisation of public enterprises (PEs) should aim at their restructuring and should not remain confined to disinvestment or transfer of ownership of PEs. The need is to professionalise the managements and reduce unnecessary interventions by Government Departments.

Broadly speaking, the consequences of privatisation can be grouped under two categories. One, the immediate problems which relate to (a) mechanisms for restructuring of ownership, management, control and other operational policies, (b) problems relating to resettlement of surplus labour, the establishment of social safety-net to reduce the hardships for retiring public sector workers and (c) provision of adequate resources and other support to make loss making enterprises become profit making enterprises. The problems are well recognised.

The second set of problems would come up after the initial transfer of PEs has been affected and CPSEs start operating as independent enterprises with or without change of ownership. These are problems emerging from operations of large sized enterprises, with the probable monopolistic situations.

From a review of the reports and recommendations of the Disinvestment Commission, it has been noted that the Commission has been in most cases ignored by the Government. This is unfortunate. When an expert group examines a problem and reports, it should be obligatory on the Government to accept the recommendation. If certain recommendations are not accepted the reasons for this must be made public and reported to Parliament. Further, the present practice of the Commission being barred to take up investigations on its own should be given up. The Commission should have the authority to report on any related aspects of disinvestment.

Under the proposed mechanism of privatisation it is expected that there would be a rapid expansion in the number of shareholders as also entry of a good number of new corporations in the capital market. India is a newly emerging capital market. The experience of the last decade has not been very encouraging for small and new investors. SEBI has certainly become more effective during the last few years. However, there still continues to be shortcomings in the regulations of capital market, which have to be attended to. There is a need to expand information base on corporations and their operations in the capital markets. This could help monitor operations of the stock exchanges for appropriate remedial measures in time.

It has been accepted in principle by the government to pay cash compensation to workers under the Voluntary Retirement Scheme (VRS). While one-time cash compensation may appear to be an attractive proposition, it may not solve the long-term problems of the workers. The emphasis should be in seeking alternatives, which provide an effective safety net that can ensure regular incomes to the retirees. The alternatives may be in (a) award of pension, (b) regular full-time or part-time employment, or (c) helping them establish independent service or manufacturing establishments.

One issue of significance is with regard to the workers who had reservations and preferences in matters of employment in the public sector. The problem may not be very serious in case of the existing workers but it should be obligatory on all large private corporations to respond to social problems of the society. Alternatives to help the weaker and socially backward sections have to be explored by the large private corporations.

Privatisation of services that leads to casualization of the labour is against the norms of labour laws. Besides exploiting the unorganised labour and denying the legitimate rights, long-term social consequences of contractualisation trends would be serious. It is, therefore, necessary that some effective institutional mechanism be established to protect casual and contractual labour.

One important reason for privatisation of PEs in India has been the continuing losses, which have to be borne by the public exchequer and thereby the common man. It is obvious that even after extensive privatisation there would continue to be certain enterprises in the public sector. One should also not rule out the possibility of new PEs coming into being in case of market failures. Additionally, in most of the privatized enterprises government is likely to remain as a dominant shareholder. The government may not be able to totally isolate itself from the working of these enterprises. The minimum expectation would be that government provides positive support to the internal structural changes in the enterprises and help the new managements to achieve higher productivity for the massive national capital that has already been invested. Government must also develop an objective and efficient system of monitoring and advice. It is also necessary to develop a proper system for identification and creation of professional groups who could be available to solve problems by all large corporations irrespective of their being in public, private or cooperative sectors. It is envisaged that if proper internal restructuring of CPSEs is attempted, the twin objectives of protecting public interest and efficiency can be combined effectively.

Public enterprises in India by the very nature of their origin enjoy a monopoly and a dominant place in the respective areas of their operations. Monopolies have a tendency to ignore research and development (R & D) and continue their economic activities with obsolete technologies, high cost operations and use of outdated and depleted capital and machinery. This results in high costs and the enterprises being left out of the modern trends in industry. In absence of any internal and external commercial threat, monopolies tend to perpetuate inefficient low quality production with little capabilities to compete globally. The change over from public ownership and control to private economic interests need to ensure that private monopolies are not established in place of public monopolies. There are fears that privatisation of public monopolies would be followed by an upward revision of tariff. Such price revisions could easily eliminate losses without improvements in productivity. To protect consumers and long-term national and industry interests, it is, therefore, essential to establish an industry-based authority to regulate and issue guidelines for conduct of dominant and large business enterprises.

For a smooth and successful transition from a planned to an open market economy it is essential that all sections concerned with the change be brought together for a healthy and meaningful system of consultations. The interaction has to be among various parties; such as, employers and workers' organizations and central and state governments. Information and the logic of the proposed steps at re-arrangement of the regulatory mechanisms must be shared without any reservation. This could help avoid unnecessary resistance to change and keep the process of change within broad perspective of development.

Annex - A

View point of the labour

1. Five major trade unions and a public sector officers' association[1] besides some individual trade union leaders and academics were contacted, who have been dealing with different aspects of labour in India. Detailed discussions with the senior trade union functionaries were extremely rewarding. Thers is a high degree of similarity in their responses, which probably reflects the closeness of the views expressed with the reality. The following is a brief point-wise summary of the views expressed by the TU leaders.

Privatization

2. Trade Unions (TUs) have expressed their disapproval of the government's unilateral decision to promote policies towards privatization of Indian public sector. They were not involved in a meaningful way in the disinvestment process either. The privatization of public enterprises, which happen to be large in size, can only mean a transfer of the public property to Indian Big Business or Transnational Corporations. Operational aspect of the proposed scheme for restructuring of public enterprises is downsizing of labour. The TUs believe the 'exit policy', 'golden handshake', privatization, closures and downsizing are all aimed at weakening of the bargaining power of labour. Each form of privatization has direct adverse implications for the labour. TUs do not accept the basic premise that public sector enterprises have always to be running under loss. They point out that the real reason for PSEs being in red is the utter neglect of PSEs in matters of appointing competent professionals. Most PSEs do not have full strength of their management boards and consequently PSEs are administered as a remote control system by bureaucrats from ministries. The TUs also underline that PSEs are directed by the government to adopt pricing policies which are wholly unrealistic and are the main cause of losses. TUs argue that since PSEs are in the nature of monopolies, left to independent operation, none of the enterprises would be in loss.

3. TUs are not prepared to accept that privatization policy is a 'home grown' product. The inspiration of this has come from foreign-based multilateral bodies like the World Bank and IMF. These policies have been thrust on the Indian government. TUs question both the assumptions and the analyses as outlined in the cryptic decisions and directives to pursue

---

[1] These were: (1) Mr. Chandi Das Sinha, Secretary Indian National Trade Union Congress (INTUC) & Editor, The Indian Worker; (2) Mr. Raj Kishan Bhakt, Member, Executive Committee, Bhartaiya Mazdoor Sangh (BMS); (3) Mr. Umraomal Purohit, General Secretary, Hind Mazdoor Sabha (HMS); (4) Mr. Tapan Sen, National Secretary, Centre of Indian Trade Unions (CITU); (5) Mr. K.L. Mahendra, General Secretary, All India Trade Union Congress (AITUC); and (6) Mr. Ashok Rao, Secretary General, National Confederation of Officers' Associations of Central Public Sector Undertakings (NCOA).

privatization of PSEs. TUs argue that while the main responsibility for the public sector losses is that of bureaucracy and political leadership, it is the labour that has been asked to pay the price. TUs say, "Common workers are totally disturbed by privatization and VRS". The situation is worse in case of State level PSEs. On the one had, NRF is not extended to them; and on the other, they just sell away the units to private parties.

VRS

4. TUs' opposition to the new economic policies is essentially due to the expected adverse effect on employment. Retrenchment or voluntary retirement in the Indian context implies, on the one hand, absence of unemployment insurance, and on the other lack of alternative jobs. Public sector employment gives them, particularly those in the lower rungs, the opportunity to lead a life of dignity and self-respect. The restructuring of PSEs is forcing them to choose a different vocation and that too unexpectedly. In most cases those who accept VRS are in their mid-life when adjustments at the personal and family levels are extremely difficult to make.

5. A few workers who were young in age, and possessed engineering degrees, opted for VRS and were able to get jobs in the private sector. A small proportion of the retrenched workers did eventually get jobs in the small-scale private sector, since this sector is labour intensive. These jobs, however, meant half the earlier income with usual insecurity, as small-scale sector is prone to high degree of mortality. Practically, all of them were critical of the way VRS is being implemented. Their response is best summed up in one of the studies of Maniben Kara Institute as "...vast majority of the workers who opted for VRS and resigned their jobs are having a bad time. Many of them were left with only a small portion of the lump sum, the major portion having gone in repayment of loans or expenses on marriages or having spent on petty unnecessary items."[1]

Inadequate VRS amount

6. Not only the VRS amounts are small, they get smaller when adjusted against loans already availed, like house building advance, etc. It is an unfortunate reality of the Indian system that workers face a variety of social pressures once they receive the severance payment. Moreover, not having used to handling relatively large amounts, they fall prey to spending on durables or end up extending sticky loans to friends and relatives or invest in unproductive and risky investments. Unlike in the West, ordinary people are not at all aware of the way stock markets function and often get lured by sudden booms in share prices.

7. The VRS amount is measly and needs to be increased in multiples. At the least, the VRS benefits should be calculated at the rate of 90 days salary for each completed year of

---

[1] Maniben Kara Institute, Voluntary Retirement Scheme and Workers' Response, Friedrich Ebert Stiftung, New Delhi, 1994, p. 35.

service.[1] This was attempted by Air India and some quasi-government institutions like the Coffee Board. It would perhaps also be appropriate for the VRS benefits to take the form of pension in entirety.[2] A government organisation could be associated with administering the pension scheme for all PSEs. This is because there have been cases in PSEs where persons who retired have altogether not received their pension payments.

Non-payment of VRS amount

8. It was pointed out that there was no guarantee that the promised amounts would be paid-out and gave the instances of NTC and IDPL, where workers were retrenched but did not receive the full VRS payment. "In Cement Corporation of India and Hindustan Steelworks Construction Limited, workers and officers opted for VRS but they were not paid the VRS amount. Now, while they continue to be in employment, they are not getting salaries."[3] Further, in the sick industries, those who opted for VRS did not receive their provident fund dues and gratuity payment. "The concerned PSEs do not have the funds to make the payments", they say.[4] This led the TUs to underline that organisations should not be allowed to offer VRS unless they have adequate funds.

Non-voluntary dimension of VRS

9. TUs point out that in a good number of cases VRS has become non-voluntary in nature because in the new scheme, where the PSEs would be given loans by banks to fund the VRS and the loans would be guaranteed by the government, those who opt for the VRS in the stipulated time period get 45 days salary for each year of service that they put in. After the stipulated period they get only 15 days salary, as then the Industrial Disputes Act becomes applicable. This forces workers to apply within the time limit set by the organisation.[5] "In Hindustan Steel Construction Limited, (HSCL) even intimidating tactics have been employed to compel the workers to take VRS. They have been told either they take VRS or lose it altogether". The voluntary nature of VRS should be restored.[6]

---

[1] That a VRS benefit calculated at the rate of 90 days salary for each completed year of service is reasonable was argued in S.K. Goyal, Madhya Pradesh: Implementation of Public Sector Restructuring Programme: A Poverty Impact Assessment Study, prepared for the Asian Development Bank, June 1998. An alternative calculation could be five years of emoluments. See: Ruddar Datt, "Public Sector and Privatization", The Indian Economic Journal, January-March 1992,No. 3, pp. 1-38.

[2] The pension benefits could be calculated as arising from a corpus based on funds that would become available if 90 days salary were to be paid for every completed year of service. The provident fund benefits and the gratuity payment would of course be received in lump sum amounts. The purpose of a pension is to rule out the possibility of those taking the VRS landing in dire straits through the inability to manage VRS benefits. The pension would additionally have to be indexed.

[3] Mr. Tapan Sen, CITU.

[4] Mr. Chandi Das Sinha, INTUC.

[5] The ex-gratia payment includes pay plus dearness allowance.

[6] This view was supported, apart from the Trade Unions, by Ruddar Datt. op. cit.

Retraining of workers

10. A vast proportion of funds in the NRF has been spent on VRS with very little going into retraining the workers.[1] One of the TU representatives even went to the extent of saying that "they have not trained 500 people to date. There is no redeployment."[2] Another said, "Retraining is a farce".[3] Very little is spent on retraining exercises.[4] It is a matter of serious concern that TUs are not convinced of the industrial training capabilities of the institutions that have been assigned the task.[5] Adequate provision needs to be earmarked in the NRF for purposes of retraining and redeployment. Retraining has to be provided while the worker was still at his job and not after he had been retrenched. Similar should be the case with redeployment.

11. Priority should be given for creating employment opportunities instead of downsizing public enterprises. First and foremost is to find ways to revive sick PSEs instead of concentrating on VRS. A revolving fund for the revival of sick industries should be created. The fund could be generated through disinvestment by LIC, UTI, GIC, etc. in private sector companies.[6] The fund could take the form of share capital in a corporation meant for the revival of sick industries. It was pointed out that the institutions often pump money to revive the stock markets yet the market continues to be a bottomless pit. Instead of referring sick PSEs to the BIFR, which is not taking any decisions,[7] an attempt should be made to handover the units to workers to be run as co-operatives.

---

[1] In 1992-93 almost the entire sum allocated to NRF, was spent on VRS (Maniben Kara Institute, 1994: 15). It is important to note that a similar view was expressed by the Committee on Public Undertakings. The Committee said: '... the trend so far has been to expend major chunk of the amount on VRS which is not in keeping with the original concept of setting up of the Fund". COPU Report (1998-99), op. cit., p. 4.

[2] Mr. Raj Kishan Bhagat, Member Executive Committee, Bharatiya Mazdoor Sangh.

[3] Mr. Tapan Sen, CITU.

[4] The Government indeed admitted that "(D)ue to financial constraints sufficient funds have not been available for various schemes envisaged under the NRF resolution." They, however, tried to explain the low expenditure on retraining by saying that expenditure on VRS would be high as the cost of VRS per employee is approximately Rs. 0.2 million while the cost of retraining is about Rs. 8,000 per employee. See: Lok Sabha Secretariat, Committee on Public Undertakings (1998-99) First Report, p.41.

[5] For instance, it was pointed out that "(T)he needed infrastructure, the methodologies relevant to the older retrenched workers and the institutional material required just do not seem to be available". See: Ashok Chandra, op. cit.

[6] Interestingly, COPU (1998-99) in response to the government's reply that investments in PSEs are made on their commercial consideration, reminded the government that:
    ... the responsibility for rehabilitation of existing PSUs, irrespective of whether they are in the infrastructural or in the non-infrastructural areas rests with the Government ... it would be unfair to hold a view that investments should not be made even for revival of a sick PSU just because it is in the non-core or non-infrastructural sector. See: COPU (1998-99), First Report, p. 5.

[7] With regard to the treatment meted out to the sick PSEs, COPU (1997-98) categorically stated that:
    Other than introducing the legislative measure for referring the sick PSUs to BIFR, no major initiatives have been taken by Government to cope with sickness in the public sector. See: Lok Sabha Secretariat, Committee on Public Undertakings (1997-98), Sickness in Public Undertakings, Eleventh Report, p. 80.

12. TUs highlighted the plight of workers of sick PSEs such as Hindustan Steelworks Construction Limited, Cement Corporation, National Project Construction Corporation, Indian Drugs and Pharmaceuticals Limited and Tannery and Footwear Corporation of India, who have not been getting their salaries regularly. Restoration of budgetary support, they say, is inevitable if regular payment of salaries has to be ensured.[1]

Contract labour

13. TUs had some very revealing things to say about reduction in public enterprise employment. While the number of workers in PSEs are being reduced, the reduction does not mean that the work is being done by a reduced workforce, but that part of the work is being done by casual and contract labour. Privatization is thus leading to exploitation as regular jobs are getting converted into low paid jobs depriving the workers social security and other essential benefits like housing, medical and children's education.

14. TUs assure that they are prepared to extend full support. Unfortunately, they say, this can be done only if they are involved in the ongoing processes in a meaningful and sincere manner.

---

[1] Significantly, Annual Report of the Ministry of Industry informs that the improved compensation package announced by the Minister of Finance in the 1998-99 budget for those seeking VRS from sick companies was still being worked out at the end of the year. See: India, Ministry of Industry, Annual Report: 1998-99, p. 178.

Bibliography

Ahluwalia Isher Judge (1996): "Economic Reform in India; Issues Ahead", in Ahluwalia, Isher Judge and Albert Berry, Perspectives: Focus on Indo-Canadian Business and Economic Issues, The Conference Board of Canada, Canada, pp. 1-25.

Aizenman Joshua (1998): "Privatization in Emerging Markets", Working Paper 6524, National Bureau of Economic Research, Cambridge, April.

Anderson Christopher W., Anil K. Makhija, and Michael H. Spiro (1997): "Foreign Ownership in the Privatization Process: Empirical Evidence from Czech Privatization", Working Paper (University of Pittsburgh).

Bajaj J. L. (1994): "Divesting State Ownership: A Tale of Two Companies", *Economic and Political Weekly,* Vol. 29, No. 35, pp. M120-M128.

Baruah Sriparna B. (1993): "Textile Mills of Assam: Is Privatisation the Answer?", *Economic & Political Weekly,* No. 31, pp. 1569-1571.

Batra G. S. and B. S. Bhatia (1994): "Liberalisation of Indian Economy : An Evaluation of Recent Public Sector Reforms and Privatisation Strategies", *Journal of Institute of Public Enterprises,* No. 1, pp. 52-62.

Beesley M. E. and S. C. Littlefield (1989): "The Regulation of Privatized Monopolies in the United Kingdom", *Rand Journal of Economics,* 20, pp. 454-473.

Bhalla G. S. (1968): *Financial Administration of Nationalised Industries in the United Kingdom and India,* Meenakshi Prakashan, Meerut.

Bhat K. S., "Non-Privatisation Reforms in State Level Public Enterprises", Institute of Public Enterprises, (Mimeo).

Bhattacharya Sisir (1993): "The Problematic of Defining New Terms of Discourse on Privatisation", *Indian Journal of Social Science,* No. 4, pp. 351-370.

Bhaya Hiten, "Public Sector: Colossus with Feet of Clay?" *Economic & Political Weekly,* 1983, No. 22, pp. M-50 - M-66.

Bhouraskar D. M. (1993): "Privatisation Policy", *Economic & Political Weekly,* No. 34, p. 1747.

Bishop Matthew R. and John A. Kay (1989): "Privatization in the United Kingdom: Lessons from Experience", *World Development,* 17, pp. 643-657.

Boubakri Narjess and Jean-Claude Cosset (1998): "The Financial and Operating Performance of Newly-Privatized Firms: Evidence from Developing Countries", *Journal of Finance,* 53, pp. 1081-1110.

Boycko Maxim, Andrei Shleifer, and Robert W. Vishny (1996): "A Theory of Privatisation", *Economic Journal,* 106, pp. 309-319.

Breman Jan (1996): *Footloose Labour: Working in India's Informal Economy,* Cambridge University Press.

Centre for Monitoring Indian Economy, Infrastructure in India, August 1995.

Chalam K. S. (1996): "National Renewal Fund and Welfare of Working Classes", *Economic & Political Weekly,* No. 49, pp. 3165-3167.

Chandra Ashok (1999): "Retraining and Redeployment: NRF Initiative and Challenge in Training", *The Indian Journal of Labour Economics,* No. 1, pp. 31-47.

Chaudhuri Sudip (1979): "FERA: Appearance and Reality", *Economic & Political Weekly,* April 21, 1979, No. 16, pp. 734-744.

_____(1979): "Financing of Growth of Transnational Corporations in India: 1956-75", *Economic & Political Weekly,* August 18, No. 33, pp. 1431-1435.

_____(1994): "Public Enterprise and Private Purposes", *Economic & Political Weekly,* No. 22, pp. 1338-1347.

Committee of Public Sector Trade Unions (1999): Declaration at the Extended Meeting in New Delhi on June 15-16.

Cowlagi V. R. S. (1994): "The National Renewal Fund: Promise, Performance, and Prospects", *Vikalpa,* No. 4, pp. 3-14.

D'Mello Bernard (1991): "Public Sector and Public Interest", *Economic & Political Weekly,* Vol. 26, No. 3, p. 107.

Dalvi M. Q. (1995): "Should Indian Railways be Privatised?", *Economic & Political Weekly,* No. 2, pp. 103-112.

Das Debendra K. (Ed.) (1994): *Privatisation of Public Sector Undertakings: Rationale and Feasibility,* Deep and Deep Publications, New Delhi.

Das Debendra K. and Vishnude Bhagat (Ed.) (1994): *Economics of Privatisation: Issues and Options,* Deep and Deep Publications, New Delhi.

Datt Ruddar (Ed.) (1993): *Privatization Bane or Panacea,* Pragati Publications, Delhi.

Datt Ruddar (1992): "Public Sector and Privatization", *The Indian Economic Journal,* January-March 1992, No. 3, pp. 1-38.

Dayal Ishwar, "Emerging Demands on Trade Unions", *Indian Journal of Industrial Relations,* No. 2, pp. 206-219.

Dewenter Kathryn and Paul H. Malatesta, "Public Offerings of State-owned and Privately Owned Enterprises: An International Comparison", *Journal of Finance,* 1997, 52, pp. 1659-1679.

Dhameja Nand (1991): "Privatisation in India: Various Problem Areas", *MDI Journal of Management,* No. 1, p. 119.

_____ (1993): "Privatisation Experiences: Lessons for Developing Countries", *Productivity,* No. 4, pp. 683-695.

_____ (1997): "Public Sector Growth and Finance: Emerging Trends", *Indian Journal of Public Administration,* No. 3, pp. 527-538.

Disinvestment Commission, Disinvestment Strategy and Issues, December, 1996.

Disinvestment Commission, Report I, February, 1997.

Disinvestment Commission, Report II, April, 1997.

Disinvestment Commission, Report III, May, 1997.

Disinvestment Commission, Report V, November, 1997.

Disinvestment Commission, Report IX, March, 1999.

Disinvestment Commission, Report X, June, 1999.

Disinvestment Commission, Report XII, August, 1999.

Dubey Rameshwar (1998): "Implementation of Employee Assistance Programme under NRF: A Case Study", *Manpower Journal,* No. 4, p. 65.

Dutta Soumyendra K. (1993): "Privatisation — Whether A Panacea?", *Indian Journal of Economics,* No. 290, pp. 291-296.

Edadan Narayanan (1997): "Privatisation Strategies in Developing Countries - External Debt and Domestic Economic Perspectives", *Economic & Political Weekly,* No. 27, pp. 1608-1619.

Edgren Gus (Ed.) (1998): *The Growing Sector: Studies of Public Sector Employment in Asia,* International Labour Organization and Asian Employment Programme (ARTEP), New Delhi.

Evans-Clock C. and A. Samorodov, *The Employment Impact of Privatisation and Enterprise Restructuring in Selected Transition Economies,* International Labour Organization, Geneva.

Frank Andre Gunder (1992): "Privatisation: Sham Debate", *Economic & Political Weekly,* No. 8, p. 432.

Ghosh Arun (1992): "A Glimpse at a Public Sector Enterprise", *Economic & Political Weekly,* No. 7, pp. 317-18.

_____ (1993): "Public Goods and Rush for Privatisation", *Economic & Political Weekly,* No. 41, pp. 2181-2182.

_____ (1994): "Ideologues and Ideology: Privatisation of Public Enterprises", *Economic & Political Weekly,* No. 30, pp. 1929-1931.

_____ (1997): "Break-Up and Privatisation of SEB in Andhra Pradesh - An Upcoming Scam", *Economic & Political Weekly,* No. 29, pp. 1782-1785.

Ghosh D. N. (1991): "Incoherent Privatisation, Indian Style", *Economic & Political Weekly,* No. 21, pp. 1313-1316.

Ghosh Jayati (1995): Abhijit Sen and C P Chandresekhar, "Privatising Natural Resources", *Economic & Political Weekly,* No. 38, pp. 2351-2353.

Ghuman B. S. (1994): "Privatisation: The Case of Punjab State Road Transport Undertakings", *Productivity,* No. 4, pp. 686-692.

Gidadhubli R.G. and Rama Sampat Kumar (1993): "Privatisation in East European Countries", *Economic & Political Weekly,* No. 24, pp. 1216-1219.

Gill Sucha Singh (1996): "Punjab: Privatising Health Care", *Economic & Political Weekly,* No. 1, pp. 18-19.

Gokarn Subir and Rajendra Vaidya (1993): "Deregulation and Industrial Performance: The Indian Cement Industry", *Economic & Political Weekly,* Nos. 8- 9, pp. M-33 - M-41.

Gouri Geeta (1991): *Privatisation and Public Enterprise: The Asia-Pacific Experience,* Oxford & IBH Publishing Co. Pvt. Ltd., New Delhi.

_____ (1992): "Privatisation - A More Balanced Approach", *Journal of Institute of Public Enterprises,* No. 3, pp. 201-210.

_____ (1996): "Privatisation and Public Sector Enterprises in India - Analysis of Impact of A Non-Policy", *Economic & Political Weekly,* No. 48, pp. M-63 - M-74.

Goyal S.K., *Monopoly Capital and Public Policy,* Allied Publishers, Delhi, 1979.

_____ (1979): Impact of Foreign Subsidiaries on India's Balance of Payments, Indian Institute of Public Administration, Delhi (mimeo). The study was prepared for the UNCTC-ESCAP Joint Unit, Bangkok.

_____ (1980): "A Preliminary Survey of Excess Industrial Capacities with the Indian Corporate Sector (Some Implications of Industrial Policy Statement of July 23, 1980".

_____ (1982): "New Industrial Licensing Policy - An Empirical Assessment". Both are working papers of the Corporate Studies Group, Indian Institute of Public Administration, Delhi.

_____ (1983): "The New International Economic Order and Transnational Corporations", in ICSSR and Institute for Social Science Research in Developing Countries, New International Economic Order: Problems and Perspectives.

Goyal S. K., et. al. (1983): *Functioning of Industrial Licensing System,* Indian Institute of Public Administration, Delhi, (mimeo) 1983.

Goyal S. K., et. al. (1994): *Small Scale Sector and Big Business,* Indian Institute of Public Administration, Delhi, (mimeo).

_____(1987): "Spectrum of Public Sector in India", in Shastri Indo-Canadian Institute, Issues in Public Sector Analysis.

_____ (1998): *Madhya Pradesh: Implementation of Public Sector Restructuring Programme: A Poverty Impact Assessment Study,* prepared for the Asian Development Bank, June.

Guha B. P. (1996): "Voluntary Retirement Schemes in Indian Industries", *Indian Journal of Industrial Relations,* No. 3, p. 378.

_____ (1996): *Voluntary Retirement: Problems and Prospects of Rehabilitation,* Shri Ram Centre for Industrial Relations and Human Resources, Delhi.

Guhan S. (1991): "Fiscal Deficit and Public Enterprises", *Economic & Political Weekly,* No. 49, p. 2840.

Gupta Anand P. (1996): "Privatization and India's Economic Reforms, Center for Institutional Reform and the Informal Sector", IRIS-India Working Paper No. 15, University of Maryland, May.

_____ (1996): "The Political Economy of Privatization in India", IRIS-India Working Paper Number 17, Center for Institutional Reform and the Informal Sector, University of Maryland, July.

Gupta D. P. (1990): *Industrial Sickness and the Role of Reconstruction Agencies,* Chanakya Publications, Delhi.

Gupta G. S. (1998): "Privatisation: Theory, Practices and Issues", *Indian Economic Journal,* No. 2, pp. 96-106.

Hirway Indira (1995): "Safety Net of the National Renewal Fund: Some Basic Issues", *Indian Journal of Labour Economics,* No. 2, pp. 185-200.

Holberton Simon (1996): "Power Behind the Golden Shares", *Financial Times,* May 4, p. 8.

Huibers Fred and Enrico C. Perotti (1998): "The Performance of Privatization Stocks in Emerging Markets: The Role of Political Risk", Working Paper (University of Amsterdam).

Huizinga Harry (1997): "Privatization, Public Investment, and Capital Income Taxation", *The World Bank,* January.

Husain Aasim and Ratna Sahay (1992): "Does Sequencing of Privatization Matter in Reforming Planned Economies", International Monetary Fund Staff Papers, 39, pp. 801-824.

India, Department of Public Enterprises (1995-96 and 1997-98): Public Enterprises Survey.

India, Ministry of Commerce (1992): Committee on Free Trade Zones and 100 per cent Export Oriented Units, Final Report, (Chairman: P.L. Tandon).

India, Ministry of Commerce (1974): Report of the Committee on Engineering Exports, (Chairman: Mantosh Sondhi).

India, Ministry of Commerce (1980): Report of the Committee on Export Strategy: 1980s, Final Report, (Chairman: P. L. Tandon).

India, Ministry of Commerce (1978): Report of the Committee on Import-Export Policies and Procedures, (Chairman: P.C. Alexander).

India, Ministry of Commerce (1984): Report of the Committee on Perspective Plan and Strategy for Export of Engineering and Capital Goods, (Chairman: D.V. Kapur).

India, Ministry of Commerce (1984): Report of the Committee on Trade Policies, 1984 (Chairman: Abid Hussain).

India, Ministry of Finance (1985): Report of the Committee to Examine Principles of a Possible Shift from Physical to Financial Controls, (Chairman: M. Narasimham).

India, Ministry of Finance (1984): Report of the Committee to Review Policy for Public Enterprises, December. (Chairman: Arjun Sengupta).

India, Ministry of Industry (1996): "Statement on Industrial Policy", July 24, 1991, Handbook of Industrial Policy and Statistics.

India, Ministry of Industry (1992-93 and 1997-99): Annual Reports.

India, Ministry of Industry (1978): Report of the Study Group on Industrial Regulations & Procedures, (Chairman: G.V. Ramakrishna).

India, Planning Commission (1964): Committee on Distribution of Income and Levels of Living: Report, (Chairman: P.C. Mahalanobis).

India, Planning Commission (1989): Report of the Eighth Plan Working Group on the Management of PSEs, (mimeo) (Chairman: V. Krishnamurthy).

India, Planning Commission (1956): Second Five Year Plan.

India, Report of the Industrial Licensing Policy Inquiry Committee, 1969 (Chairman: S. Dutt).

India, Report of the Monopolies Inquiry Commission, 1965 (Chairman: K.C. Dasgupta).

India, Report of the Tenth Finance Commission (for 1995-2000), December 1994.

Institute of Public Enterprise (1995): Seminar on "Restructuring of State Level Public Enterprises", June 30-July 1, Hyderabad.

Iyer Ramaswamy R. (1985): "The Macro-Economic Study of the Public Enterprise Sector'", *Economic & Political Weekly*, No. 21, pp. M-65 - M-74.

Iyer Ramaswamy R. (1998): "The Privatisation Argument", *Economic & Political Weekly*, No. 23, 11, pp. 554-556.

_____ (1990): "Privatisation Debate: An Alternative Framework", *Economic & Political Weekly*, No. 27, pp. 1491-1492.

_____ (1990): "Public Enterprises as State and Article 12", *Economic & Political Weekly*, No. 34, pp. M-129 - M-134.

_____ (1991): "Fiscal Deficit and Public Enterprises", *Economic & Political Weekly*, No. 44, pp. 2538-39.

_____ (1991): *A Grammar of Public Enterprises: Exercises in Clarifications*, Rawat Publications, Jaipur.

_____ (1992): "Fiscal Deficit and Public Enterprises: Some More Grammar", *Economic & Political Weekly*, No. 6, pp. 295-296.

_____ (1994): Public Enterprise and Private Purposes, *Economic & Political Weekly*, No. 34, pp. 2246-48.

_____ (1995): "Uncertain Future of Public Enterprises", *Economic & Political Weekly,* No. 34, pp. 2121-22.

J. M. (1993): "Privatisation: Magic Ward or Budgetary Cop-out?", *Economic & Political Weekly,* No. 52, pp. 2865-2867.

Joshi Vijay and I. M. D. Little (1994): *India Macroeconomics and Political Economy 1964-1991,* World Bank, Washington, D.C.

Joshi Vijay and I. M. D. Little (1996): *India's Economic Reforms 1991-2001,* Oxford University Press, Delhi.

Kabra Kamal Nayan (1985): "Nationalisations in India: A Study in Policy Options - 1947-1980", Indian Institute of Public Administration, New Delhi (Mimeo).

Kalirajan K. P. and R. T. Shand (1996): "Public Sector Enterprises in India: Is Privatisation the Only Answer?", *Economic & Political Weekly,* No. 39, pp. 2683-2686.

Katz Barbara G. and Joel Owen (1993): "Privatization: Choosing the Optimal Time Path", *Journal of Comparative Economics,* 17, pp. 715-736.

Kay A. J. and D. J. Thompson (1986): "Privatisation: A Policy in Search of a Rationale", *Economic Journal,* March.

Khambata Farida and Dara Khambata, "Developing New Capital Markets in the Third World: Privatization & Emerging Stock Markets", *Foreign Trade Review, 88,* No. 2, p. 132.

Khasnabis Ratan and Sudipti Banerjea (1996): "Political Economy of Voluntary Retirement - Study of Rationalised Workers in Durgapur", *Economic & Political Weekly,* No. 52, pp. L-64 - L-72.

Kikeri Sunita, John Nellies and Mary Stirley (1994): "Privatisation: Lessons from Market Economies", *World Bank Research Observer,* 9 (2), pp. 241-72.

Kikeri Sunita, John Nellis, and Mary Shirley (1992): "Privatization: The Lessons of Experience" *World Bank,* Washington, D.C.

Kole Stacey R. and J. Harold Mulherin (1997): "The Government as a Shareholder: A case from the United States", *Journal of Law and Economics,* 40, pp. 1-22

Kulkarni G. R. (1979): "Management Problems in the Public Sector", *Economic & Political Weekly,* No. 9, pp. M-3 - M-12.

Kumari Anita (1993): "Productivity in Public Sector", *Economic & Political Weekly,* No. 48, pp. M-145 - M-162.

Kurtz Mariann (1995): Privatisation and Development Scenario Papers on Privatisation, Draft, Price Waterhouse LLP for USAID, Washington, D.C. (Office of Economic and Institutional Reform. Center for Economic Growth).

Kurup N. P. (1994): "Muddle of Partial Privatisation of Banks", *Economic & Political Weekly,* No. 37, p. 2402.

La Porta Rafael and Florencio Lopez-de-Silanes (1997): "Benefits of Privatization - Evidence from Mexico", Private Sector, *World Bank,* Washington, DC: June, pp. 21-24.

Lok Sabha Secretariat, Committee on Public Undertakings (1987): Accountability and Autonomy of Public Undertakings, Thirty-second Report, Eighth Lok Sabha, Department of Public Enterprises, Ministry of Industry, New Delhi.

Lok Sabha Secretariat, Committee on Public Undertakings (1987-88): Sickness in Public Undertakings, Eleventh Report.

Lok Sabha Secretariat, Committee on Public Undertakings (1998-99): First Report: Sickness in Public Undertakings.

Lok Sabha Secretariat, Committee on Public Undertakings (Eleventh Lok Sabha), Tenth Report.

Lok Sabha Secretariat, GOI (1981-82): Committee on Public Undertakings (COPU), 49th Report, New Delhi.

Lok Sabha Secretariat, Public Accounts Committee (1993-94): Disinvestment of Government Shareholding in Selected Public Sector Enterprises during 1991-92, Seventy fifth Report, 1994.

Majumdar Sumit K. and Abuja Gautam (1997): "Privatisation: An Exegesis of Key Ideas", *Economic & Political Weekly,* No. 27, pp. 1590-1595.

Majumdar Sumit K. (1996): "Assessing Comparative Efficiency of the State-owned, Mixed, and Private Sectors in Indian Industry", *Public Choice,* pp. 1-24.

Mani Sunil (1992): "New Industrial Policy: Barriers To Entry, Foreign Investment and Privatisation", *Economic & Political Weekly,* No. 35, pp. M-86 - M-94.

_____ (1995): "Economic Liberalisation and the Industrial Sector", *Economic & Political Weekly,* No. 21, pp. M-38 - M-50.

Maniben Kara Institute (1994): *Voluntary Retirement Scheme and Workers' Response,* Friedrich Ebert Stiftung, New Delhi.

Manickavasagam V. and A. R. Alagappan (1998): "Reservation Policy in PSUs: How Effective", *Economic & Political Weekly,* No. 15, pp. 823-824.

Marathe Sharad S (1989): "Regulation and Development: India's Policy Experience of Controls Over Industry", Second Edition, Sage Publications, New Delhi.

Martin B., "The Social Employment Consequences of Privatization in Transition Economies: Evidence and Guidelines", Interdepartmental Action Programme on Privatization, Restructuring and Economic Democracy - Working Paper IPPRED-4, International Labour Organization.

Masud Javed (1991): "Privatization and Deregulation in Pakistan (Policy Framework and Strategy)", Paper presented for the Planning and Development Division, Government of Pakistan, July.

Megginson William L. and Jeffry M. Netter (1998): "From State to Market: A Survey of Empirical Studies on Privatization", presented at Global Equity Markets, Paris, France, December 10-11.

Mehta Ankit and Shachi Trivedi (1996): "Reshaping the Economy: Implications of Privatization in India", *Indian Economic Journal,* No. 2, pp. 104-116.

Mehta S. S. (1995): "Exit Policy and Social Safety Net", *Indian Journal of Labour Economics,* No. 4, pp. 603-609.

Mishra R. K., "Safety Net, National Renewal Fund and State Level Public Enterprises in India: A Case Study of Hyderabad Allwyn Limited", Institute of Public Enterprises, (Mimeo).

Mishra R. K., "SLPE Reforms and Privatization in Various States", (unpublished notes), Institute of Public Enterprise, Hyderabad.

Mishra R. K. and B. Ratan Reddy (1994): "Scope for Reform and Privatisation of SLPEs in Orissa", *Asian Economic Review,* No. 3, pp. 725-736.

Mishra R. K. and R. Nandagopal (1989): "Financial Implications of Privatisation of Public Enterprises in India", *MDI Journal of Management,* No. 2, p. 31.

Mishra R. K. and R. Nandagopal (1991): "Privatisation of State Transport Undertakings in India: Scope and Modalities", *Journal of Institute of Public Enterprises,* No. 1, pp. 33-46.

Mishra R. K. and R. Nandagopal and Mallikarjuna Rao (1993): "State Transport Undertakings in India: Reforms and Privatisation Strategies", *Finance India*, No. 4, pp. 899-915.

Mishra R. K., Nandagopal R. and A. Lateef Syed Mohammad (1993): "Sale of Public Enterprise Shares: Frittering Away Nation's Wealth", *Economic & Political Weekly*, No. 48, pp. M-163 - M-168.

Misra B. M. (1993): "Privatisation of Public Enterprises in India — Some Issues", *Indian Economic Journal*, No. 2, pp. 71 - 88.

Modi Sanjay, K. C. Singhal and Umesh C. Singh (19965): "Workers' Participation in Trade Unions", *Indian Journal of Industrial Relations*, No. 1, pp. 40-58.

Morris Sebastian (1991): "Holding Companies, Performance Contracts and Task Orientation in Public Sector", *Economic & Political Weekly*, No. 48, pp. M-137 - M-144.

Mukherjee A. (1998): "Indian Capitalist Class and Congress on National Planning and Public Sector 1930-47", *Economic & Political Weekly*, No. 35, pp. 1516-1528.

Mukherjee Aditya (1976): "Indian Capitalist Class and the Public Sector, 1930-1947", *Economic & Political Weekly*, No. 3, pp. 67-73.

Mukul (1991): "Workers Against Privatisation", *Economic & Political Weekly*, No. 30, pp. 1781-1785.

_____ (1991): "Uttar Pradesh: Workers' Struggle Halts Privatisation Moves", *Economic & Political Weekly*, No. 43, pp. 2460 - 2462.

_____ (1992): "Uttar Pradesh: Workers Challenge Privatisation", *Economic & Political Weekly*, No. 1-2, pp. 25 - 27.

Muraleedharan K. P. (1996): "Implementation of Voluntary Retirement Scheme - Some Issues", *Productivity*, No. 2, p. 278.

Nagraj R. (1991): "Public Sector Performance in Eighties; Some Tentative Findings", *Economic & Political Weekly*, No. 50, pp. 2877-2883.

_____ (1993): "Macroeconomic Impact of Public Sector Enterprises: Some Further Evidence", *Economic & Political Weekly*, No. 3 & 4, pp. 105-109.

Nandakumar P. and S. Ravishankar (1994): "Empirical Study of Membership Participation in Trade Union Activities: An Indian Perspective", *Indian Journal of Industrial Relations*, No. 1, pp. 69-78.

Nandrajog M. L. (Ed.) (1999): *National Renewal Fund - A Look Ahead*, International Labour Organization, New Delhi.

Narayanan M. S. (1994): "Industrial Sickness; Review of BIFR's Role", *Economic & Political Weekly*, No. 7, pp. 362-376.

Nellis John, "Time to Rethink Privatization in Transition Economies?", Discussion Paper Number 38, International Finance Corporation, *The World Bank*, Washington, D.C.

Nigam Raj K. (Ed.) (1995): *Economic Reforms and Public Sector in India* (with update on Policy Reference for Public Sector Enterprises), DC Publications, New Delhi.

Papola T. S. and Alakh N. Sharma (1996): "Structural Adjustment, Poverty, Employment and Safety Nets: The Indian Experience", *Indian Journal of Labour Economics*, No. 3, pp. 591 - 623.

Parekh H. T. (1988): "Public Minority Participation in Equity of Public Sector Companies", *Economic & Political Weekly*, No. 23, pp. 1162-1163.

Parikh Kirit S. (1992): "Privatisation and Deregulation: Irrelevant Hypotheses", *Economic & Political Weekly*, No. 9, pp. 483 - 484.

Paul Samuel (1985): "Privatisation and the Public Sector: Relevance and Limits", *Economic & Political Weekly*, No. 8, pp. M-4 - M-8.

_____ (1992): "Privatisation and Deregulation", *Economic & Political Weekly*, No. 26, pp. 1339 - 1340.

Pillai Manmohan (1993): "Macroeconomic Impact of Public Sector Enterprises Comment", *Economic & Political Weekly*, No. 22, pp. 1121-1122.

Pradhan B. K., D. K. Ratha and Atul Sarma (1990): "Complementarity Between Public and Private Investment in India", *Journal of Development Economics*, 33, pp. 101-106.

Raghavan S. N. (1994): *Public Sector in India Changing Perspectives, Asian Institute of Transport Development,* New Delhi.

Raju P. L. N. (1991): "Privatisation of Passenger Road Transport System — Methods and Scope", *MDI Journal of Management,* No. 1, p. 59.

Rangarajan C. (1997): "Disinvestment: Strategies and Issues", Reserve Bank of India Bulletin, February No. 2, pp. 125-129.

Rao K. V. (1991): "Rationale and Framework for the Privatisation of State Level Public Enterprises in India", *Journal of Institute of Public Enterprises,* No. 1, pp. 47 - 56.

Rao S. L. (Ed.) (1996): *Reforming State-Owned Enterprises,* National Council of Applied Economic Research, I. P. Estate, New Delhi.

Rao S. L. (1994): "Labour Adjustment As Part of Industrial Restructuring: Human Dimensions of Liberalisation", *Economic & Political Weekly,* No. 6, pp. 313-320.

Ratnam C. S. Venkata (1992): "Social and Labour Issues in Privatisation - An Overview", *Indian Journal of Industrial Relations,* No. 2, pp. 139 - 154.

_____ (1993): "Adjustment through Privatisation: The Indian Agenda", *ASCI Journal of Management,* No. 4, pp. 165 - 186.

Reddy T. Chandramohan, V. M. Selvaraj and S. V. Udhayakumar (1991): "The Privatized Worker in the Milieu of Collective Action", *Indian Journal of Industrial Relations,* No. 1, p. 92.

Reddy Y. Venugopal (1992): *Public Enterprise Reform and Privatisation,* Himalaya Publishing House.

Reddy Y. Venugopal, Geeta Gauri, and J. M. Mauskar (1995): "Regulatory Policies and Practices: the Case of Reorientation", presented at Asian Conference on The Emerging Role of the State in the Transport Sector in the Perspective of Economic Liberalisation, (Unpublished).

Reddy Y. Venugopal, T. Koteswara Rao and R. K. Mishra (Eds.) (1990): *Towards Public Enterprises: Towards A White Paper,* Institute of Public Enterprise and Booklinks, Hyderabad.

Roy A. K. (1994): "IISCO Privatisation: The Real Issue", *Economic & Political Weekly,* No. 20, pp. 1171-1172.

Rudra Ashok (1991): "Privatisation and Deregulation", *Economic & Political Weekly,* No. 51, pp. 2933-2936.

_____ (1992): "Privatisation and Deregulation", *Economic & Political Weekly,* No. 20-21, p. 1100.

_____ (1992): "Privatisation and Deregulation", *Economic & Political Weekly,* No. 30, p. 1628.

Rutledge Susan L. (1995): "Selling State Companies to Strategic Investors - Trade Sale Privatizations in Poland, Hungary, the Czech Republic, and the Slovak Republic", CFS Discussion Paper Series Number 106, *The World Bank,* January.

Sankar T. L. and Y. Venugopal Reddy (1990): "Red Herring of Privatisation", *Economic & Political Weekly,* Nos. 7-8, pp. 407-408.

Sankar T. L. and Y. Venugopal Reddy (Ed.) (1989): *Privatisation: Diversification of Ownership of Public Enterprises,* Institute of Public Enterprise and Booklinks Corporation, Hyderabad.

Sarma Atul, "Restructuring and Privatisation of Public Enterprises in India", Indian Statistical Institute, New Delhi.

Sastry K. S. (1987): "Privatisation of Public Enterprises", *Productivity,* 1987, No. 1, p. 141.

Saxena A. P. (1993): "Privatisation: Cure or Curse?", *Economic & Political Weekly,* No. 21, p.1036.

Sen Anindya and Soumyen Sikdar (1997): "Privatization and the Choice of Organization Form", *Decision,* Nos. 1-4, pp. 15-20.

Sen Anindya (1998): "Privatization and Surplus Generation", *Indian Economic Journal,* No. 2, pp. 133-139.

Shirley Mary and John Nellis (1991): Public Enterprise Reform The Lessons of Experience, EDI Development Studies, *The World Bank,* Washington D.C.

Sidhu Hina (1995): "Privatisation of State Level Undertakings in Gujarat", *Decision,* Nos. 1-2, pp. 99-112.

Singh Gurdeep and B. S. Bhatia (1991): "Privatisation of Public Enterprises Concept, Approach & Issues", *Journal of Institute of Public Enterprises,* No. 4, pp. 279-283.

Singh Shrawan Kumar (1993): "Disinvestment of Public Sector Equity - An Analysis", *Yojana,* No. 17, pp. 6-9.

Srinivasan T. N. (1991): "Indian Development Strategy: An Exchange of Views", *Economic & Political Weekly,* Nos. 31-32, pp. 1850-1852.

_____ (1991): "Reform of Industrial and Trade Policies", *Economic & Political Weekly,* No. 37, pp. 2143-2145.

_____ (1992): "Privatisation and Deregulation", *Economic & Political Weekly,* No. 15, pp. 843-848.

Srivastava V. K. L. (1988): "Pricing Policies of Public Enterprises in India", in Mathur, B.L. (ed.): Public Enterprises: Policy and Performance, Arihant Publishers, Jaipur, Chapter IX, pp. 95-105.

Standing Conference of Public Enterprises (1989): Approach Paper to the White Paper on Public Enterprises, New Delhi.

Standing Conference of Public Enterprises (1990): Blueprint of SCOPE's White Paper on the Public Sector, New Delhi, April.

Standing Conference of Public Enterprises (1990): Reports/Recommendations of Various Committees on Public Enterprises, New Delhi.

Stiglitz Joseph E. (1986): *Economics of the Public Sector,* W.W. Norton & Company, New York, London.

Swamy Dalip S. (1994): *The Political Economy of Industrialisation,* Sage Publications, New Delhi.

Syed Ayub (Ed.), *The Swraj Paul Factor,* Palakmati Printers Pvt. Ltd, Bombay.

Tandon Pankaj (1997): "Efficiency of Privatised Firms - Evidence and Implications", *Economic & Political Weekly,* No. 50, pp. 3199-3212.

Tornell Aaron (1999): "Privatizing the Privatized", Working Paper 7206, National Bureau of Economic Research, Cambridge, July.

Trivedi Prajapati (1993): "What Is India's Privatisation Policy?", *Economic & Political Weekly,* No. 22, pp. M-71 - M-76.

Tulpule B. (1992): "Exit Policy in Public Sector", *Economic & Political Weekly,* No.7, pp. 319-321.

Ubha Dharminder Singh and J. S. Pasricha (1991): "Should India Go for Privatisation?", *Journal of Institute of Public Enterprises,* No. 4, pp. 271-275.

Wagle Subodh, Girish San & Shantanu Dixit (1997): "SEB Privatisation: Transcending the Issue of Ownership", *Economic & Political Weekly,* No. 40, pp. 2561-2562.

World Bank (1994): "India: Recent Economic Developments and Prospects", Report Number 12940-IN, Washington, D.C.

_____ (1991): "Report and Recommendation of the President of the International Bank for Reconstruction and Development and International Development Association to the Executive Directors on a Proposed Structural Adjustment Loan/Credit to India", November.

_____ (1989): *India: An Industrialising Economy in Transition,* A World Bank Country Study.

Press Reports

"6,000 opt for VRS at Sail", Statesman, September 6, 1998.

"AP's economic restructuring programme — A trailblazing start", Hindu Business Line, August 17, 1998.

"BHEL may face resistance from workers", Hindu Business Line, August 22, 1999 .

"BHEL VRS achieves target before deadline", Business Standard, July 28, 1999.

"CCEA approves guidelines for operating national renewal fund", Economic Times, October 29, 1992.

"Cong will give statutory powers to divestment panel", Financial Express, August 24, 1999.

"IPCL staff to boycott LS polls over disinvestment", Hindu Business Line, August 30, 1999.

"MFL workers up in arms against privatization", Financial Express, August 23, 1999.

"Minority Shareholders to Have Greater Say in SBI", Economic Times, March 15, 1996.

"PSU disinvestment: Manmohan admits lack of experience", Hindustan Times, August 13, 1993.

"Simultaneous Examination of PSU cases - DPE seeks BIFR's opinion", Hindu Business Line, Internet Edition, June 28, 1999.

"Standing Committee of Public Enterprises seeks review of Contact Labour Act following Supreme Court directive to Air India for absorption of contract labour", Business Standard, Internet Edition, February 11, 1998.

"State-owned units want the government to contest the Supreme Court ruling on contract labour", Business Standard, Internet Edition, January 14, 1998.

"TRAI as the govt might... Unless legislative lacunae is fixed, the regulator will remain a toothless wonder", Economic Times, June 27, 1999.

"TRAI moves HC to define role & reach", Economic Times, July 28, 1999.

"TRAI reduced to playing role of tariff setter: Sodhi", Financial Express, August , 23, 1999.

"SAIL cites 7 plus points of VRS", Economic Times, September 2, 1998.

Gupta Uttam, "Don't Throw the Baby at BIFR Doorstep", Financial Express, Monday, December 25, 1995.

Hakeem M.A., "Reform has Bypassed Public Sector", Financial Express, Monday, June 5, 1955.

4

Privatization in Nepal

Dr. Narayan Manandhar* & Dr. Pushkar Bajracharya**

1. Brief background of privatization

1.1 Introduction

Unlike in other countries where nationalization was primarily responsible for state ownership of business and industries, Nepal's experience presents a different story. The lack of development of the private sector, the prevailing economic dogma of state intervention and the availability of foreign aid in the form of turn-key projects have heavily contributed to state-ownership of business and industries in Nepal.

From the sixties to the early eighties, there was an upsurge in the establishment of public enterprises. During this period, the number, scope and size of investment in public enterprises expanded tremendously. They have expanded from a mere holding in a commercial bank in early 50's to a total number of 61 public enterprises by the end of mid 70's. Enterprises have permeated to almost all sectors of the economy, namely, manufacturing, public utilities, banking, trading and social services. However, the contribution of public enterprises in terms of GDP share is little over two per cent. Compared to an average of 11 per cent for developing economies, the share is substantially lower in Nepal (World Bank, 1995). This is due to the structure of the economy itself. Nepalese economy is still dominated by agriculture, carried on mostly in small-scale unorganised private farms.

However, compared to gross domestic investment, the share of investment in public enterprises is very large. This is about 43 per cent of GDP and is nearly double that of developing economies. Large-scale manufacturing establishments are still dominated by public enterprises. Public enterprises even today have remained an important source for employment. In 1996, public enterprises absorbed around eight per cent of the total employment in the organised sector of Nepal. The growth of employment in public enterprises is presented in Figure 4.1.

The expansionary drive for establishing public enterprises came to a halt only in the Sixth Five Year Plan Period (1980-85) when the series of review studies on public enterprise performance carried in the Fifth Five Year Plan period (1975-80) presented a bleak picture (CCC, 1977). Not only was the performance of public enterprises unsatisfactory, even the government was having difficulty in managing, supervising and controlling them. This led government to take a restraining policy on public enterprises which, basically, meant that it

* Exective Director, Industrial Relations Forum, Nepal.
** Professor, Tribhuwan University, Nepal.

was going to exercise voluntary restraint in the establishment of public enterprises. The word "selling" of public enterprises also appeared, for the first time, in the Sixth Plan Document.

In 1985, attempts were also made, albeit unsuccessfully, to float shares of some public enterprises. However, the lack of public response plus the turning of privatization into a political issue led the government to doubt the privatization policy itself. The Seventh Five Year Plan Period (1985-90) was a period of homework and preparation for privatization.This was indicated by the series of seminars and workshops held on privatization. It was also a time when the government created a Privatization Cell within the Ministry of Finance. But no serious attempts were made to privatize public enterprises.

Figure 4.1
Growth of employment in public enterprises

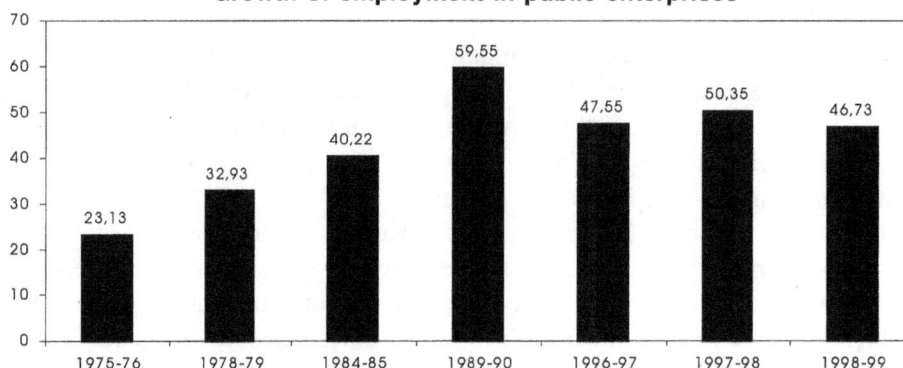

Source: Various issues of annual report on Targets and Performance of Public Enterprises Published by MoF.

The People's Movement for Restoration of Democracy in 1990 and the subsequent ascent of Nepali Congress Government in 1992 saw a new beginning in the chapter of privatization in Nepal. The period also marked a beginning for a new economic thinking from a pro-public sector, government led development to a pro-private sector, and market oriented liberal thinking.

1.2 The genesis of privatization

As mentioned above, although attempts to privatize public enterprises can be traced back to the Sixth Five Year Plan Period (1980-85), concerted effort to privatize came only at the time of Nepali Congress (NC) government in 1992.The NC government came up with a five-phased privatization programme to privatize as many as 51 public enterprises. Privatization strategies were divided into four categories, namely, those requiring (1) immediate privatization, (2) privatization with preparation, (3) liquidation and (4) restructuring. By 1994, the government was able to privatize eight units and to liquidate two more. Similarly in 1994, to speed up the privatization programme, the government also enacted the Privatization Act. However, the policy was heavily criticised by the opposition and also by members within the Nepali Congress party itself. Basically, the criticisms were levelled as follows:

* selling the assets of the country to foreigners; primarily; meaning the growing role of foreigners in the Nepalese economy;
* concentrating economic power in the hands of a few rich business houses;

* lack of transparency in privatization deals;
* under-valuation of assets;
* short-term orientation of privatization policy; and
* undermining the diplomatic relationships of the country, meaning, foreign aided public enterprises, demonstrating friendly bilateral relationships, have been sold off.

The mid-term poll of 1994 and the subsequent formation of a series of coalition governments resulting from a hung parliament situation, put a brake on the privatization movement in the country. A major setback was felt during the nine-month period of United Marxist-Leninist (UML) Government in 1994/95. However, during the coalition government of Nepali Congress in 1996 and 1997, the privatization process gained some momentum. Five more public enterprises were privatized.

1.3 Reasons for privatization

Excepting smaller political parties primarily with leftist orientation, there is some sort of political consensus on privatization amongst the major political parties in Nepal. However, they differ considerably on the degree of emphasis given to and the mode of privatization. For example, Nepali Congress Party has taken privatization as a matter of "(internal) necessity" while the second largest party, UML has taken it as "(an external) compulsion". It is a matter of necessity because, for long, public enterprises have drained national resources. The economic liberalisation strategies pursued by the nation, supported and assisted by World Bank and IMF, made privatization a crucial component. Later on, the World Bank and ADB linked various loan components the conditionality of privatization. Opposite stands taken by two major political parties are mentioned in Table 4.1.

Table 4.1: Stands taken by Nepali congress and UML

Nepali Congress Party	*UML Party*
* Privatization is a means to increase foreign direct investment in the country. * Privatization is a national necessity. * Privatization will increase the role of the private sector and limit the role of the government. * The Privatization Act is adequate to address the needs of privatization programme. * Apart from those enterprises deemed necessary to be under public ownership and management, all other enterprises will be Privatized.	* Privatization should be done to promote national investment. * Privatization is not a priority issue. * It is a wrong notion to believe that private sector is the most efficient and effective mode of operation; the role of the statemust not be minimised in the name of privatization. * The Act is not adequate to address the needs of privatization programme. * Privatization should be done in a selective manner based on national interest, productivity enhancement, employment creation and the interests of workers nd workers.

Source: Information summarised from the party paper published in Privatization Policy and Process in Nepal, *SCOPE*, 1997

While pursuing the privatization policy, the government has broadly enunciated three major policy goals: they are (1) reducing financial and administrative burden (2) improving operational efficiency of the privatized enterprises and (3) involving public participation in the ownership and management of public enterprises.

1.4 Reduction of financial and administrative burden

Public enterprises have consistently drained rather than developed national resources. Their poor performance track record has been a drag on national treasury. Every year, the government is injecting a huge sum of money in the form of capital, loan and subsidy into public enterprises. On an average, the flow of funds to public enterprises accounts for 30 percent of the budget deficit. For the period 1979-1998, the total net flow of funds, between government and public enterprises, was found to be negative, meaning, there was more flow of funds from the government to the public enterprises than the other way round (Figure 4.2). For the same period, the flow of funds from government grew at a rate of 23 percent per annum. However, the flow of funds from public enterprise was 17 per cent per annum only. Clearly, there is increasing financial burden on the government.

For the last four decades, the average rate of return from public enterprises was calculated to be around 1.46 per cent. In fiscal year 1997/98, the capital employed in public enterprises reached to the tune of Rs. 81 billion. However, the gross profit figure was reported to be 1.62 per cent only. Figure 4.3 depicts the rate of return from public enterprises for the period 1963-1998. There is a consistent fall in the performance of public enterprises compared to rising investment (Figure 4.4). Ironically, it is the trading and manufacturing public enterprises, which are contributing to the massive financial drain.

Figure 4.2
Flow of Funds

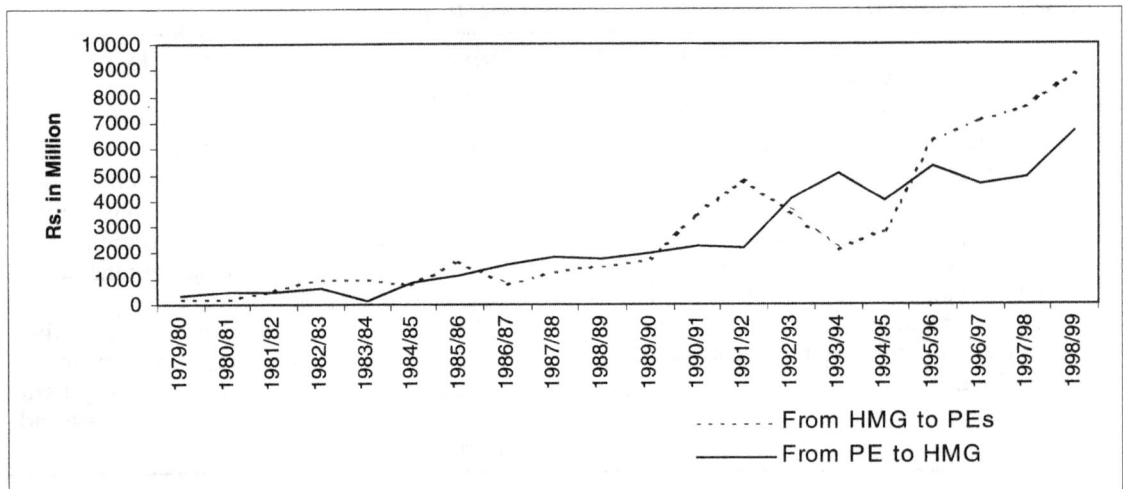

Source: The Economic Survey, MoF.

Figure 4.3
Average Rate of Return from Public Enterprises

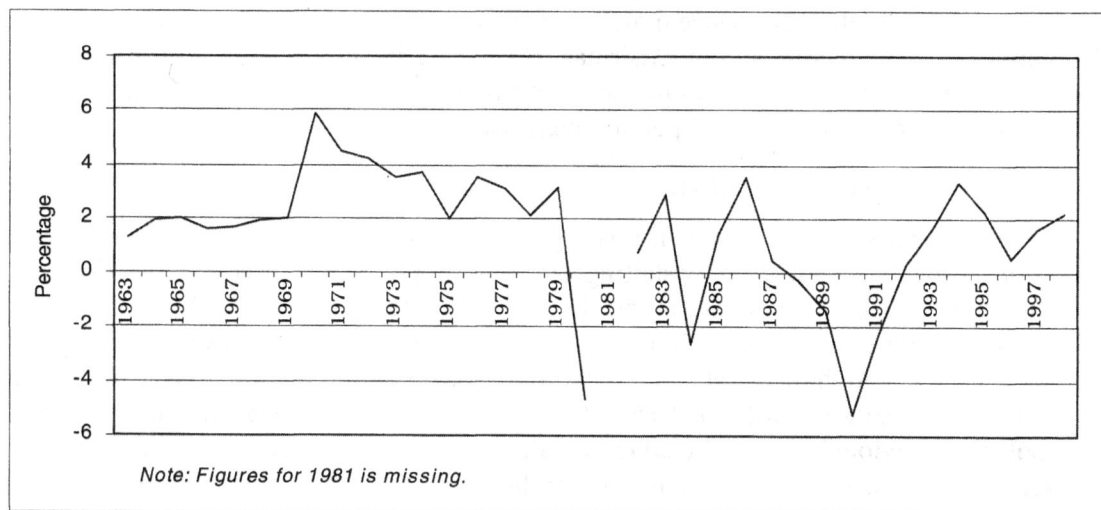

Note: Figures for 1981 is missing.

Source: Data updated from *Improving Public Enterprise Performance: An Empirical Study of Behaviour and Performance of Public Enterprises in Nepal,* Ph.D. Dissertation by Narayan Manandhar, unpublished, University of Birmingham, UK, 1993.

Figure 4.4
Growth of capital employed in public enterprises

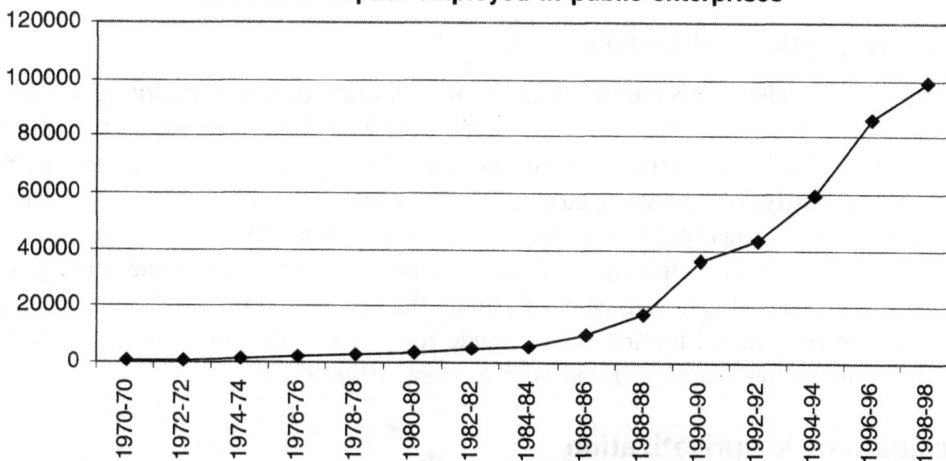

Source: The Economic Survey, MoF.

A large portion of the public enterprise capital structure is composed of loan capital, particularly, external loans. This accounts for 74 per cent of the total capital and is about 27 per cent of the total foreign debt of the country. Clearly, the poor financial health of public enterprises has posed a serious budgetary pressure.

Obviously, financial burden also entails administrative burden. Literally, public enterprises are self-governing autonomous units. Yet their supervision, monitoring and evaluation responsibilites rest with the government. At present, 42 assorted public enterprises are spread over eleven ministries with the Ministry of Industry holding more than a dozen enterprises. The Ministry of Finance, through its Corporation Coordination Division, supervises budgetary allocation and approval, performance monitoring and evaluation. The burden of administration also implies periodic recruitment of Chairman, Board of Directors and General Managers in public enterprises, which also invites public criticism of political patronage, appointments and interference in the management of public enterprises.

1.5. Improving operational efficiency

Public enterprises are renowned for their gross inefficiency in Nepal. Due to government protection, obsolete technology, over staffing and constant political interference, the efficiency of public enterprises is, probably, at the lowest level. This is very much evidenced by indicators like poor capacity utilisation, high prices, low quality and/or unreliability of goods and services. Due to bureaucratic structure of public enterprises, there is a dearth of entrepreneurial talent and spirit. The lack of hard budget constraint, managerial incentives and monopolistic behaviour has contributed to operational inefficiency and large-scale corruption in public enterprises. This is also one reason for their poor financial health. It is expected that privatization will increase the productivity of these enterprises and, this in turn, will help to create more employment opportunities, better wages and working conditions, lower prices, better quality products and services and increased government revenue from taxation. The government has placed high hopes on privatization.

1.6. Involving public participation

Privatization is also conceived as a mode of economic decentralisation. It is conceived particularly with a focus on private sector development in Nepal. In the privatization Act, privatization is defined in the broadest term, as "an act to infuse participation by any means, either wholly or partly, of private sector or of the workers or workers, or of all desirous groups." Two ideas are conceived within this public participation rubric. First is the involvement of the private sector either in the form of share ownership or simply in the management of the enterprise. The second is to reduce or eliminate the "crowding out" effects of government investment in the economy. Mention is also made for privatization as a tool to invite foreign direct investment in the country (*Economic Survey,* 1998/99).

2.   Preparations for privatization

2.1   Institutional arrangement

As per the provisions made in the Privatization Act, the Privatization Committee has been formed under the chairmanship of the Minister or the State Minister of Finance. The other members of the Committee are:

1.   Chairman of the Finance Committee (House of Representatives)
2.   Two members of the Parliament nominated by the government
3.   A member from the National Planning Commission

4.   Secretaries from the Ministry of Finance, Ministry of Law, Justice and Parliamentary Affairs, Ministry of Labour and the line ministry of the concerned enterprise to be privatized

5.   President of the Federation of Nepalese Chambers of Commerce and Industry and

6.   Division Chief of the Corporation Coordination Division/Ministry of Finance who is to act as the Member Secretary.

If deemed necessary, the Committee can invite the chief of the enterprise, the representative from labour and any other distinguished economists in its meetings.

The function of the Committee is to undertake necessary actions and decisions with regard to privatization of public enterprises. On the basis of its study, the Committee recommends to the Cabinet. However, the final authority to privatize rests with the Cabinet.

Previously, technical committees were conceived to assist the Privatization Committee in reviewing and prioritizing public enterprises for privatization. Now, the Privatization Cell performs the duty of the Secretariat of the Privatization Committee. The Cell also acts as a monitoring and regulatory agency. In August 1999, nearly after seven years of privatization, the Cell has initiated a monitoring study on the performance of privatized units.

Since 1998, Adam Smith Institute, a British consulting firm, is assisting the Privatization Cell with the support of Department for International Development (DFID), UK. In the past, there were also financial supports from UNDP/World Bank, USAID and DANIDA.

2.2 Privatization process

The Privatization Cell initiates the process of privatization. The idea of privatizing any public enterprise is forwarded to the Cell either by the concerned line ministry, or the Finance Ministry or the Privatization Committee. The Cell undertakes a detailed study on privatization and recommends the same to the Committee. Once the decision to privatize is taken by the Committee, tender calls are made through public notification explaining the mode and conditionality of privatization. Interested parties are supplied with the Information Memorandum containing necessary information about the units to be privatized. To have serious investors only, the memorandum is made available only against a deposit of Rs. 200,000, of which, 90 per cent is refundable. The deposit money is reduced to Rs. 10,000 if any workers wishes to participate in the bidding process. However, the money is not refundable. This provision has been made to invite workers buyouts.

Article 10 of the Privatization Act spells out six criteria for evaluating bid proposals. They are:

(1) Attractiveness of the price offered
(2) Management of the enterprise without changing its nature
(3) Retention of the service of existing workers and workers
(4) Enhancement of employment opportunities
(5) Managerial experience and expansion of the enterprise by preparing good business plans and making further investments.

In order to avoid controversy, attractiveness of the price offered has been the primary criteria for privatization. This is evidenced by two facts: the offer of enterprises to the highest bidder and the closure of a number of privatized units after privatization.

In the past, decisions were made on the basis of highest bidding. This process has led to the choice of wrong buyers. Therefore, in order to improve the bidding process, two-envelope system has been introduced. Under this system bidders are asked to submit two proposals - one technical and the other financial. In the first stage, screening is done on the basis of technical proposals and after that the financial bids of qualified bidders are considered.

The bids are opened in front of the representatives of bidders. At first, only technical details of the bidders are considered. The Secretary of the line ministry heads the negotiation team. If necessary, bidders are also asked to improve on their bids. At the second stage, financial proposals are considered and the team, comprising the ministers from the Finance Ministry and the concerned line ministry negotiates with bidders. This team submits its findings to the Privatization Committee, which in turn refers it to the Cabinet for final approval.

As per Article 11(A) of the Privatization Act, the government is bound to publish, within one month from the day of signing of the privatization agreement, the information on privatization deal for public knowledge. This is to ensure transparency in privatization deals.

2.3 Speed of privatization

The speed of privatization is very important in determining the outcome of privatization. The speed by which privatization decisions are made also reflect the determination and commitment of the government towards privatization. When the government launched the first phase of privatization; the decision was made within four months of the tender call. The speed was pretty fast.

However, frequent changes in coalition governments, particularly, during 1995-98 have put a drag on privatization deals. Not only were no programmes announced during these three years period; even the decisions made regarding the privatization of Nepal Tea Development Corporation and Butwal Power Company have been delayed considerably. This in turn has put privatization debate into much more controversy. The delayed decisions have cost not only in terms of amounts foregone and government's liability to inject more subsidies but also the psychological costs of deteriorating morale of workers and the management. It is said that after eighteen months of delay in the privatization decision of Tea Development, the government is incurring huge losses by way of deterioration in the condition of the tea estates. The company is running at an annual loss of Rs. 20 million. The government's uncertainties on the privatization decision have affected the performance of many public enterprises enlisted for privatization. There is a perceptive fall in the performance of public enterprises like Himal Cement Company, Rastriya Banijya Bank, Industrial District Management, Gorkhapatra Corporation and Tea Development Corporation after these enterprises was enlisted for privatization.

2.4   Valuation of enterprises

Three types of valuation methods have been used to evaluate the relative worth of privatized units. These methods were: liquidation values, net assets value and the cash flow value. During the first phase of the privatization programme with the support of UNDP and World Bank, Deloitte Ross Tohmatsu of New Zealand was involved in the valuation of enterprises. There is considerable controversy over the valuation of the privatized enterprises. The Annual Report of the Auditor General (1998) has accused that eleven enterprises have been sold off, on an average, with an undervaluation of 29.29 per cent. There are also cases where enterprises have been sold at less than their liquidation value. The valuation controversy seems to have occurred in almost all privatized units. This is because privatized units hold immensely unutilized assets in the form of real estate. The valuation of land has been a critical issue.

2.5   Social protection and safety nets

As provided in Article 14 of the Privatization Act, three policy measures have been undertaken to mitigate privatization related labour problems. They are:

1. *No redundancy clause.* The workers have been guaranteed continuity of their services in privatized enterprises. Where continuity of the services cannot be guaranteed, the government provides necessary retrenchment compensation.

2. *Guarantee of accrued salary and benefits.* The workers willing to continue their services will be guaranteed salaries and benefits "no less favourable" than what they earned under government ownership.

3. *Availability of shares at a discount price.* In all privatized units, the government has allocated five percent of the total shares to workers at a discount of 25 per cent payable on an installment basis. Apart from these three provisions, the government has reduced the deposit money to Rs. 10,000 if the workers wish to participate in the bidding process.

One distinct feature of privatization is that a large majority of the shares ranging from 51 per cent to 72 per cent of the total share ownership is being passed on to a single or a small group of entrepreneurs. Public share participation has been limited from 25 per cent to 30 per cent. Two factors seem to have underscored the block share transfer to a private party. The first is lack of capital market development in Nepal. The poor financial condition of public enterprises cannot attract a large number of public investors. Even in the case of share offering by privatized units, the public response is very poor. The second factor is the need to inject private entrepreneurs in the privatized enterprises. Obviously, giving substantial management control to a minority group entails the sacrifice of distributional goal. However, it is necessary to have commercial goals like rapid expansion through capital injection, productivity, growth and new technology and innovations. Increasing operational efficiency is also one of the avowed goals of the government.

Workers' participation in terms of share ownership is limited to the extent of five per cent in almost all privatized units. It is difficult to understand why five per cent across the broad was applied to all privatized units. The underlying reason may be that workers may not be able to afford to buy the shares.

3. Approaches to privatization

The Privatization Act provides six broad options to privatization, namely, selling of shares, formation of cooperatives, sale of assets, lease, management contracts and other modalities deemed appropriate by the government. The privatization experience to date shows that a number of privatization modalities ranging from outright sale of assets and business to liquidation to management contract and lease out have been tried. However, these modalities have evolved not out of planned thinking but out of a desire to experiment and, moreover, as criticisms mounted, to look for a softer and safer approach to privatization. If this had not been the case, the government would have never privatized a relatively large unit like Harisiddhi Bricks and leased out a smaller unit like Bhaktapur Bricks. Similar is the case with Raghupati Jute Mills and Biratnagar Jute Mills. The former was privatized while the latter was given on management contract.

3.1 Sale of assets and business

The "Sale of Assets and Business" method was used for the three enterprises disposed under Phase I, namely, Bhrikuti Paper, Harisiddhi Bricks and Bansbari Shoe Factory. Under this method, the companies were liquidated, the government took up their liabilities; and assets and business were sold to private parties. They were given a block share of 70 per cent while the public and workers were offered 25 per cent and five per cent of the total shares. There is some modification in the sale of Bansbari Shoe. Only machines and business of the company were sold off, the prime land and buildings were excluded from the sale. The factory was to be relocated outside Kathmandu valley within five years of privatization. The three companies that came into existence in the post privatization period were, legally, new entities. Even their names had been changed to Sri Bhrikuti Pulp and Paper Nepal Ltd., Letherage Bansbari Tannery and Shoe Factory and Harisiddhi Bricks and Tile Factory.

The sale of assets and business method gave way to problems of liquidating public enterprises and settling their old liabilities. Even after seven years of privatization, the liquidators of these first three companies have not been able to finish their tasks. Furthermore, some investors are claiming tax rebates and tax holidays, to be made available under the Industrial Enterprise Act, on the ground that these units are new industrial ventures. The problems associated with the sale of assets and business in these three units led government to draft the Privatization Act in 1994 and also to ease future privatization programme and look for newer modalities of privatization.

3.2 Sale of shares

The complications associated with the sale of assets led the government to go for selling of shares in subsequent rounds of privatization. This approach is being tried in nine out of 16 privatized units. Under this method, the companies continue to exist under their old legal identity but government ownership is passed on to new owners. Again, block shares ranging from 40 per cent (Nepal Lube) to 70 per cent (Balaju Textile) were transferred to a group of businessmen.

Some new options were tried even within the sale of share method. For example, in the case of Nepal Film Development Company, besides 51 per cent shares allocated to the private party, 24 per cent was allocated to persons related to the film industry. This was done to bring in the expertise of professionals involved in the film industry. Similarly, in the case of Raw Hide, shares were distributed to a consortium of ten tanneries with an upper limit of 17 per cent of the shares. In fact, this is a kind of cooperative method of privatization. However, due to dispute amongst partners, the company has been closed since the date of privatization.

In the case of Nepal Bank Ltd., the government sold off 10 per cent of its 51 per cent holdings thereby keeping itself as a minority shareholder. Out of this ten per cent, five per cent was sold to the workers and five per cent to a joint venture private bank.

The privatization of the Agriculture Tools Factory presents another variant within the sales of share method. Sixty-five per cent of its total shares were sold to an workers of the company. On the face of it, it does look like an workers buyout. However, the reality presents a different story. It is known that the real owners of the company were different. By bidding the company on behalf of an workers, they were taking the advantage of concessionaire bidding fee of Rs. 10,000 applicable to workerss. Dispute between investors led to the closure of the factory.

Mention should also be made here of the two recent cases of privatization debacle. The first is the privatization of Nepal Tea Development. It was offered for three options, namely, (1) sale of 65 per cent block shares to a private party (2) lease out the 5100 acre of land with 65 per cent block shares offer for other assets (3) establish each tea estate as an autonomous entity and offer 65 per cent block shares. The government opted for the second method and the company was offered to Mr. K. C. Palaniswami from south India. Mr. Palaniswami offered Rs. 226.5 million plus Rs. 27 million as annual royalties. He deposited five per cent of the bid money (Rs. 13.30 million) but failed to deposit remaining 95 per cent within a grace period of 28 days, giving the reason that money transfer could not be made due to administrative procedures of the Reserve Bank of India. As per the contract, the government forfeited the deposit money and cancelled the privatization agreement. On September 1999, the government asked the remaining bidders to make a fresh bid without retreating from their original offers.

The second debacle is the privatization of Butwal Power Company. Butwal Power is a public company having 97 per cent of government shares ownership. The government has offered 75 per cent of its shares. This is the largest offer made by the government running over Rs. 1 billion. The privatization of this single unit may overshadow all the privatization transactions made in the past. Although 12 parties took interest in the company, only two companies, one Norwegian Interkraft and the other, an Anglo-American Consortium company, called Independent Power Company (IPC) bid to take over the company. After much pushing and pulling from donor agencies. The government has decided to call for a fresh financial bid from parties. Earlier, the parties had submitted their proposals with some conditionality attached to their proposals, which ran counter to the government's tender call.

3.3 Liquidation

Two companies, namely, Tobacco Development Company and Jute Development Company were liquidated in 1993. These two companies were sick industries supplying inputs, namely, tobacco and jute respectively to another state-owned cigarette and jute industry. Market potentialities of these two companies had dried out because the companies were supporting farmers through government subsidy. The only possible option was to close down the companies.

On August 1999, the government decided to liquidate the ropeway and trucking business of Nepal Transport Corporation while it will continue trolley bus and railway services. This is the first time the government has opted for a partial closure after a prolonged strike by the workers. The government is also closing Timber Corporation of Nepal.

3.4 Lease out

Bhaktapur Bricks is the lone case of company lease-out. The government used to own two brick factories. Earlier, the government had privatized Harishiddhi Bricks. This second company was leased out to a private party for ten years with an annual rental charge of Rs. 14,50,000 subjected to an increment of 10 per cent per annum. Nearly after two years in operation, after the inability of the party to run the factory, the government cancelled the lease agreement and once again took over the control of the factory.

3.5 Management contract

Biratnagar Jute Mills presents another lone case of failed management contract. However, the story of the Mills is a somewhat different. It is the first industrial venture of Nepal. Established in 1936, it was a blend of government, foreign and private investment until 1995 when the UML government decided to buy all the shares of the Indian Party and increase the government's holdings from 12 per cent to 46 per cent. The private party is still the majority shareholder in the company. However, because of dispersion of shares amongst Rana families, the responsibility of managing the company has always been with the government. In December 1996, the government decided to give up the company under management contract for five years to a private party on a profit sharing ratio of 80:20 between the government and the private party. After managing the company for sixteen months the party gave up. The Board of the company gave another management contract for five years to a new private party, this time with a profit sharing ratio of 60:40. Again, after operating the company for ten months, the second party also gave up and the company has closed down since May 1999. The company presents two successive failure cases of management contracts. The government has made a fresh call to lease out the company. It is known that three parties have made their bids.

4. Economic and social effects of privatization

The government has envisaged privatization programme to build competitive edge of the economy by bringing in private capital and management and by reducing the "crowding out" effects of public sector investment. Private sector has been identified as the key player, and private sector participation in economic development is being encouraged and motivated. In the Ninth Five-Year Plan (1997-2002), the government has envisaged its role only as a facilitator. The government has planned to reinvest the money realized from privatization in social sectors like education, health and drinking water. In a way, privatization is an ambitious programme expected to have far and wide reaching economic and social effects. It may be true that the total size of the public sector may be small vis-a-vis the total national economy compared to many developing countries. However, due to predominance in a number of important areas, the public sector has come to play a crucial role both in the lives of people as well as the economy. From this perspective, privatization has attracted widespread concern and reactions.

However, the total impact of privatization on the economy is expected to be minimal. Compared to the total public enterprise sector, the scale of privatization is very much limited. Nearly out of five dozen public enterprises/institutions, the government has Privatized sixteen units and this includes two liquidations. In 1996, the total capital employed in public enterprises was Rs. 86 billion; however, the total amount effected by privatization was around Rs. 800 million only. This is less than one per cent of the total capital employed. Similarly, the employment effect is less than 10 per cent of total employment in public enterprises. Furthermore, out of fourteen Privatized units excluding two liquidations, four units have been closed due to operational difficulties. Some units like paper, textile, jute and brick factories are struggling to survive. The sale of shares in Nepal Bank Ltd. has not affected its performance or the style of management and operational strategies. Bhrikuti Paper, previously much quoted as a successful case of privatization, has already applied for a sick industry status. This has led to queries about the efficacy of the privatization programme.

In spite of these expected minimal effects, there is growing outcry and criticism against the privatization programme. This is primarily because public enterprises are the organized sectors of the economy where vested interest groups like trade unions, management, government bureaucracy and politicians are more vocal and strongly organized than anywhere else in the economy. The urban character of public enterprises also adds to their political clout. In the following sections, some possible economic and social effects of privatization are analyzed. Basically, employment effects are considered under social effects.

4.1 Economic effects

4.1.1 Deficit reduction

At macro economic level, the government has made claims that privatization programme has been able to help curtail budget deficits by way of "not having to support loss-making public enterprises". During the fiscal years 1992 to 1994, there has been a marginal reduction in budget deficits from Rs. 11.96 billion to Rs. 10.55 billion. This reduction was accompanied by an increase in the net flow of funds from public enterprises to the government during this period from Rs. 473 millions to Rs 1.19 billion. However, the reduction in budget deficits henceforth has not been found to be consistent. Rather there has been a continuous increase in budget deficits and negative fund flows from public enterprises to the government. Definitely, the privatized units were not the ones taking away the chunks of government subsidy and capital transfer. There are some other factors to blame.

Another interesting aspect of privatization is the utilization of privatization sales proceeds. By 1997-98, the government had raised Rs. 731 million from the privatization programme. Out of this Rs. 671 million, was spent on the payment of gratuity, discharging loans and other liabilities. The remaining balance of Rs. 60 million was deposited in the Privatization Fund. Interestingly, there are also cases where privatization liabilities are much more than the sales proceeds. The Auditor General also reports that an outstanding amount of Rs. 156 million still remains to be collected from private parties. Nearly, half of this amount is composed of interest and penalty charges and in some cases, these charges have exceeded the principal amount due (Auditor General Report, 2056).

4.1.2 Investment

One perceptible change brought about by the privatization programme is the increase in private sector investment. Either to augment the production capacity or to restructure or renovate the production process, private sector investment has been made as one of the main conditionalities of privatization. This has been incorporated in business plans and is also one of the criteria for evaluating privatization proposals. For example, in the privatization proposals, Bhrikuti Paper, Leatherage Bansbari and Harishidhi Bricks were to substantially increase their production capacity. In case of Leatherage Bansbari, the factory had to be relocated outside Kathmandu Valley. This implies further investment in land and building.

Table 4.2 provides a picture of post privatization investments in the privatized units.There has been an investment of Rs. 928 million, 80 per cent of which was made by Bhrikuti Paper alone. It has tremendously increased its capacity from 13 MT per day to 88 MT per day. Similarly, Harishidhi Bricks is also expected to double its capacity after privatization. Another interesting feature of investment is that a large portion of this investment is made out of loan capital. This is evidenced by a huge increase in the loan capital of privatized units. Privatization has increased financial risks for units. The recent crisis in Bhrikuti Paper and Harishidhi Bricks is related to loan financing.

Privatization programme has also brought some foreign direct investment (FDI). This has happened in Bhrikuti Paper and Leatherage Bansbari. However, the amount is not

Table 4.2 Provides a picture of post privatization investments in the privatized units.

significant. The proposed privatization of Butwal Power is expected to bring in substantial FDI to the country.

Table 4.2: Investment in Privatized units   *(Rs. in million)*

Privatized Units	investment
1. Bhrikuti Paper	728.0
2. Harishidhi Bricks	120.0
3. Leatherage Bansbari	43.8
4. Raghupati Jute Mills	36.0
5. Nepal Film	10.0
6. Balaju Textile	0.5
Total	938.3

Source: Information collected from company sources and field visit.

4.1.3 Outputs

With increased capacity in some privatized units, production has also gone up. As stated above, most perceptible changes were seen in Bhrikuti Paper where the capacity has increased more than seven times.

Saving a few enterprises, which are now closed, generally, the output of privatized units have increased. This increased output is closely related to capacity increment. There is also a perceptible change in the quality of outputs. Bhrikuti Paper has introduced 40 gm. newsprint, duplex board poster paper and pulp for export. It has also saved energy by introducing husk boilers. Similarly, Harishidhi Bricks has introduced floor tiles in its production line. Nepal Bitumen has introduced emulsion products, Lube Oil has applied for ISO besides changing its production items and packaging system.

There has also been reorientation in the products of some privatized units. Leatherage Bansbari has stopped production of shoes and has basically concentrated on export of wet blue hides. Similarly, Nepal Film has concentrated on the processing and sale of films. After production of two films in joint collaboration with other parties, it has literally stopped film production. Balaju Textile has given up textile production and is occupied with the shop towel production made available under US quota system. In future, it is planning to divest into a hospital business in collaboration with Apollo Hospital of India. The unutilised land of Balaju Textile is being invested as share capital of Apollo Hospital. This conversion of textile business into a hospital business may stir further controversy in the privatization programme.

4.1.4 Productivity

It is difficult to measure productivity changes before and after privatization. This is because many privatized units have reoriented or diversified their production. It is particularly difficult to have a composite measure of productivity index when enterprises produce a wide variety of outputs with different measurement scales. In spite of these difficulties, a crude measure of productivity is used here to measure the before-after changes in productivity.

Productivity is simply defined here as the units of outputs divided by the total number of workers. This gives an approximate measure of labour productivity. Where the enterprises produce different groups of products like in the case of Harishiddhi Bricks, which produces bricks, roof tiles and floor tiles, only the major product line is used to compute the productivity index. This computed productivity measure is indexed using the year of privatization as a base year, (i.e., 100). The results are presented in Figure 4.5 and 4.6. In Figure 4.5 the largest productivity gain is seen in Balaju Textile. This result must be read with caution as the rise in productivity index is due to the production of shop towel from 1995/96. Before that, it was producing cloth. The production of shop towel is simpler and faster compared to the production of cloth. Therefore, production after 1995/6 is comparable to the production before that period.

Bhrikuti Paper shows a consistent increase in productivity after privatization. The productivity in Harishidhi Bricks is in fact on the decline. However, this is not taking into account the production of roof and floor tiles. In Figure 4.6, productivity has increased in all three units after privatization, namely, Nepal Bitumen, Nepal Lube and Nepal Foundry.

Figure 4.5
Productivity growth in Harishiddhi Bricks, Balaju Textile and Bhrikuti Paper

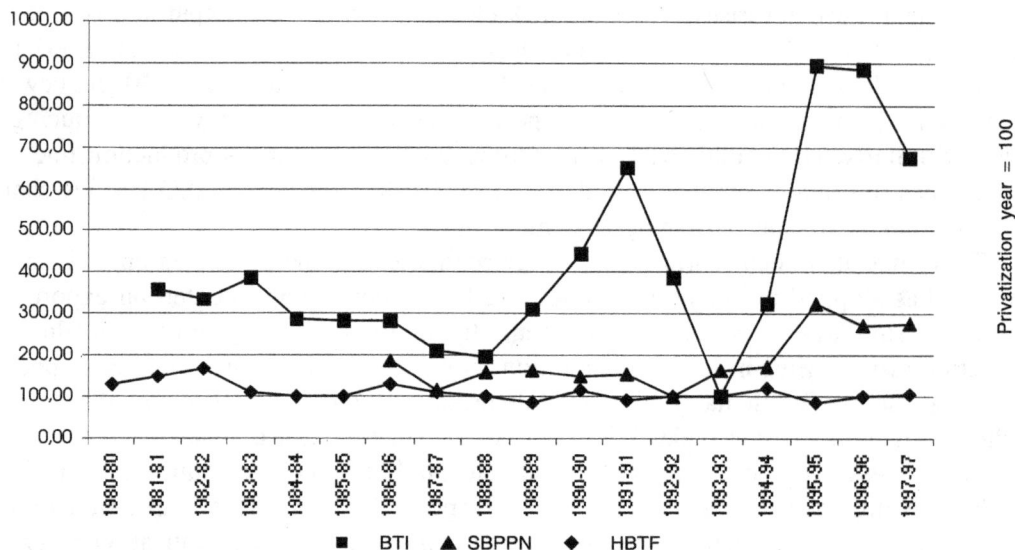

Source: The Economic Survey, MoF.

4.1.5 Price

Generally, the prices of products produced by the privatized units have sharply increased after privatization. In some cases like bricks and textiles, the price has increased by more than 50 per cent. The abrupt increase in price, subsequent to privatization, reflects the inherent inefficiency of public sector pricing policy. The price rise also reflects the operation of market forces hitherto suppressed under public sector regime. The consequence of the price rise on consumer welfare must be carefully interpreted. As far as input prices are concerned, they have benefited suppliers. The land compensation paid to farmers by Harishiddhi Bricks has increased considerably after privatization.

Figure 4.6
Productivity growth in Nepal Bitumen, Nepal Lube and NFL

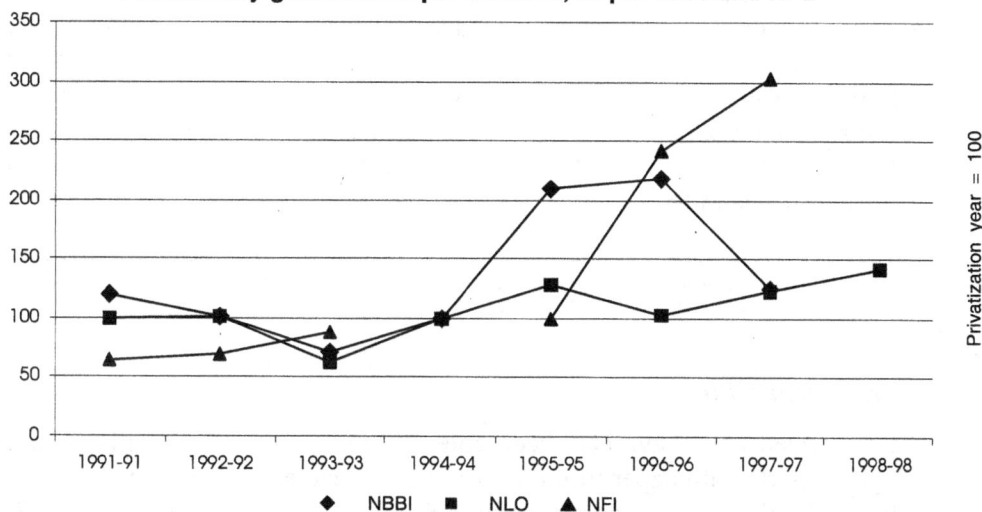

Source: The Economy Survey, MoF.

Public enterprise operation in Nepal has an urban character, that is, they serve limited urban population. Therefore, the real benefits of price control and subsidization has gone to the well-to-do urban consumers. In case of high competition from imports, the chances of increasing price are quite limited as in textile and paper products, as both industries are, at present, severely under competition from imports.

4.1.6 Profit-loss situation

The increase in capacity and output of privatized units are not reflected in their profitability situation. Apart from smaller units like Nepal Bitumen, Lube Oil and Nepal Foundry, most other privatized units are under financial strain. As stated above; Bhrikuti Paper has already applied for a sick industry status. The closure of many privatized units is also an indication of the fact that the financial condition of these could not improve even in the hands of the private sector. The inefficiency of public enterprises must be related to market conditions, production technology, and source of financing and management factor rather than ownership per se. However, if the profit and loss situation of privatized units is to be compared with the profit-loss situation immediately before privatization, many enterprises have been able to reduce losses, if not increase their profits. However, three units privatized under the first phase have not been able to improve their financial condition. The available data on profit and loss situation in the privatized units are given in Table 4.3.

Table 4.3: Before after profit/Loss situation of Privatized units

(Rs. in million)

Privatized units	Before privatization	After privatization
1. Nepal Lube	+0.60 (1993/94)	+5.38 (1997/98)
2. Nepal Bitumen	+0.68 (1992/93)	+3.07 (1997/98)
3. Leatherage Bansbari	- 2.23 (1992/93)	+1.13 (1997/98)
4. Nepal Foundry	+3.88 (1995/96)	+0.83 (1998/99)
5. Nepal Film	-4.81 (1992/93)	+0.25 (1997/98)
6. Bhrikuti Paper	+8.7 (1991/92)	-228 (1997/98)
7. Harishiddhi Bricks	+0.04 (1991/92)	-20.28 (1995/96)
8. Bhaktapur Bricks	-12.25 (1995/96)	-7.5 (1997/98)
9. Raghupati Jute Mills	-75.30 (1991/92)	-3.18 (1997/98)
10. Balaju Textile	-1.2 (1991/92)	-0.21 (1997/98)

Source: Information collected from company sources and various issues of annual report on *Targets and Performance of Public Enterprises* (Yellow Book) published by MoF.

4.1.7 Export potentialities

Some privatized units have also been able to generate export potential. For example, Bhrikuti Paper exports pulp paper to India. Similarly, Leatherage Bansbari exports wet blue leather to India. Balaju Textile is surviving on US quota for shop towel. Probably, Raghupati Jute Mills is the only enterprise that exports 80 per cent of its jute to India, and export predominates its sales. The post privatization scenario of Raghupati Jute Mills has totally changed. During government ownership, the company used to have inputs supplied from local farmers and such input prices were subsidized by the government. Its outputs were sold to the two state-owned cement industries. Now, the privatized Raghupati Jute Mills is in a reverse order, it is importing jute inputs from Bangladesh and exporting its outputs to India. The Government of India's policy to have all food materials and 75 per cent of cement packed in jute bags has also helped Raghupati Jute Mills to survive, otherwise, jute market has been on the decline since a considerable period of time. In terms of export performance, therefore, there has been a notable positive improvement in privatized units.

4.1.8 Capital market development

Public participation in privatized units through share ownership has contributed to the development of the capital market in the country. The total number of shareholders in the privatized units is around 32,000. This is a significant figure in comparison to the total of 300,000 shareholders in the country. A large number of shareholders are in Nepal Bank, Harishiddhi Bricks, and Nepal Film. Although the absolute number of shareholders in privatized units has increased, public response to share holding is not that encouraging. The shares offered by Harishiddhi Bricks are being converted into debentures. The poor public response is reflected by the downward trend in share prices of privatized units. In the case of

Harishiddhi Bricks, its share price has plummeted from Rs 19 to Rs 2.90. The most taxing part is that the company has not been able to hold annual general meeting even after seven years of privatization. Some details on share markets of privatized units are given in Annex 1.

4.2 Social effects

4.2.1. Employment effects: quantity

It is very difficult to pin point the exact effect of privatization on total employment, because both positive and negative factors are simultaneously at work. First, there is "no reduction clause" which seeks to stabilize the employment level. Second, voluntary retirement scheme has been introduced in some privatized units before and after privatization. Third, there are also cases where existing workers have resigned after privatization and new replacements have been made. This gives a neutral effect on total employment figures.

Some of the privatized units have been closed after privatization. If one includes employment figures in these closed units, then the total effect is substantial. Jobs of about 3,200 people have been directly affected by the closure of four units, namely, Bhaktapur Bricks, Biratnagar Jute Mills, Agriculture Tools, and Raw Hide. Whether this closure is due to privatization or due to some other exogenous factor is a matter of debate. Even in the existing public enterprise sector there is a gradual decline in employment opportunities (Figure 4.1).

However, if one excludes the closed units and seeks to analyze the total employment figure, then the total effect is marginal. That is, there are not many changes in employment figures. The available figures on employment before and after privatization are given in Table 4.4.

Table 4.4: Total employment in Privatized units: before and after

Privatized units	before	After privatization 1995*	1998**	1999***
1. Bhrikuti Paper	297	379	578	580
2. Harishidhi Bricks	595	600	454	526
3. Leatherage Bansbari	484	closed	70	97
4. Nepal Film	107	48	54	51
5. Balaju Textile	108	103	101	35
6. Nepal Bitumen	55	60	45	56
7. Nepal Lube	102	95	91	95
8. Nepal Foundry	61	-	20	52
9. Raghupati Jute Mills	1479	-	1446	1750
Total	3228	1285	2859	3242

Data Source:
* Study conducted by DEAN, 1995
** Study conducted by IRF, 1998
*** Field visits

The terminal data on post privatization employment in 1995, 1998 and 1999 is also presented in Table 4.4. Interestingly, the total employment declined sharply in 1995 and, there after, there has been a gradual rise. In 1995 there was about 60 per cent decline in total employment, in 1998 and 1999 the figure was reduced to 13 per cent and one per cent respectively. This confirms the fact that, in the short run, privatization may heavily shed jobs. But it need not be so in the long run. From the table it is also worth noting that large positive changes have taken place only in a couple of units, namely, Bhrikuti Paper and Raghupati Jute Mills. Large reduction in Letherage Bansbari is due to relocation of the factory and stoppage of shoe production. In 1999, the total employment in the privatized units increased, albeit marginally.

4.2.2 Employment effects: Quality

The total employment effect masks the qualitative changes in employment, namely, the nature and type of job losses, the level of job security, changes in terms and conditions of employment, trade union and collective bargaining situation. Observations on these matters are described below.

Redundancy clause and job security: The government has sought to guarantee the continuity of the services of workers including their seniority and privileges in privatized units. In case of their retirement, the government is to provide reasonable compensation and benefits. Apart from a few units, "no redundancy" clause was applied in almost all privatized units. In spite of this arrangement, feeling of job insecurity is high amongst workers. A number of factors have contributed to this job insecurity.

First, in spite of the "no redundancy" clause, a large majority of workers, previously working under public ownership, has voluntarily opted for retirement (Annex 2). In some cases this happened before privatization, as in the case of Nepal Foundry or after privatization as in the case of Leatherage Bansbari where almost all workers opted for voluntary retirement. The large-scale exodus of workers working under public ownership must have exerted a considerable strain on workers who decided to continue after privatization. In fact, the feeling of job insecurity is high in every sector of employment in Nepal.

Second, there is a negative effect of the voluntary retirement scheme. In privatized units where workers opted for voluntary retirement, they were mostly senior, experienced and qualified staff members who saw more job prospects outside the enterprise. The re-hiring of some retired staff members is an evidence of this fact.

Although, the validity of the argument is very questionable, Letherage Bansbari is now arguing that it cannot continue its shoe production simply because the company lacks qualified personnel to undertake shoe production. However, in the privatization programme, the company is the first one, which had opted for voluntary retirement before privatization. Almost 100 staff members were laid off before the company was handed over to new owners. The exodus of experienced and qualified manpower has further burdened privatized units with having to work with inefficient staff members who naturally are inclined to be more insecure about their jobs.

Third, in many privatized units, there is a tendency to bring new personnel, more often foreigners, with high salary and perks under contracts. Apart from feeling of job insecurity emanating from contractual arrangement, there is also a deep psychological conflict between the new hires and existing workers. The recruitment of non-Nepali managers hàs been a contentious issue in privatized units. The prevalence of nepotism is another factor for the deteriorating morale of workers who had decided to continue services after privatization.

Fourth, during the course of the interview with some trade union leaders (details provided in the next chapter), new owners were also reported to harass workers, probably, as a way to get rid of them. This could also be the reason why workers opted for voluntary retirement after privatization. Existing workers may not have been fired, as it was not possible under "a redundancy clause" but unfavorable terms and conditions, like frequent transfers to the inconvenient places or to unsuitable jobs or strict control and monitoring of behavior may have led them to give up their jobs. Workers simply cannot tolerate new management methods.

The "no redundancy clause" is also found to be masking the real problem. In some cases, it appears that it is not a part of the "job security" arrangement, rather it comes as government's inability to pay separation benefits like gratuity, pensions and other facilities to retiring workers. During the course of interview with some of the staff members they responded that many workers are happy to quit the enterprise if only they are paid their gratuity money. In sick enterprises like Hetauda Textile Industry and Biratnagar Jute Mills, a large number of workers are ready to quit their jobs at any time if they are paid gratuity and other separation benefits.

The "no redundancy clause" has also come under heavy criticism from new owners. The new investors feel that having to carry on with existing workers, their hands are effectively tied in improving management of privatized units. In the privatization of Raghupati Jute Mills, the new management had taken up the company only after keeping all personnel costs at zero. Thus, all existing personnel obligations were nullified before privatization. Similar proposals have been forwarded for the privatization of Biratnagar Jute Mills. As the real purpose and effectiveness of "no redundancy clause" has been found to be self-defeating, the policy needs to be explored further before its application across the board.

Type of job losses: Irrespective of the "no redundancy clause" job losses have occurred in almost all privatized units. However, the categories of people whose jobs were affected are not the ones at the top level or at the bottom level. Basically, it is the people at the middle level like the administrators, accountants, supervisors and other personnel. As new managers sought to curtail personnel costs, these people were directly affected by the privatization process. However, it is difficult to single out privatization as a single factor behind this kind of middle level job squeeze. Generally, the pyramidic organizations are downsizing throughout all kinds of organizations. Since public enterprises have the hierarchic bureaucratic structure, obviously, the privatization process takes a great toll on them.

Contractualization of jobs: There is a growing tendency amongst the new managers to go for contractual, temporary, daily wage, piece rate wage hiring in the privatized units.

This is a way to avoid long-term risk and commitment of carrying a permanent labour force. This is also a way to avoid possible labour agitation and trade unionism. The rigidity of Nepali labour law is also partly responsible for this type of managerial behavior. This system is widely reported in the case of Balaju Textile, Leatherage Bansbari and Raghupati Jute Mills. In the case of Raghupati Jute Mills, the present labour discontent is with temporary appointment. After freezing all employment under public ownership, the new management has given permanent status to 100 workers only although it claims that the process of giving permanent status to all workers is under way. However, Lube Oil presents an exceptional case where nearly 50 per cent of the total workers were given permanent status immediately after privatization. This was done to diffuse job insecurity feelings. Under public sector regime, it could never have been possible. There are strict rules and cumbersome procedure to make workers permanent.

The contractual arrangement of jobs, particularly, at the top management level seems to have affected Bhrikuti Paper. There had been, at least, three changes in the top-level management. As new management takes time to learn the business, frequent changes in management have disturbed smooth operation. Changes in top management also affects the whole team as new people come in to take new positions and old members have to be repositioned somewhere else. Management changes, often taken as a chronic problem of public enterprise management, also seem to prevail in the private sector in Nepal.

Salaries and benefits: Apart from continuity of services, workers in the privatized units were also guaranteed "no reduction" in salaries and facilities received during public sector ownership. The available information of privatized units showed some increase in salaries and benefits of workers. However, the increase in salary and benefits is being compensated by increase in work hours or reduction in other facilities and leaves. The new managers have also introduced performance based incentive schemes. During the course of interviews with staff members from Film Development, it was stated that the new management has literally taken the meaning of "no reduction in salaries and benefits". Workers often compare their salaries and benefits with other public sector workers and claim that "no reduction" necessarily does not mean "increase". Some reported positive and negative changes in salaries and benefits received by the workers after privatization are presented in Table 4.5.

The story of new hirees is a bit different. As many of them are hired on contract or temporary basis, they seem to enjoy fairly good salaries and benefits. Their proximity or close relations with the new management may have helped them enjoy better facilities. This is a contentious issue in all privatized units. This is also a matter of conflict between the newcomers and existing staff members.

Trade unions and collective bargaining: Labour relations deteriorated sharply immediately before and after privatization. Union activities have subsided in the privatized units. Labour strife, agitation and protests are still going on in some enterprises listed for privatization. In cases like Bhrikuti Paper, the new owners could not take over the company even after months of privatization. In the case of Leatherage Bansbari, almost all workers took voluntary retirement after factory relocation dispute. This dispute cost substantial money

Table 4.5: Reported positive and negative changes in salaries and benefits

	Positive	*Negative*
1. Bhrikuti Paper	* 15% increase in house rent allowance * 12.5 percent increase in special allowance * 70% increase in DSA * 40% increase in life and insurance premium * One month's salary as bonus	* Reduction in leaves. * Salaries have been reviewed only after revisions in the minimum wage. * Workers are uncertain about their PF and insurance.
2. Harishiddhi Bricks	* 8% salary increment * Unification of annual leaves * Transport facility * Incentive system based on performance slabs	* Officer level salary has not been increased.
3. Leatherage Bansbari	* 8% increase in salary with some increase in overtime benefits	
4. Nepal Film		* No increase in salary and benefits
5. Balaju Textile		* Reduction in benefits * Workers are more worried about jobs than salary increments.
6. Raghupati Jute Mills	* Increase in daily wage rate of Rs 80 per day on average. * Medical benefits. * Gratuity paid to employees	* Workdays increased from 6 to 7 days a week. * Reduction facilities. * Freeze in employment.
7. Nepal Foundry	* 10-15 % increase in salary * Technical allowance, production allowance	
8. Nepal Lube	* Collective Bargaining * 26% Bonus distribution	

Source: Information collected from field visit interviews.

to the government in terms of gratuity payment to retiring workers. The workers of some closed units like Biratnagar Jute Mills, Agriculture Tools and Bhaktapur Bricks are still fighting for their lost jobs, salaries, provident fund and gratuity. The need for the government to undertake responsibility to pay gratuity or other termination benefits without any commensurate change in the price of the enterprise may have affected seriously the actual realization of privatization sales proceeds. There is a sincere need to value the price of enterprise on the basis of workers retention or retirement or other pertinent conditionalities. Otherwise, the agreement is expected to lose only from the transaction.

Primarily three factors influence the growing labour tensions in public enterprise. First is the poor financial condition of public enterprises themselves. A decade or two back, jobs in public enterprises were more secure and more rewarding than anywhere else. Their wage rate was far above the market wage rate. Now, with continued deterioration of performance, public enterprises can no longer afford to provide the same sort of facilities and privileges to its workers.

Thus, workers' morale and job satisfaction have declined. Second, overstaffing is a major phenomenon of public enterprise management in Nepal. Added to this overstaffing, political appointment and patronage of staff members have led to over politicization of the labour force in general and trade unions in particular. The managers are also lax in dealing with trade union activities. Therefore, trade unionism is more active in public enterprises than in the private sector. Given this state of affair, privatization acts as a fuel to the fire. The findings of a survey of trade unions and workers are presented in Annex 3.

It is interesting to note that although, labour strife was ripe immediately before and after privatization, it seems to have died down after privatization. The only reported strike, after privatization was in Lube Oil. This was solved through the collective bargaining process. In the case of Bhrikuti Paper, although two unions operate, no strike has been reported ever since the private sector took the enterprise under its control. The management reported that the union was very cooperative with new owners. Instead of strikes and agitation, trade unions and workers seem to be worried about the closure of the company and of losing their jobs. They are more worried about financial losses, corruption, inefficiency, and frequent management changes. Similar feelings were reported in the case of Balaju Textile and Nepal Film. Ironically, the industrial sickness seems to be contributing in containing labour strikes and disputes in Nepal.

In the case of Nepal Film and Balaju Textile, trade union activity totally disappeared after privatization. This has come after nullification of trade union activities. However, in regard to Balaju Textile, about one dozen labour dispute cases are being lodged at the Labour Court. In Leatherage Bansbari, the presence of trade union has been totally eliminated as all workers are under contractual terms. In the case of Raghupati Jute Mills, there are as many as four unions. With the recent reopening of the company, labour rivalry may have contributed to the multiplicity of unions. Four general conclusions can be deduced from the observation of trade unionism in privatized units:

(a) There is a large-scale exodus of workers due to management actions against trade union activists. Trade unions are suppressed in privatized units.

(b) The use of contract, temporary and daily wage earners are other methods of avoiding trade unionism

(c) Where trade unions are relatively strong, new investors manage them in a better way than in public enterprises

(d) The poor conditions of privatized units and the fear of losing the job have contributed to seal off collective labour disputes.

5. Privatization: Future programmes and strategies

It is true that within a relatively short period of time Nepal has made some progress in introducing a new concept like privatization. However, it is also true that the history of privatization in the country has been somewhat checkered with different governments giving different emphasis and priority to the programme. From the study of privatization programme, it appears that most of the programmes were implemented by or during the government of Nepali Congress. The other political parties have either ignored or given minimum importance to privatization. The increasing concern shown towards privatization from various quarters especially by the workers and the media reflects a dismal scenario of the whole privatization process. The various flaws and anomalies have also been pointed out in the Auditor General's Report. Two privatization debacles, namely, the privatization of Tea Development and Butwal Power Company, have recently slackened the process of privatization. However, they have not deterred the government from pursuing ambitious privatization targets. As far as the objectives, targets and strategies of privatization are concerned, they appeared to be adequate and clean. However, operational problems and implementation barriers have significantly slowed down the process.

The assessment of impacts and the experiences of the past privatization programme have not instilled proper confidence in the public. The evaluation of the privatization programme in the Eight Five-Year Plans showed some progress. Some positive signs were also noted in the case of Bhrikuti Paper though the initial euphoria did not last long enough. Bhrikuti Paper, the most lauded for its capacity expansion and production increase after privatization, has recently applied for 'a sick industry' status. This does not augur well for the entire privatization process.

Some subtle changes in the premises and approaches can be noted in the Ninth Plan. It specifies that privatization programme has been implemented as an alternative to improve effectiveness in the utilization of resources invested in the public sector and orienting them towards economic consolidation. Further, privatization has been defined as a long-term process. The reasons attributed for this are the prevailing state of natural monopoly, huge investment requirements, a bleak prospect for attracting adequate private sector investment and the problem associated with a large number of workerss in the public enterprise. The plan has clearly identified the existing problems of privatization as follows: lack of adequate resources and credible investors, unnecessary politicization, vast amount of unproductive assets in the public enterprises, heavy debt burden, determination of the price to be obtained from the sale, ignorance, dilemma and low level of awareness among concerned policy makers towards the realities, their control-oriented cultural extremity, financial and other concessions and incentives required to be provided to the privatized enterprises, overstaffing and changes to be initiated in staff attitude towards work etc.

5.1 Planned privatization

The privatization committee has either approved or planned 12 additional enterprises for privatization. However, no efforts seem to have been initiated. It shows that privatization programme appears to have lost direction after the initial thrust, and regrouping of activities and programmes is essential to give a new direction and purpose to the programme. These should clearly embrace strategies of adequate social dialogue and ensuring proper transparency.

5.2 Future programme

Despite considering the privatization as a long-term process, the Ninth Plan has laid down an ambitious privatization plan. The attainability of this plan is questionable. Out of 46 remaining public sector enterprises, the Plan has spelled out to initiate the privatization process in 30 units.

The list of units to be privatized is not only long but includes some of the largest public sector organizations. Further, there exist diverse emphasis and priorities in the programme. However, the multilateral donor agencies are pushing for the privatization of the two public sector-banking institutions, namely, Rastriya Banijya Bank and Nepal Bank Ltd., and two public utilities, namely, Nepal Telecommunication Corporation and Nepal Drinking Corporation.

The government is facing difficulty with the privatization of two enterprises, namely, Butwal Power Company and Nepal Tea Development Corporation. In Butwal Power, new financial proposals have been asked from the two bidders. In respect to Tea Development, recently, a proposal is reported to have been accepted by the Privatization Committee. Due to bickering and inability to take specific decisions, privatization process has significantly slowed down. Hence, it may not be out of place to conclude that it will take much longer time to carry out the proposed privatization programme. Lack of transparency in privatization process has been one of the complaints often aired. Therefore, significant improvements are required not only to smoothen the pace of privatization but also to win the confidence of workers and people.

The Ninth Plan has also defined the long-term strategy of the government in respect of future privatization programmes. It has emphasized to promote private sector participation in the production and distribution of goods and services and other economic and social sector investment and management being currently undertaken by the government. For ensuring efficiency and optimization of resource utilization the government has outlined following activities to be privatized in the Ninth Plan period: Postal service, civil aviation, highways, bridge, irrigation, canal, hospital, school, campus, university, media, drinking water sewerage, transportation system, tax collection at the local level, traffic control system, sanitation and security, forest management, river training and embankment, disaster management, fire control, distribution of medicine, supply of food, fertilizer, energy and petroleum products; study and research on mining and geology; control of school examinations, training management for human resources, management of physical resource and services of the government, management of printing press of the government, security, maintenance and regular management of temples and other religious sites, management of national parks, parks and livestock farm, places of archaeological importance, national library, reading room, conference-hall, museum, zoo, management of Hanumandhoka and other historical places, stadium and sports facilities, parade ground, management of expedition and trekking permits, management of transit facilities, management of national debt, and printing and publication of the government.

Adam Smith Institute (ASI), the advisers to the Privatization Cell within the Ministry of Finance, have attempted to categorize privatization targets. It has identified three enterprises as the big targets, namely, Royal Nepal Airlines, Nepal Telecommunication and Rastriya Banijya Bank. ASI has tried to categorize other significant targets into three groups, probably, to prioritize privatization in that order/category.

5.3 Policies and strategies

The policies and strategies defined in the plan appear to be clear. They have been defined taking into consideration the lacunae in previous efforts and experiences. The primary emphasis is to create a consensus by keeping people well informed. Other strategies include selection of appropriate modality, selection of corporations, selection of investor, effort to get fair price, encouragement of FDI, sound negotiation on privatization terms and conditions, policies to protect the interest of workers, monitoring of privatized units, enactment of appropriate laws and by-laws and amendment of the Privatization Act. A particular note of two policies may be made - protecting the interest of workers and generating transparency in the privatization process. The only issue is how these goals will be attained. The plan document is not very specific on this. To have effective implementation of the policies and strategies, obviously detailed operational policies are required.

6. Recommendations for minimizing social effects

Due to the limited scale of the privatization programme itself, so far, the social effects of privatization have also been limited in Nepal. However, given the ambitious nature of the privatization programme and the deteriorating scenario of labour relations in the public enterprise sector, there is a need to rethink the process of privatization for mitigating the social effects. This is more so in a country where social security provisions are minimal and the spectre of unemployment is high. Moreover, with the reinstitution of multi-party democracy, labour can no longer be treated as a residue element in the privatization programme. The clout of trade unions has increased tremendously in the public sector. Even when the government is able to suppress the labour movement in a particular privatized unit, its bullying can have a negative impact on other enterprises enlisted for privatization.

Already, labour relations in public enterprises in Nepal are at the lowest level. This is because (1) of deteriorating conditions of public enterprises in general, (2) overstaffing and under utilisation of capacity in public enterprises and (3) labour problems induced by the privatization programme. Labour relation's problems are severe in public enterprises due to management laxity and a strong and equally politicised labour force. At present, labour unionisation is higher in government owned industries than in private sector industries. The problem has also been aggravated by the existence of multiple unions within a public enterprise making it difficult to have a concerted voice of labour.

Inadequate measures to inform, educate, consult and involve workers in the privatization programme have further aggravated the situation. Although redundancy studies were carried out during the first phase of the privatization programmes, no such studies were reported in other privatization programme. The closure of some units after privatization has killed workers trust and confidence in the privatization programme itself. This is one reason for labour relation's problems before, after and during privatization.

The government's policy to mitigate the problems of labour relations through no redundancy clause in privatization agreements, guarantee of working conditions after privatization and the allocation of five percent workers' shares at discount price have hardly helped to contain the problem. The present study reveals that trade union antagonism against privatization is running high. At the time of this study, labour strikes were underway in some privatized units like Agriculture Tools, Biratnagar Jute Mill and Bhaktapur Bricks. In the following sections we will consider some measures to mitigate the problems of labour relations in the privatization programme.

6.1 No redundancy clause

Experience has shown that privatization is particularly hard on workers and trade unions. Although in the long run, with increased efficiency, privatization may help to increase employment opportunities, in the short term it freezes or sheds jobs. The heart of the dilemma is as an ILO report states, "it is difficult for affected workers to agree to a logic that dictates the necessity of losing their jobs in the overall interest of the survival of an organization with which they have long been associated" (ILO, 1991).

Although "no redundancy clause" has been used as a helping tool in assuring workers and trade unions of their job security after privatization and containing labour strife at the time of privatization, the reluctance of new owners to carry on with old workers and a prevalence of widespread feeling of job insecurity among workers after privatization has given rise to doubts on the effectiveness of this clause. Instead of giving a choice to workers to stay on with their jobs or leave the organization, the new owners need to be given a free choice in recruitment of workers once privatization has taken place.

Clearly, the new owners who decide to carry on with the existing workers or who help to generate additional employment opportunities should be given some tax incentives, preferential treatment or other facilities. Only after deciding to take in the workers, can a "no redundancy clause" be revoked as privatization conditionality. To give further flexibility to new owners, such a clause can have a time bound stricture like "no workers can be fired for five years". This will also give workers an ample time to rethink on their career.

Those workers who cannot be adjusted in privatized units should be given an option either to have a generous voluntary retirement package or readjusted to some other units. The other units could be both public and private organizations. Here again, some incentives can be offered to the organizations helping to absorb privatization redundancies. The inability of government to pay separation benefits to the workers must not, in any way, be a factor behind the "no redundancy" scheme. The liabilities from separation of workers must be determined in advance.

6.2   Training and reintegration

Training and reintegration are required to deal with the labour surplus arising out of privatization. Although reintegration, meaning readjustment of workers to other state-owned units have been tried in the past, training measures have hardly been used. Surplus workers could be assisted with various skill-oriented training programmes that can be adjusted to new employment opportunities. They can also be assisted to find new job opportunities or supplied with credit facilities for self-employment.

6.3   Workers' education

There is a total absence of information, education and consultation in the privatization programme. In the absence of education on the possible consequence of privatization on workers' job security, working conditions, their rights and obligations in the enterprise, room for politicization of the privatization programme grows. Together with the slow process of privatization, lack of education programme has sharply deteriorated the performance of public enterprises enlisted for privatization. Moreover, trade unions are campaigning on their own to counter possible privatization. Workers seem to be quite aware of the fact that they can survive only to the extent that the organization survives. If liquidation is a better option, it is better to close the unit than pretend to save jobs through privatization measure. Creating confidence in the system is crucial for the success if the only option left is to carry on with the existing situation. It is equally important to deal with scepticism as with over and unfounded assurances like better wages and working conditions after privatization. Similarly, it is as necessary to inform workers and trade union representatives about the benefits of privatization as much as the costs of no privatization.

It is also necessary to promote social dialogue between workers and employers. At present, the privatization programme is totally driven by the government, that too, with an objective of lessening its administrative and financial burden. Ironically, privatization has been pre-dominantly a public sector affair with the government taking all the initiatives and responsibilities for privatization. Although, provision has been made to accommodate the President of the Federation of Nepalese Chambers of Commerce and Industry (FNCCI) in the Privatization Committee, labour representation is discretionary. This is also one of the factors leading to employee discontent with the privatization programme.

6.4   Workers buyouts/ownership plans

The present mode of injecting five percent workers share ownership in the privatization programme is very much questionable, as workers have shown less interest in shares than in job security. First, the offer of five percent shares is more of a symbolic gesture than a mechanism to allow worker participation in ownership and management of the privatized unit. Second, workers have shown little interest in buying the shares of sick units.

The government's lack of interest to realize distributive goals of privatization is being reflected also by the block share transfer to a nucleus of private party. This is necessary in view of the poor financial condition of many privatized units and also to invite further investments and have a controlling interest in enterprise management to attain operational efficiency. However, save a couple of privatized units, operational efficiency goals largely remain to be achieved. The closure or sick industry status of privatized units provide evidences for this. Now, the government is reasoning that privatization per se may not be a factor behind the closure or problems of privatized units. If this is true, then it is also equally true that to achieve successful privatization programme it must be accompanied or supported by "other policies". These other policies are a matter to be further investigated. At this stage, it could be said that other policies are squarely lacking in Nepal's privatization drive.

However, again where workers' involvement in the programme is crucial or gaining the trust and confidence of the trade union is a precondition for a successful privatization programme, the workers themselves may be asked to run the enterprise. Sri Lanka has taken a good step by calling its privatization programme as "peoplisation". Given the poor financial condition of public enterprises and their bleak prospects, workers may not be interested in running the enterprise. Still the option could be tried in many enterprises where there is little physical asset base but more human resources as in the case of research, consultancy and training related enterprises.

6.5 Restructuring programmes

A number of restructuring programmes can be introduced before privatization is pursued. Restructuring may involve wholesale structural changes, management change, financial restructuring and operational restructuring. The basic aim of restructuring is to improve the status of the enterprise to get better price and improve the viability of the organization. This has been practised in many countries and has also been rewarding. But in Nepalese perspective, the chances of success appear to be poor due to the absence of performance evaluation and merit based rewarding system in practice. A few experiences have only proven even management contract is no guarantee to improve the organization. So, the scope for proper restructuring may be limited. However, various activities may be initiated which is quite feasible even in the Nepalese situation. This could start from undertaking redundancy study as was done in the first phase of the privatization programme. From the study one can conclude that necessary steps should be taken to deal with redundant work force, determination of skills that are really going to be made redundant, determining the actual financial liability of the government, possibility of internal transfers, training and retraining needs and finding out ways to deal with union antagonism. Freezing recruitment in public enterprises could be another approach to prepare the enterprise for privatization. Delinking public enterprise jobs from the civil service or amongst the public enterprises could also help to mitigate the problems of inter enterprise comparison of jobs or doing away with the ascribed social status in having public enterprise jobs. Curtailment of opportunities for moonlighting and corruption in public enterprise jobs can also help to mitigate the problems of giving undue status to public enterprise jobs. Alternatively, the government can also ask private sector jobs to provide comparable social security so that workers in public enterprise do not feel better off both financially and psychologically. Even the new private sector management may have to be trained or at least, given an orientation on the management of the enterprise. This does not mean to inculcate the same old habits. In a country where entrepreneurship skills are squarely lacking, such training programmes do help a lot in the government's determination to develop private sector through privatization process.

6.6 Regulation and monitoring

Privatization in no way diminishes the government's responsibility toward public enterprises, before, during or after privatization. Just having concluded a successful deal does not end the government's responsibility towards privatization. At present, the government seems to be driven more by the agenda of "shedding the load" of managing sick public units. This is a mere transfer of load from the public to the private sector. The government has failed to regulate and monitor privatized units. The low priority given to regulation, monitoring and evaluation of privatization is very much evidenced by the fact that (1) Rs. 156 million remains to be still collected from seven privatized units (2) the government has not taken over the privatized unit which has been closed for so many years and (3) the liquidator has not finalised its accounts even after eight years of privatization (Auditor General's Report 2056). Because of the lack of proper, timely and adequate regulation and monitoring system, even the government does not have proper access to the performance information of privatized units. A system must be enforced to make new owners comply with the conditionalities of privatization.

Annex 1: Information on capital market situation of privatized units

Privatized units	Face value (Rs)	Market price (Rs)	No of Shareholders	Number of workers holding shares
Nepal Bank	100	360	8104	6483
Harishiddhi Bricks	10	2.90	7094	
Nepal Film	100	62	7009	Almost all workers hold shares
Bhrikuti Paper	100	63	3986	some 200 to 300 workers own shares
Leatherage Bansbari	100	53	2198	
Balaju Textile	-	-	1663	14 workers
Raghupati Jute Mills	-	-	936	
Nepal Lube	100	340	462	82 workers, some had sold their shares.
Biratnagar Jute Mills	-	-	171	
Nepal Bitumen			110	Workers have not taken shares due to losses.
Total			31,733	

Source: Information collected from Security Exchange Centre.

Annex 2: Nature of job losses in privatized units

Privatized Unit	Description of job losses
1. Nepal Film	Out of 107 workers, 60 workers resigned after privatization
2. Balaju Textile	Nearly 50 percent of the total workers left the job
3. Raghupati Jute	The unit was Privatized after bringing the workers at zero level. Out of Mills 1750, 100 workers have been given permanentstatus.
4. Nepal Foundry	Nearly all people opted for voluntary retirement, workers were given 35 days salary for every year of service. Three people joined after privatization.
5. Leatherage Bansbari	100 workers were given voluntary retirement prior to privatization, another 154 opted for voluntary retirement after privatization and in 1995, after locational dispute all the workers left the job and opted for voluntary retirement.
6. Harishidhi Bricks	Out of 602 workers, 84 people get retirement- 20 workers under age limit and 64 workers opted for voluntary retirement. Management has reduced the years of service from 25 years to 20 years to get voluntary retirement.
7. Nepal Bitumen	Some voluntary retirement but not of significance.

Source: Information collected from field interviews.

Annex 3 - Privatization: Workers' perceptions and responses

During the course of the study, a sample of workers and trade union leaders, numbering a total of fifty, from privatized units were interviewed to solicit their opinion and suggestions on privatization. Only those workers who opted to continue their services after privatization have been selected for the interviews. These workers were expected to have a better perception of "before-after" privatization scenario than the new workers who joined the units after privatization. The workers were also handed a structured questionnaire to collect their opinions. The summary of responses are given below and the results of the survey is presented in the box.

1. Should public enterprises be privatized?

Trade union leaders and workers were generally found to be antagonistic to the privatization move. This feeling was observed in almost all the interviews. However, in the administered structured questionnaire, only 52 per cent of the total respondents were found to hold negative attitude towards privatization. Nearly 38 per cent viewed that public enterprises should be privatized. A similar number of respondents also expressed that privatization is appropriate for increasing the competitive capacity of enterprises. Privatization is referred as a solution to the growth of corruption, inefficiency and lethargy in government management. The main agenda of privatization should be to improve the work performance of public enterprises.

Those who held negative attitude towards privatization reported that they were against privatization because:

(1) of the problems faced by workers in some privatized units like Agriculture Tools and Bhaktapur Bricks

(2) poor results from the privatization programme and

(3) the benefits of privatization have gone into the hands of a few people.

Respondents also suggested that if there is to be privatization then it should be selective such as privatization of sick units or privatization with specific measures. They also concluded: where management improvement is possible, privatization measure should not be opted.

2. Were the goals of privatization achieved?

Nearly half of the total respondents opined that the results of privatization were poor or worse than what used to be at the time of government ownership. Another half responded, that the results were positive. Respondents also seemed to believe that none of the three goals of privatization programme have been achieved. Although some private gains may have accrued to a few people, by and large, privatization has been used to shed the burden of the government to the private sector. Respondents were also firm in their view that increasing operational efficiency should be the single goal of the privatization programme.

3. What is the appropriate modality of privatization?

Privatization should be carried out on the basis of national interest. The choice of a modality should be based on the nature and type of concerned enterprise. Privatization must be seen in the total perspective of the industrialization process in Nepal. These were some specific recommendations from workers and trade union activists. In the structured questionnaire, nearly 66 per cent reported that workers should be involved in the privatization process. However, 22 per cent also reported that selling of shares is the best option. Guaranteeing the security and condition of workers, transparency in financial deals and handling of labour management issues were regarded as the main issues to be considered in the privatization programme.

4. What is the effectiveness of workers' safety measures made in the privatization programme?

Respondents believe that the safety nets made in the Privatization Act are not only inadequate but a sort of hoax. If adequate safety nets had been made, the new management in Raghupati Jute Mills would never ask to fire all the workers before takeover. They strongly suggested that there should be a provision in the privatization agreement not only spelling out "what the new management is expected to do" but also "the consequences of not doing so". Concerns were also expressed by respondents over the exit of talented and skilled manpower from the company under the so-called "voluntary retirement scheme". Therefore, they recommended tying-up employee share ownership with their employment in the enterprise. That is, the issue of shares should be made conditional for employment in privatized units. Respondents opined that the guarantee of jobs is a more attractive proposal than an issue of workers share at discount price and on an installment basis.

The workers complained that the use of "golden handshakes" in the Nepal Drinking Water Corporation has been used as a substitute for the compulsory retirement scheme. In case of Nepal Film, previously agreed twelve-installment facility on workers' shares has been reduced to one installment payment. This, they say, is to harass the workers. Similarly, in Bhrikuti Paper workers were told that they could sell their shares only after five years. Trade union leaders questioned "what is the point in holding these useless shares?" In many units, either employee shares were not issued at all or where they have been issued, employee response has been poor. In totality, workers participation through share-ownership has not been an effective mechanism.

5. What are the benefits of privatization to workers?

Many workers felt that in a situation where workers do not even get their salaries, it is very difficult to see how privatization will increase their welfare.

They further stated that the salaries and benefits of higher-level staff members or of the workers close to the management have definitely increased. But the general workers feel ever greater job insecurity. Therefore, job security should be the primary concern in privatization.

If there exists the problem of over-staffing in public enterprises, it should be adjusted with capacity increment, better utilization of manpower and, if necessary, surplus workers should be readjusted or reintegrated into other stae-owned enterprises. Respondents held that in no way should privatization be a part of the retrenchment programme.

Some of the reported changes in salaries, benefits and other facilities provided to workers are given in Table 3.1. Basically, respondents viewed that the capacity, sales, profits and working conditions have improved but there has been a further deterioration in worker exploitation, working hours, leaves, job security and union activities.

Table 3.1 Workers' perception of post privatization changes

Dimensions of changes	New Addition	Increased	Same	Reduced	Abolished
Salary/allowances		9	13	10	
Leaves		1	20	12	
Other facilities			11	15	1
Working conditions	2	10	11	4	
Working time	1	7	16	2	
Number of Workers	2	1	7	17	
Job Security		11	17	16	
Union Activities	2	4	5	9	2
Worker Exploitation	1	17	8	2	
Industry Capacity	2	9	11	4	
Capacity Utilization	2	5	8	8	
Sales	1	8	10	3	
Profits	1	19	7	5	
Bonus			9	6	2
Social Security (Insurance, pension, gratuity)	2		8	8	3

Source: Field visits

6. What is the effect of privatization on trade unions?

Trade union leaders perceived that the nature of industrial relations has changed after privatization. Under public ownership, unions could place indiscriminate demands, this is not possible in privatized units. Due to closure of many privatized units and also due to the near collapse situation of some privatized units, trade unions have to think twice before they take industrial actions. Trade union activities are now more specific and concentrated in privatized units than in public enterprises. Compared to public enterprises, the problems of multiplicity of unions in privatized units is less severe. Workers believe that trade unions need not necessarily oppose privatization moves. They can also support privatization provided adequate job security measures are incorporated in the privatization programme.

7. Is there workers' involvement in the privatization programme?

By and large, workers and trade union leaders reported that worker's involvement, consultation and participation are totally missing in the privatization programme. If they ever exist, it is only in the form of "notification" to trade unions. Any inquiry by the union is treated as " a confidential matter" and there is a tendency amongst officials to hide or misinform the union on privatization. For example, the union came to know about the privatization of Tea Development only after getting information from the internet. Similarly, in the case of Nepal Film, Balaju Textile and Bhrikuti Paper, the government took no consultation and advice from workers.

8. What possible social security measures can be adopted in the privatization programme?

Respondents said that there is no social security measure for workers in the privatization programme. Security of the jobs was the major concern of respondents. Some suggested that life insurance policy equivalent to five years salary, as being provided in the Lumbini Sugar Mills, be adopted as a social security measure for workers.

9. What are the perceptions of the workers on foreign direct investment in privatization?

Respondents opined positively that privatization could increase the inflow of FDI in the country, however, such inflows must not accompany the inflow of foreign workers as well. FDI must be used to promote employment opportunities in the country rather than the inflow of capital per se. Respondents opined that enough caution be exercised regarding the type of capital to be invited. Inflow of debt capital may put the country at risk. They opined that the sharp reduction in equity capital in privatized units is not a sign of good financial health. The respondents were also critical of the lack of professionalism on the part of Nepali entrepreneurs. They opined that FDI may bring in professional management in the enterprises but priority should be given to national investors. Some respondents opined that the government should hold a policy of 51:49 ownership ratio in the case of FDI.

Annex 4 - List of Persons Visited for Interviews

A. Officials and Managers

1. Mr. Omkar Shrestha
   Hon'ble Ministry for Industry
2. Mr. Mahesh Acharya
   Hon'ble Minister for Finance
3. Mr. Pradeep Shrestha
   President, FNCCI
4. Mr. Rajendra Dahal
   Editor, Himal Magazine
5. Mr. Tanka Khanal
   Privatization Cell
6. Mr. Douglas Clarke
   Adam Smith Institute
7. Mr. Bishnu Rimal
   Secretary General, GEFONT
8. Mr. Keshav Shrestha
   Manager, Bhrikuti Paper & Pulp
9. Mr. Prakash Shrestha
   Marketing Manager, Harisiddhi Bricks
10. Mrs. Shanti Shrestha
    Personnel, Harisiddhi Bricks
11. Mohan Chandra Ghimire
    Manager, Raghupati Jute Mill
12. Manoj Upadhyay
    GM, Biratnagar Jute Mill
13. Ananda Nepal
    DGM, Biratnagar Jute Mill
14. Sundar M. Shrestha
    Adm. Officer, Balaju Textile
15. Ramesh Pokharel
    Chief Adm. Officer,
    Bhrikuti Paper & Pulp
16. Tara Nath Mainali
    Manager, Nepal Foundry Industry
17. Dinesh Rai
    Nepal Lube Oil

B. Workers and Trade Union Activists

Raghupati and Biratnagar Jute Mill

18. Dev Narayan
19. Kushum Mainali
20. Asha Kumar Chetri
21. Ramanda Yadav
22. Kul Bdr. Shrestha
23. Bhakta Bdr. Shrestha
24. Basu Dev Dulal
25. Tika Ram Poudel

Nepal Film Development Company

26. Mr. Ratna Kaji Tuladhar
27. Mr. Prakash Man Singh Pradhan
28. Mr. Shyam Nepali
29. Mr. Deepak Man Shrestha
30. Mr. Kiran Oshi
31. GEFONT
32. O. Koirala, Sunsari
33. Hem Raj Regmi, Nepalgunj
34. Madhusudan Katiwada, Makwanpur
35. Kamal Gautam, Bhairahawa
36. Keshav Dawadi, Hetauda
37. Rajiv Ghimeri, Jhapa
38. Umesh Upadhyay, Kathmandu
39. Manohari Sivakoti, Kathmandu
40. Maiya Pode, Kathmandu
41. Ramesh Badal, Kathmandu

DECONT

42. Suresh Kunwar, Kailali
43. Tej Bdr. Basnet, Kathmandu
44. Devendra Lamsal, Sunsari
45. Ghanashyam Subedi, Bhojpur
46. Usha Khadka, Makwanpur
47. Rishav Ghimire, Lalitpur
48. Raj Kumar Bhandaari, Solu
49. Ravi Lal Shrestha, Nawalpur
50. Raghu Nath Adhikari, Bara
51. Ramesh Sedai, Kavre

NTUC

52. Shyam Bdr. Malla, Udayapur
53. R. K. Pandey, Ilam
54. Chandra Thakur, Mahottari
55. G. R. Bhatta, Makwanpur
56. Lok Raj Subedi, Lumjung
57. Jagdish Pd. Sharma, Tanahu
58. Giri Raj Ojha, Banke
59. Youba Raj Lama, Kailali
60. G. Khadka, Chitwan

Bibliography

Arya, Ramesh C. Privatization (1994): *A Case Study of Raw Hide Development,* published in The Kathmandu Post, Dec 20 and 21.

Auditor General's Office, Annual Report of the Auditor General, 2055 (1998) and 2056 (1999).

CCC, (1977): *Performance of Public Enterprises in Nepal:* Macro Study, Kathmandu.

CRPS and DEAN (1995) *Case Studies of Privatized Public Enterprises of Nepal,* Kathmandu: Council of Retired Public Servants and Development Associates Nepal (unpublished).

CRPS/DEAN (1995): *Rastrasewak, an issue on privatization in Nepal,* Vol. 1 No 3, summer.

Galal (1994): A. et al *Welfare Consequences of Selling Public Enterprises: An Empirical Analysis,* Oxford University press.

Huq Muzammel (1997): *The Impact of Ownership on Grameen Bikas Banks Current and Future Performance,* Institutional Reform and the Informal Sector, University of Maryland College Park, March.

ILO 1991, *Privatization: Role of Employer's Organization* by C. S. Venkata Ratnam, ILO, Geneva 1991.

ILO 1997, *Lessons from Privatization: Labour Issues in Developing and Transitional Countries* edited by Rolph Van Der Hoeven and Gyorgy Szirac Zki.

Management Association of Nepal (MAN) (1998): *Byavasthapan, Special Issue on Privatization,* No 6, Feb.

Manandhar, N. (1998): *Public Enterprises and Privatization,* Kathmandu.

Manandhar, N. (1993): *Improving Public Enterprise Performance: An Empirical study of Behaviour and Performance of Public Enterprises in Nepal,* Ph. D Dissertation, University of Birmingham UK.

Ministry of Finance (1991): Policy paper on the Privatization of Public Enterprises, Kathmandu.

Ministry of Finance (1999): A Report on Performance of Privatized Enterprises, unpublished Report

Ministry of Finance (1998/99): Economic Survey.

Ministry of Finance, *Performance Targets and Achievement of Public Enterprises,* Various Annual Reports.

Ministry of Finance, *Privatization of Public Enterprises: Facts about Privatization,* Progress of the Privatization Programme and Conditions of Privatization Agreements, 1994 (in Nepali).

Ministry of Finance (1992): *Privatization Strategy.*

Ministry of Finance (1992): *Privatization Strategy,* prepared by Frank Cook, July.

Nepal Administrative Staff College, " Report on High Level Workshop on Privatization, August 8-11, 1988, Kathmandu and also see the report on Seminar on Privatizing Public Enterprises, 1990.

Regmi, Jaya Ram (1996): Nepal Country Paper on Privatization in *Privatization of State Owned Enterprises:* Experiences of Asian and Pacific Economy, published by APO, Tokyo, Nov.

Report submitted by the Committee composed of three Mps to Review Privatization Programme, 1995 (in Nepali).

Sharma and Robin (1995): *Privatization: Lessons of Experience,* Kathmandu.

Society for Constitutional and Parliamentary Exercises (SCOPE), *Privatization Policy and Process in Nepal,* Kathamandu, April 1997.

Swanson & Dan (1994): *Evaluation of Privatization in Nepal,* Kathmandu, USAID/INTRADOS.

UNDP (1992): *Privatization Strategy, Kathmandu,* UNDP/Ministry of Finance.

World Bank (1995): *Bureaucrats in Business: The Economics and Politics of Government Ownership.*

5

Privatization in Pakistan

DR. A.R. KEMAL*

1. Introduction

Despite frequent changes in the governments since 1985, five regularly elected and six care takers, there has been consensus on the continuation of privatization policy and as such it is expected to be cornerstone of all the future government policies, at least in the near future[1]. Instead of arguing the merits or demerits of the privatization policy, we explore policy measures that help the levels of efficiency and at the same time have the minimal adverse social impact.

A large number of public sector units have already been divested and a number of other public enterprises including telecommunications and thermal power stations have been placed on the privatization list. Nevertheless, serious doubts have been expressed about transparency of the bidding process and the impact of privatization on efficiency, investment, production, prices, employment and fiscal deficit. Accordingly, there is a need to identify constraints in realising various objectives of privatization with a view to suggesting concrete policy measures that may be taken to overcome the constraints.

Divestiture of assets is not new to Pakistan though the motivation for divestiture has not been the same in different time periods. During the 50s and the 60s, public sector used to invest in non-traditional activities especially where the gestation period was long and private sector was reluctant to invest. While a large number of private sector units were nationalized and public sector expanded at a rapid rate in the 70s, an effort to divest public sector enterprises were made during the mid-eighties. However, the efforts to divest shares worth Rs 2 billion of various profit making public enterprises in the mid-eighties and 14 loss making industrial units for divestiture in 1988 did not succeed. Similarly, out of the six profit-making corporations identified for partial divestiture in 1990, only 10 per cent shares of Pakistan International Airlines could be divested. The slow pace of privatization led to the establishment of a Privatization Commission on January 22 1991, which offered 105 industrial units, four banks, and two development financial institutions for sale. Subsequently, initiatives were undertaken for privatization of thermal power units of the Water and Power Development Authority (WAPDA), private sector managment of some sections of Pakistan Railways and

---

* Chief Economist, Planning Commission, Pakistan.

[1] The new government has announced that public enterprises shall be made more efficient. It does not suggest if privatization policy still continues or shall be abadoned.

partial divestiture of the Telecommunications Corporation of Pakistan (TCP). At present, as many as 46 industrial units, including all the remaining manufacturing units with the exception of Pakistan Steel, have been placed on the privatization list. Furthermore, two banks and six non-bank financial institutions; four units in the oil and gas sector; Karachi Electric Supply Corporation; six thermal power units and three area electricity boards of WAPDA; Pakistan Telecommunications; Pakistan Shipping Corporation and National Tanker Corporation; and Pakistan Railways are also on the privatization list.

During 1991-92, 69 manufacturing units and two commercial banks were successfully privatized. So far 91 industrial units, majority shares of two major banks and three non-bank financial institutions (NBFIs), 10 per cent shares of Pakistan International Airlines, 12 per cent shares of Pakistan Telecommunication and 26 per cent of Kot Addu power station have been divested. All in all 106 units have been divested, and so far government has received Rs. 59.6 billion through the sale of these enterprises. Total employment in the manufacturing units, which were privatized by sale of assets and where the management was transferred, was around 35,000, out of which 63.3 per cent opted for golden handshake scheme. If the retrenched workers are also taken into consideration, employment in privatized units may have gone down by at least three-fifth.

2.   Rationale for privatization

Objectives of privatization at different points in time have varied. During the period 1988-90, privatization was pursued to divest 14 loss making manufacturing units and raise funds by selling shares of profit making units for retiring public debt and thus reducing debt servicing (See Rothschild, 1990). Privatization Commission in 1991 did not explicitly spell out the basic rationale for privatization. Nevertheless four major objectives that could be discerned from various statements issued by the government are:

- Improvements in the level of efficiency in the production processes;
- Reduction in the debt burden of the government and fiscal deficit;
- Broad-basing equity capital; and
- Releasing resources for the physical and social infrastructures.

Whereas in the initial stages of its establishment Privatization Commission did not spell out the objectives of privatization, it has recently come up with a very clear Mission Statement contained in the Privatization in Pakistan (1998):

"Privatization is envisaged to foster competition, ensuring greater capital investment, competitiveness, and modernisation, resulting in enhancement of employment and provision of improved quality of products and services to the consumers and reduction in the fiscal burden".

The objectives of privatization outlined in the publication cited above are:

- Creation of market based economy
- Promoting the expansion and efficiency of private sector enterprises
- Encourage competition, specially by abolishing the monopolies and promote integration of the domestic economy into the world economy

- Support wider capital ownership and encourage employee owner relationship
- Establish and develop capital markets for mobilization of domestic savings
- Reverse the flight of capital abroad and repatriate capital already transferred
- Mobilization of private sector resources for future investments
- Promote economic flexibility
- Maintain or create employment
- Improve the quality of goods and services
- Maximise receipts from privatization to pay off public debt and reduce the public sector deficit
- Substantially reduce the size and scope of the public sector
- Substantially reduce the financial drain of public enterprises on the government
- Decrease the opportunities for misuse and corruption of public property by government officials and public sector managers.

These objectives are indeed laudable but quite ambitious. Though, privatization is neither necessary nor sufficient for realization of some of these. For example, mobilization of savings, reversing the flight of capital and promotion of savings and investments do not need privatization and they can not be achieved just by pursuit of privatization. In the following we examine the arguments that privatization lead to reduction in fiscal deficit, improvement in the efficiency levels, broad base the ownership and higher level of investment in the physical and social infrastructures.

2.1 Reduction in fiscal deficit

Privatization in a perfectly competitive market with complete foresight may have no impact on fiscal deficit because the expected sale price determined as the reserve price of assets would be exactly equal to the discounted flow of net benefits. If the private sector offers higher prices than the reserve price, fiscal deficit situation would improve. However, the private sector's willingness to do so, of course, depends upon the assessment of profits in the post-privatization period and willingness to share the expected higher profits with the public sector.

2.2 Increase in the efficiency levels

While private producers are forced to reduce their cost to minimum for their survival, public firms may not make sufficient efforts to reduce production costs as they are under no compulsion to ensure an acceptable return to the equity holders. Similarly, private managers have more flexibility in taking the decisions than the public sector firms. Moreover, public investments may be influenced by political considerations, thus adversely affecting the allocative efficiencies. While in a competitive framework, privatization would always help in realising allocative efficiency, X-efficiency and non-market efficiency gains, in a monopolistic framework this is not necessarily true. The cost in public monopoly at equilibrium point may not be minimal unless it is effectively regulated. Whether privatization would result in higher level of efficiency or not is an empirical question. For conflicting evidence see Stigler (1975); Wolf (1979), Baumol (1996) and Kemal (1996).

2.3 Releasing the resources for physical and social infrastructures

A well functioning and profit making public enterprises can also be divested for releasing the resources for development of infrastructures if the resources for infrastructure are not available.

2.4 Broad-basing of ownership of equity capital

Broad-basing the ownership of equity capital is for the reasons of distributive justice. But it presupposes that small investors have sufficient investible funds to buy the shares of public industrial enterprises and that unless the public enterprises are divested shares are not available to them. Both of these assumptions may not always be valid. Moreover, the assumption is that allocating a part of the shares at face value for the workers would result in improvement in the welfare for these workers.

3. Modes of privitization in Pakistan

Public enterprises may be liquidated or divested partially or completely, and the divestiture may take different forms including flotation of shares in the stock exchange market, sales through financial institutions and equity tap and outright auction.

- **Liquidation:** Public enterprises making losses due to a number of factors such as inappropriate location, poor technology, etc. cannot be divested, and as such they are prime candidates for liquidation and not divestiture. However, losses due to poor management may be overcome through transfer of management and control with or without transfer of the assets.

- **Sale of Assets:** The divestiture of public enterprises may be pursued through following four methods.

  (a) *Flotation of Shares:* The shares of public enterprises are floated in the Stock Exchange Market, and government progressively reduces its share holding in such enterprises. Such flotation has three distinct features. First, induction of private capital may result in higher levels of productivity. Second, government retains sufficient control if the firm is of strategic importance. Third, gradual divestiture would not have an adverse impact on the prices of the shares.

  (b) *Equity Tap:* The only difference in equity tap and floatation of shares is that the amount of shares being offered is not restricted. Whatever the demand, shares would be automatically supplied by the government.

  (c) *Sales through Financial Institutions:* Since capital markets in many developing countries are quite limited, it is feared that off-loading of shares in a big way may significantly depress the share prices. With a view to alleviating such fears, financial institutions may be appointed underwriters to avoid a run on the share prices.

   (d) *Auction:* Auction may be done through sealed bidding or open bidding. Similarly, bidding may be done for a part of the shares or for the entire company.

- **Privatization: By-passing the Sale of Divestiture:** Besides liquidation and sale of assets through any of the four methods, the public sector may take certain measures to realize the intended objectives without selling the assets.

   (a) **Franchising:** Government may offer a franchise to private sector, but control the prices.

   (b) **Repealing Monopoly**: Government may remove the restrictions on entry of the private sector in all activities.

   (c) **Contracting out**: Instead of carrying out certain services in the public sector, private contractors may be hired to do the specified work.

   (d) **Leasing**: Public assets are leased to the private sector with a view to improving productivity.

Following are the six different modes through which public enterprises in Pakistan were divested until 1997:

   (i) Divestiture through bids;

   (ii) Sale of suitable amounts of shares through the stock exchange;

   (iii) Sale to Workers' Management Group on the basis of an evaluation of assets, liabilities and net worth and matching the maximum bid received;

   (iv) Sale to *modaraba* companies, working on the Islamic profit-and-loss sharing principle, which raise funds for purchasing shares;

   (v) Management contracts with *modaraba* companies, leasing or contracting of management to private entrepreneurs for a specified period; and, finally,

   (vi) Lease management contract with the workers for a specified period to enable them to buy out the enterprises they have been working in.

The privatization policy of 1998 outlines following four modes for privatization:

- Total disinvestment through competitive bidding
- Partial disinvestment with management control
- Partial disinvestment without management control
- Sales/Lease of assets and property

These measures may be grouped into:

(i) Sale of assets through bidding to individuals, to workers-management groups, and to *modaraba* companies (those working on the profit and loss sharing principle); and

(ii) Sale of assets through the floatation of shares in stock exchange and leasing.

Liquidations have rarely been used; probably the roti corporation units are the only ones so far liquidated. Privatization Commission insisted that the units should be operated after the take over. Nevertheless, a large number of loss making units have been converted into essentially real estate.

In the eighties, government appointed financial institutions as underwriters but no unit could be divested. Similarly shares have not been put on tap. A limited number of shares of Pakistan International Airlines (PIA) and Pakistan Telecommunications have been offered for sale. PIA divested 10 per cent of the shares through the stock exchange, and Pakistan Telecommunications divested 12 per cent of its shares. Twenty six per cent shares of Kot Addu thermal power station have been divested with the change in management as well. Profitability in these organizations have increased sharply after the divestiture but not necessarily through improvements in efficiency.

The principal method of divestiture in Pakistan has been sealed bidding. Where bid was below the fixed price, the open bidding has been used. Sales have been generally to individuals or groups of individuals, but in nine specific cases sales have been made to the worker-management groups. On average the manufacturing units taken over by the worker-management groups have outperformed the units taken over by other private sector groups. In the banking sector, however, the performance of worker-management group has been inferior to the other divested bank.

Leasing, franchising, liquidation and other possible modes of privatization have been used only sparingly. A couple of railway sectors were offered to the private sector for operation but with not much success. Similarly there was a proposal to let private sector run the goods trains against the payment of track charges, but the experience has not been very successful. An exercise for unbundling of both WAPDA and railways was carried out but so far not much has resulted from such exercise.

The methods employed to privatise the public assets and their valuation, cost of disposal, and sources and timings of cash flows, and post-privatization capital structure play an important role in the realisation of various objectives of privatization. For example, the bid price offered by the prospective buyer depends on the perceptions regarding the net future benefits. In the absence of complete information, the expected profits are randomly distributed with subjective probabilities. The shape of probability distribution varies across individuals; risk averters would under-bid and risk plungers would overbid. Withholding the information has also serious implications for the levels of productivity. The firms, which is able to buy the unit at a price lower than the reserve prices,[1] may feel as if its operations are efficient but in fact they may not be, and as such may develop inertia to improving productivity. The over-bidders, on the other hand, may run into losses and cash flow problems with the result that unit may close down and overall productivity of the economy may fall.

4.   Privatization and fiscal deficit

One of the main objectives of the privatization has been reduction in fiscal deficit. Privatization is presumed to help in retiring the public debt and thus in reducing the debt

---

[1]   It assumes that reserve prices have been correctly perceived by the government agency.

servicing. At the same time the surplus of autonomous enterprises also tends to fall. If reduction in debt servicing exceeds the fall in surplus of autonomous bodies, budgetary deficit tends to fall.

The Stabilization and Structural Adjustment Programmes of IMF being implemented since 1988-89 also aim at a reduction in fiscal deficit through resource mobilization and reduction in public expenditure. Therefore, reduction in the fiscal deficit in the post-privatization period cannot be attributed to privatization only.

The fiscal deficit increased upto 8.5 per cent of GDP by 1987-88 when Pakistan signed three year Stabilisation and Structural Adjustment Program (1987-88 to 1990-91). Fiscal deficit declined to 6.5 per cent of GDP over the first two years of the program. However, despite the divestiture of a large number of manufacturing units and two banks in the 1990-93 period, fiscal deficit increased sharply though it declined to a level of around 6.5 per cent in the subsequent years. Cumulative privatization receipt of Rs 59.6 billion compared to a debt of Rs 2,500 billion is rather small. The interest payments savings by retiring Rs 59.6 billion may not even be sufficient to compensate for the decline in surplus of autonomous bodies. It may, however, be added that privatization of large banks and telecommunication can have significant influence on the fiscal deficit (Figure 5.1).

Figure 5.1
Privatization and fiscal deficit

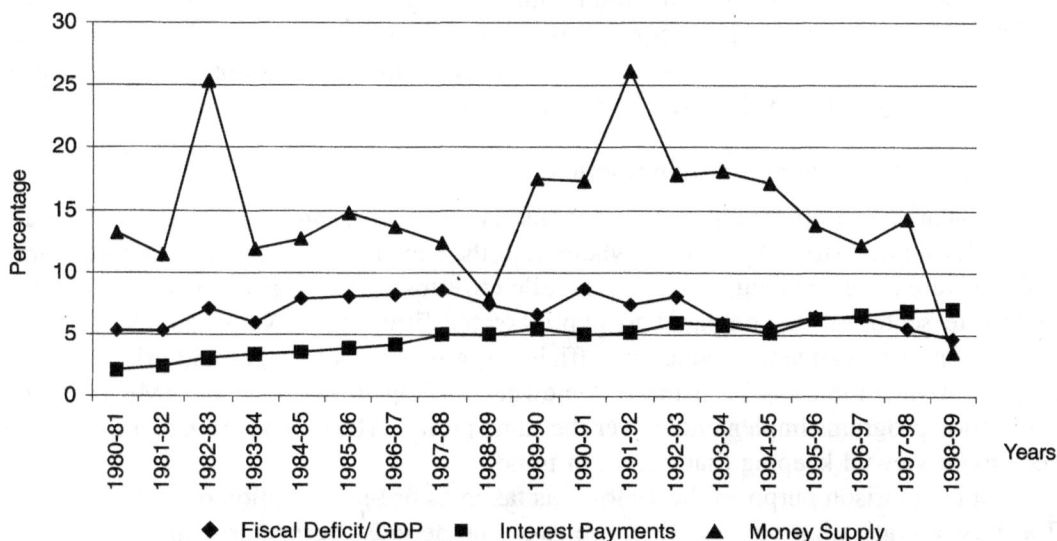

5. Privatization and levels of efficiency

While it is generally believed privatization results in higher level of efficiency such claims cannot be substantiated always. Alam (1989), Beesley (1997), Candoy (1989), Caves and Christensen (1980), CIDA (1987), Dotgson (1987), Foreman Peck (1989), Kemal (1993, 1996), Naqvi and Kemal (1991, 1994, 1998), Sen (1992), Selim (1988) and Walle (1989) have provided examples that privatization did not necessarily improve the level of efficiency. Kikeri, Nellis and Shirley (1992) have shown, on the other hand, that while in most of the cases privatization led to improvement in efficiency, at least in 25 per cent of the cases it did not. The general conclusion emerging from these studies is that the quality of management and the market structure and not privatization per se determine performance of a firm.

Competitive market structure forces producers to reduce the cost to minimum and increase the output to a level where marginal cost is the minimum. Accordingly privatization in a competitive framework results in higher levels of production and lower level of prices with favourable impact on employment, real wages and investments. On the other hand, in a monopolistic framework producers restrict the output to a level where price exceeds the marginal costs which are still falling and may lead to lower level of output, higher prices and loss of consumer surplus. By regulating the prices, a monopolist may be forced to lower the prices to marginal cost. While tradable goods industries can be regulated through changes in the import duties on competitive imports, in case of non-traded goods efficient regulation may not even be feasible.

The decreasing cost in industries results in natural monopolies and the producers make losses if production is expanded to a level where marginal cost is the minimum. Unless private sector firms are compensated for the loss, no regulation can force a firm to increase the output to a level where marginal cost is the minimum. Subsidy can be avoided if firm is allowed to restrict output and charge a price equal to the average cost. The assumption that an efficient regulatory agency capable of determining and enforcing marginal cost or average cost pricing would exist may not be valid (See Baumol, 1996).

5.1 Increase in efficiency in manufacturing

Comparison of efficiency in public industrial enterprises and private sector firms in the manufacturing industries of Pakistan where both the sectors simultaneously operated prior to the divestiture of manufacturing industries failed to substantiate higher levels of efficiency of the private sector firms compared to public sector firms. (See Naqvi and Kemal, 1991). Comparison of investment, production, efficiency, employment, wages and prices in the pre- and post-privatization has been made somewhat difficult because of the IMF deflationary stabilisation programs implemented over the same period. The comparative picture, therefore, needs to be viewed keeping that caveat in mind.

For comparison purposes the 1986-91 is taken as pre-privatization period and the 1992-97 as post privatization period.[1] Over the two time periods average growth rate of GDP has gone down from 5.44 per cent to 4.15 per cent and the compound growth rate from 5.44 to 4.13 per cent – a decline by more than one per centage point in growth of GDP. While the decline in growth rate may also have been the result of deflationary monetary and fiscal policies but at least partly it is due to privatization (Figure 5.2).

---

[1] 1991-92 year has been excluded as a privatization period.

Figure 5.2
Average and compound growth rates of GDP, investment and employment

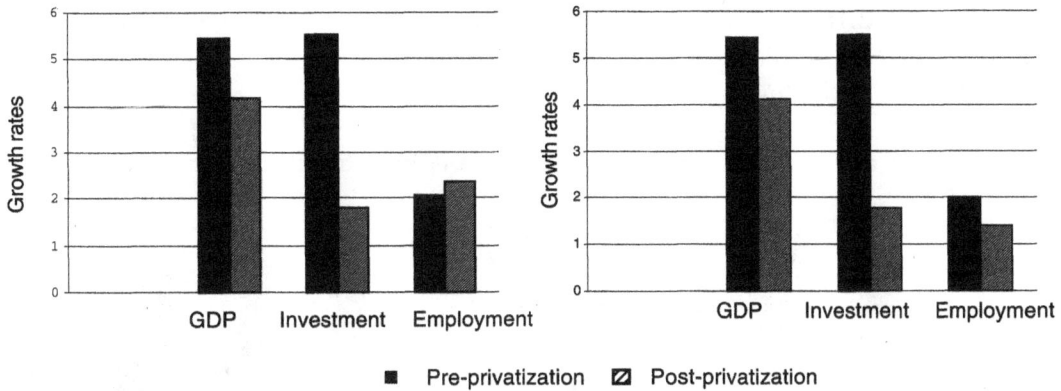

■ Pre-privatization   ▨ Post-privatization

The decline in the growth rate of investment has been even more dramatic. The average growth rate of investment fell from 5.55 per cent to just 1.82 per cent and the compound growth rate from 5.49 to 1.76 per cent. The fixed investment as a per centage of GDP has fallen from a little more than 17 per cent in the second half of the eighties to 13.6 per cent of GDP by 1998-99 only because public sector investment declined from about 9 per cent to 5.2 per cent over the same period. The private sector investment, in fact, increased from less than 8 per cent to 9.4 per cent in 1997-98 (falling to 8.4 per cent in 1998-99), but it could not compensate for the decline in public investment (Figure 5.3).

Figure 5.3
Fixed investment ratios

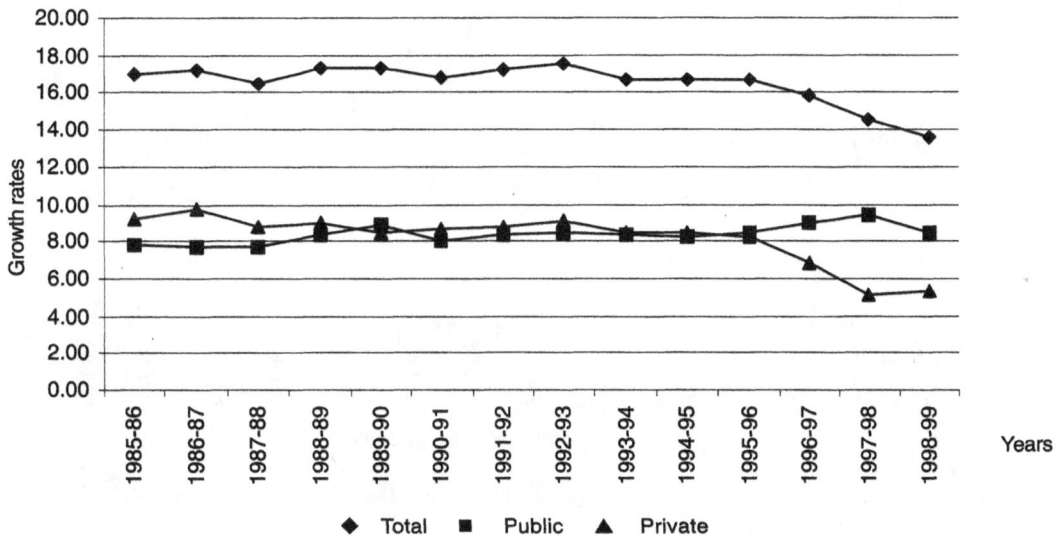

♦ Total   ■ Public   ▲ Private

The output and investment in the manufacturing sector show similar trends as observed in the aggregate GDP and investment. The average growth rate of manufacturing output over the two time periods fell from 3.85 to 3.45 per cent while the compound growth rate declined from 6.03 to just 2.16 per cent.[1] Similarly the average growth rate of investment in the large scale manufacturing sector fell from 7.44 per cent to -2.45 and the compound growth rate from 6.46 to -6.64 (Figure 5.4).

Figure 5.4
Average and compound growth rates of GDP, investment and employment

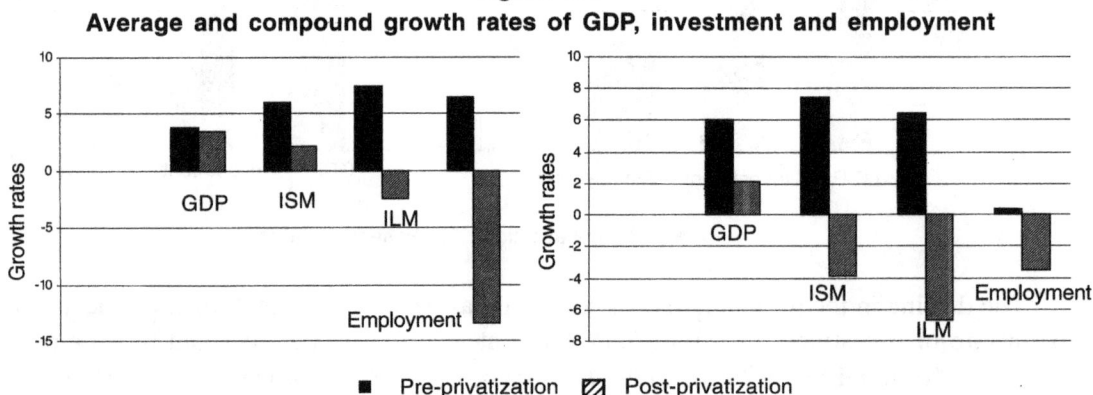

■ Pre-privatization ▨ Post-privatization

Sharp fluctuations in the investment in the post privatization period needs to be noted. Investment rose sharply during 1991-94 period ranging between 4.4 and 4.8 per cent of GDP and but since then has declined to 2.7 per cent of GDP by 1998-99 (Figure 5.5).

Figure 5.5
Investment in manufacturing

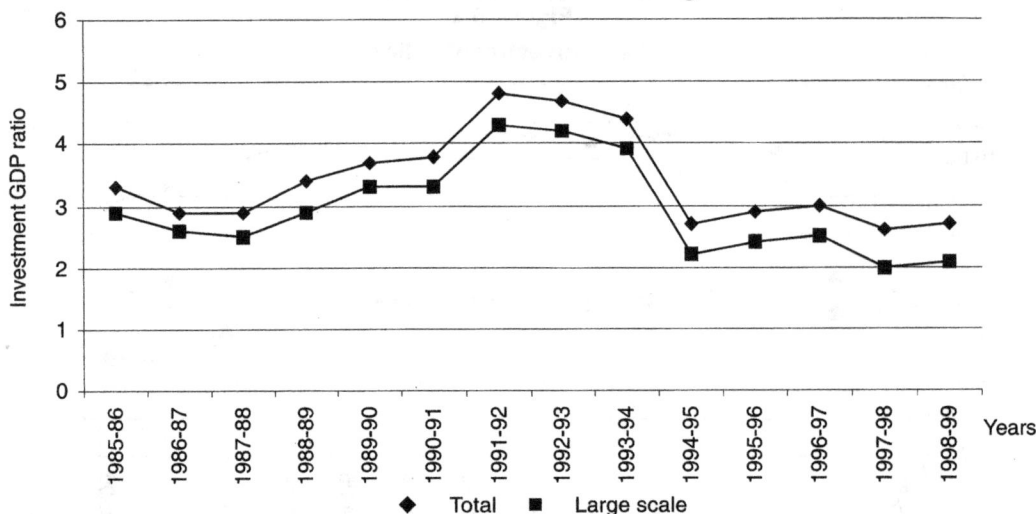

◆ Total ■ Large scale

---

[1] The difference in compound and average growth rates is a reflection of sharp fluctuations in the growth rates of the manufacturing sector.

In order to assess the growth of the industry, the data made available by the Federal Bureau of Statistics (FBS) and Provincial Bureaus of Statistics (PBS) on production, employment and employment cost has been analysed. The FBS data indicate an increased growth rates in case of vegetable ghee, nitrogenous fertilisers, soda ash, caustic soda, chlorine, switch gears and tractors and a decline in the growth rates of phosphatic fertilisers, cement, scooters, motorcycles, buses, trucks, motor cars and jeeps. Decline in output of cement and consumer durables industries seem to have been the collusion of the duopolists.

The PBS data also show a sharp increase in the growth rate of vegetable ghee, fertiliser and chemicals industries while cement and automobiles industries indicate a sharp fall in the growth rates of output. However, the real wages have been stagnant thus indicating that the workers have been untouched by any growth (Figure 5.6).

Figure 5.6
Nominal and real wages

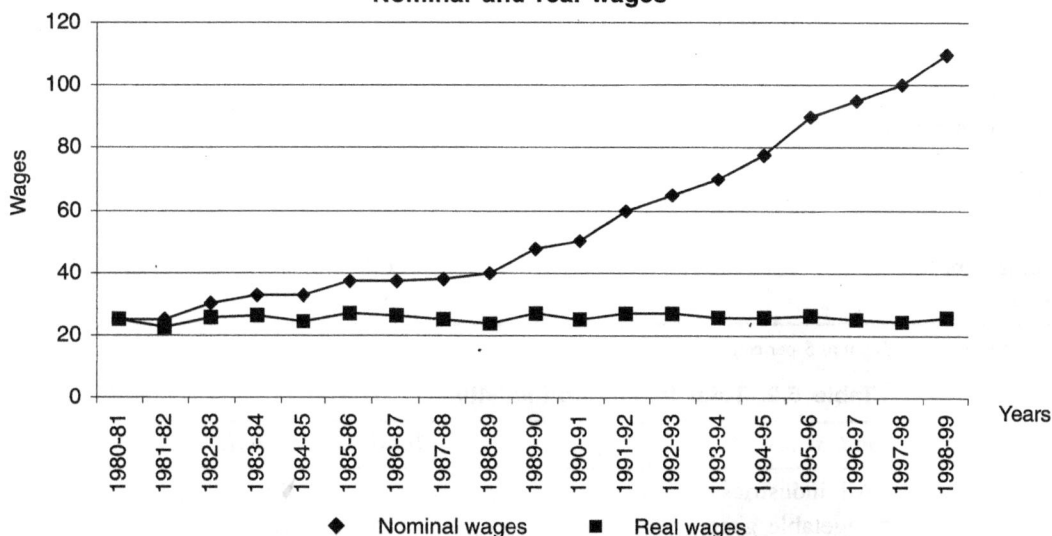

The analysis of variance and regressions reported in Kemal (1996) does not suggest any improvement in the levels of efficiency measured by the return to equity or return to fixed assets. With a view to isolating the impact of concentration and protection levels on the growth of output after privatization, growth rate of post-privatization period was regressed against the growth rates in pre-privatization period, concentration ratios and protection.

The coefficient of dummy variable is negative in eight and positive in the remaining 6 industries but in nine industries it is insignificant. The coefficient is significant and positive in nitrogenous fertilisers and switchgears, and significant and negative in scooters/motorcycles, LCVs, motorcars and jeeps. Fertiliser is a regulated industry and the automobile sector is oligopolistic (Table5.1).

Data to estimate total factor productivity are sketchy. The Census of Manufacturing Industries data show a decline in total factor productivity in the large scale manufacturing sector by 6 per cent but an increase by 2 per cent in the privatized industries over 1991-96 period. While productivity in vegetable ghee and transport equipment industries increased by 69 and 18 per cent it fell by 29 per cent in compressed gases, nine per cent in fertilizer, six per cent in cement, one per cent in agricultural machinery and 33 per cent in textile machinery (Table 5.2).

Table 5.1: Results of regression of post-privatization output against time, dummy and manufacturing output

Name of industry	Coefficient of time	Coefficient of dummy
Vegetable Ghee & oil	1.98	0.004
Nitrogenous fertilizers	8.4*	0.18*
Phosphatic fertilizers	-15.6*	0.01
Soda ash	6.1*	0.03
Caustic soda	7.5*	-0.07
Chorine	18.3*	-0.13
Cement	1.5	-0.07
Switch gears	-15.6	1.06*
Scoters/Motor cycles	10.9	-0.33
Trucks	9.1	-0.2
Buses	5.6	-0.75
LCV	11.3	-0.65*
Motor cars/Jeeps	6.8	-0.55*
Tractors	5.2	0.08

Note: * shows significant at 5-per cent level,

Table 5.2: Total factor productivity

Industries	Total factor productivity
All industries	0.94
Vegetable ghee	1.69
Compressed gases, etc	0.71
Fertilizers	0.91
Cement	0.94
Agricultural machinery	0.99
Textile machinery	0.67
Transport equipment	1.18
Total privatized industries	1.02

Public enterprises have been instrumental in diffusion of technology especially through vigorous pursuit of an indigenisation program. Whereas public sector firms would provide training facilities irrespective of the fact whether gains from training are internalized or not, private sector would not make such investments unless they are sure that gains can be internalized. This may have serious implications for productivity.

The common man would see the benefit of the privatization only if the prices fall. Besides, if the growth of production falls and prices rise, then it is clear that they are using their monopoly power. The real prices deflated through the wholesale price index of the products of the industries produced by the privatized industries have not fallen. As a matter of fact, they have gone up.

5.2 Banking sector

Pakistan has already divested two relatively smaller banks and is in the process to divest two major banks. A large number of Pakistani and foreign banks are operating simultaneously in Pakistan, and they compete vigorously with each other. It is therefore expected that performance of the privatized banks would be better.

Two privatized banks are Allied Bank Ltd. (ABL) and Muslim Commercial Bank (MCB). Former was taken over by a management group and a private investor has acquired the latter. The performance of the Muslim Commercial bank in the post privatization period has been somewhat better then that of the Allied Bank. However, any improvement in performance is overshadowed by the ballooning employment cost (Figure 5.7). Paid-up capital of ABL increased from Rs 272 million in 1991 to Rs 1063 million by 1997 and of MCB from Rs 576 million in 1991 to Rs 1820 million in 1997. Similarly deposits of ABL increased from Rs 25 billion to Rs 63 billion and of MCB from Rs 350 billion to Rs 1024 billion over the same period. The profits of both the banks have increased. In case of ABL, profit increased from Rs 100 million in 1991 to Rs. 531 million in 1995 but since then it has fallen. The profit of MCB increased from Rs 212 million in 1991 to Rs 1235 million in 1997.

Figure 5.7
Performance of the banking sector

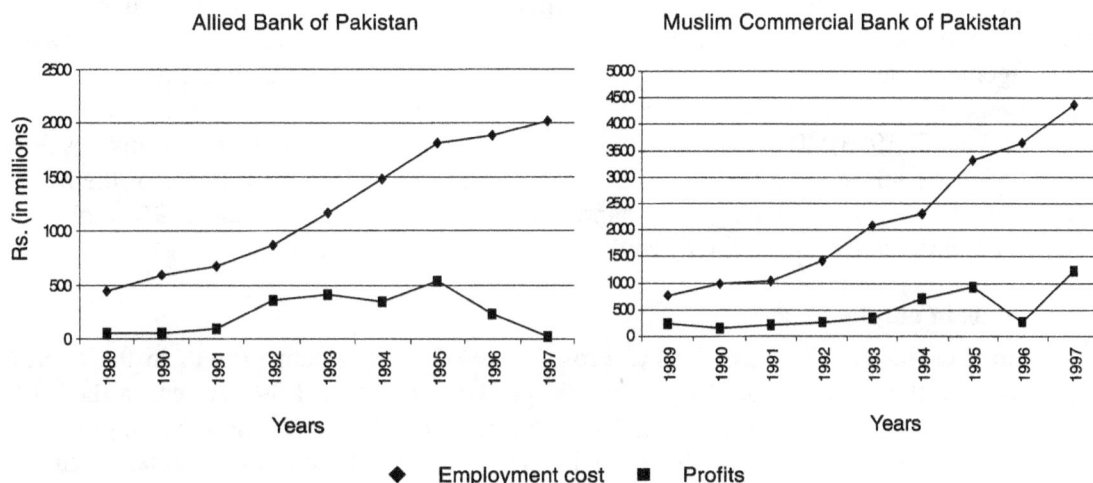

Source: Banking Statistics of Pakistan, various issues.

5.3 Power and telecommunications sector

Only 26 per cent shares of one thermal unit have been divested and the management has been transferred to the private sector. There may have been an improvement in productivity but the increase in profits has been due to higher prices, which were also guaranteed. The increase in power prices and losses of the power utility have placed a question mark over the concept of welfare. On the other hand sale of shares of telecommunications and PIA without any change in management could not have any impact on the levels of efficiency.

6. The Impact of privatization on employment

While improvements in productivity would eventually result in higher levels of well being, the impact of privatization on prices, employment and wages and other employment benefits determine the resultant impact on social fabric of the country. As mentioned earlier, privatization neither resulted in lower rate of inflation nor in the lower real prices of the products of the privatized industries.

The decision to divest manufacturing and financial enterprises, Water and Power Development Authority (WAPDA) and Pakistan Telecommunications put the job of more than 500 thousand workers at stake. There are five possible ways in which privatization may affect the labour. First, since public sector enterprises traditionally employ labour in excess of their requirements, the private sector would like to get rid of the excess labour. Second, in an oligopolistic market structure the possibility of collusion is quite distinct and as such they may restrict the output, and consequently the demand for labour would be reduced. Third, the private sector may like to opt for capital intensive methods of production, thus further reducing demand for labour. Fourth, even when more workers are required in the private sector, they may be hired on contract with a view to avoiding benefits to be provided to full time employees.

Obviously, divestiture through stock exchange without change in management would hardly affect the level of employment. However, complete or partial divestiture with change in management and enterprise restructuring prior to its sale would definitely affect the employment levels because the public enterprises are generally overmanned. (See Kemal, 1993 and Lawai, 1993). The recent restructuring of Habib Bank and United Bank resulted in loss of job for ten thousand workers. Similarly 2,225 out of 3495 employees of the heavy engineering industry have taken golden handshake/voluntary retirement and 2195 employees in vegetable ghee mills not yet privatized have taken voluntary retirement.

6.1 Trends in employment

Compared to an annual compound growth rate of 2.0 per cent growth in the overall employment in the pre-privatization period, the growth rate fell to 1.39 per cent in the post-privatization period. Increase in capital intensity over time has constrained the employment growth in addition to decline in the growth rate of output. Employment situation in the manufacturing sector, where most of the privatization has taken place, is quite worse. Whereas in the pre-privatization period, employment in the manufacturing grew at a rate of 6.5 per cent, employment in the manufacturing sector declined at a rate of 13.5 per cent. Even more disturbing is the decline in employment in the small-scale industries in recent years. The Census of manufacturing industries data indicate 9.7 per cent decline in employment in the large scale manufacturing sector over 1990-91 to 1995-96 period (Figure 5.8).

Figure 5.8
Growth rate of employment

The Provincial Bureaus data available only for two provinces viz. Punjab and Sindh indicate that except for fertilizer where employment increased at a rate of 1.37 per cent in the post-privatization period compared to a decline in the pre-privatization period, the trend is exactly the reverse in all the other industries. Employment in vegetable ghee grew at a rate of 1.66 per cent in the pre-privatization period, but declined at an annual compound rate of 4.78 per cent in the post-privatization period. Employment in the cement industry increased at a rate of 0.85 per cent in the pre-privatization period and declined at a rate of 3.84 per cent in the post-privatization period. Employment declined at a rate of 2.95 per cent in chemicals and at a rate of 2.16 per cent in automobile industries during the post privatization period (Figure 5.9).

Figure 5.9
Growth rate of employment in large scale

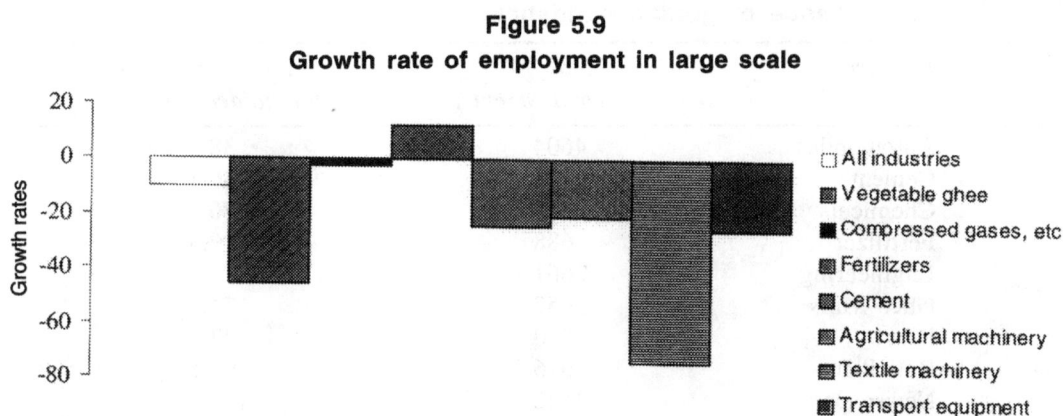

The Census of Manufacturing Industries data also shows a decline in employment in the large scale-manufacturing sector. Except for fertilizer, where employment increased by 12.4 per cent, all the other privatized industries have witnessed very sharp decline in employment. Vegetable ghee lost 45 per cent of the work force and textile machinery about three-fourth.

With a view to protecting the workers against the loss of job, the government and the representatives of the workers had reached an agreement in 1991. The agreement states:

(a) That there shall be no lay-off during the first year of privatization;

(b) That workers opting for the golden handshake will be given four months of the last salary drawn *plus* gratuity equaling to one month salary for each year of service;

(c) That worker's rehabilitation programme through overseas employment and training will be continued and adopted;

(d) That 10 per cent of the shares should be offered to the employees; and

(e) That the workers should be allowed to bid for purchase of the unit and they shall be given preference.

The agreement guarantees the job for one year. Though workers were not laid off in the first year, producers encouraged their workers to take the golden handshake and as many as 63.3 per cent of the employees in the manufacturing sector opted for golden handshake. Whereas the incidence was only 10.5 per cent in the fertilizer industries but almost everyone opted for voluntary retirement scheme in newspaper industries. In rice and roti plants it exceeded 90 per cent, in engineering, ghee and chemicals it exceeded 70 per cent and in automobiles and cement it exceeded 30 per cent. The high incidence of golden handshake may have been the result of two main factors. Firstly the workers knew that the job security was offered only for just one year and as such they did not want to take any chances. Second, since the responsibility of paying golden handshake was with the government, the new owners encouraged the workers to take golden handshake and later employ them on contract (Table 5.3).

Table 5.3: The incidence of golden handshake

Industries	Total employment	Per centage opting for golden handshake
Automobiles	4604	38.0
Cement	8289	36.1
Chemicals	6342	70.8
Fertilizer	688	10.5
Engineering	2661	77.5
Ghee Mills	5057	74.3
Rice	810	93.3
Roti Plant	676	99.1
Newspapers	1142	100.0
Miscellaneous	5056	97.3
Total	34649	63.3

Source: Privatization Commission.

As much as one quarter of the bid value has been used in the golden handshake and in some industries they have even exceeded the bid value (Table 5.4). This was necessitated by the fact that such industries were making losses and there was no way that the industry could be divested unless they were provided the golden handshake.

Table 5.4: Bid value and golden handshake payments

Particulars	Bid value (in million Rs.)	Per centage of bid value used in golden handshake
Automobiles	1032.77	12.89
Cement	6352.27	11.05
Chemicals	5320.53	15.06
Fertilizers	435.39	0.70
Engineering	193.35	51.05
Ghee Mills	620.05	56.13
Rice	237.35	39.02
Roti Plant	18.90	25.88
Newspapers	231.10	191.00
Miscellaneous	175.15	533.70
Total	14616.86	24.35

Source: Privatization commission.

A large number of units have been virtually closed and some of them have changed the manufacturing activity. Essentially in such cases all the workers have been rendered unemployed. More than half the industrial enterprises either are closed down or almost all the employees have been rendered surplus.

The worker-management groups have acquired 9 units. They are operating efficiently without any retrenchment of the workers. As regards retraining of the workers there has been virtually no progress. The workers are invariably offered ten per cent shares but they have rarely shown interest in purchasing shares in these units.

6.2 Banking Sector

ABL was transferred to the management group of the workers employed in the bank and as such there has been no reduction in the employment. Similarly, MCB did not lay off any workers. The wage bill of ABL has increased from Rs 677 million in 1991 to Rs. 2017 million in 1997 and of MCB from Rs 1048 million to Rs 4361 million over the same period. The increase at current prices over the six years period is 197.9 and 316 per cent respectively in ABL and MCB. The consumer prices over the same period increased by 104.0 per cent. Increase in employment cost in real terms may be reflecting to some extent increase in employment but mainly it is due to an increase in wages and salaries.

7. Wage rates and social protection of the workers

The interviews carried out with the manufacturers and the labour leaders show interesting views. The producers in general appreciate the privatization policy but they have divergent views on privatization of the infrastructures. While those engaged in the manufacturing activity feel that the government has no business to carry out the commercial activities like manufacturing, and they are against privatization of utilities. This is because induction of private sector in power has raised the cost of electricity to a level that they have lost comparative advantage. They are of the view that if infrastructure units have to be privatized it should be through stock exchange, and the pricing policy should be under the control of the government. They also indicate that more transparency would help the privatization process in a significant way (Figure 5.8).

Whereas the private sector maintains that they are providing even better facilities to the workers than they were enjoying in the public sector, the workers do not agree. The workers suggest that while employees' old age benefit is intact, the pension scheme for the managers and professionals has been abandoned, the number of bonuses has been slashed and increments to the salaries have been stopped. Workers also complain about the insecurity of job and pension and believe that the low paid employees are being thrown out.

The trends in nominal and real wages show interesting pattern. Whereas upto 1990-91 there was an increasing trend, the same is not observed in the post privatization period. The Provincial Bureau data indicate a very sharp decline in the real wages of the workers. The aggregate real wages have declined by 7.6 per cent in the 1990-91 to 1997-98 period compared to 37 per cent increase in the 1983-84 to 1889-91 period. The decline over the same period has been 29.1 per cent in vegetable ghee industry and 17 per cent in cement industry. However the wages increased in the fertiliser sector by 7.7 per cent over the same period.

The Census of Manufacturing Industries Data indicates a marginal increase of 2.5 per cent in the real wage rate over the 1990-91 to 1995-96 period. The increase in the industries that have been privatized is 5.1 per cent. Nevertheless in the vegetable ghee,

Figure 5.10

Labour productivity and real wages

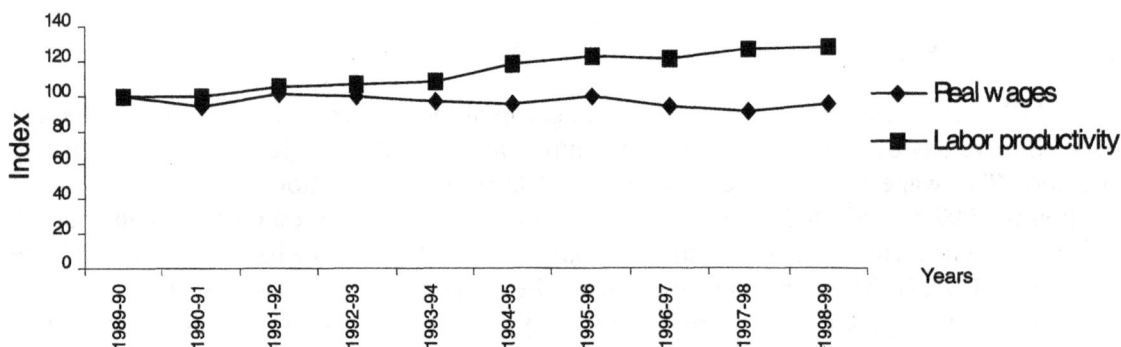

compressed gases, and textile machinery real wages declined by 12.3, 22.3 and 30 per cent respectively.

The survey carried out by Worker's Federation of Pakistan (1993) spells out the benefits to the workers of both the private as well as public enterprises. The survey shows that the fringe benefits in the private sector are lower and workload is higher compared to the public sector. Whereas 47.1 per cent public firms in the manufacturing sector operated for five days a week and another 23.5 per cent for five and a half days per week, the proportion in the private sector was only 23.5 and 15.7 per cent respectively. In the services sector 31.4 and 21.0 per cent of public firms operated for five, and five and half days, the proportion in the private sector was 10.1 and 5.8 respectively including a high probability that workers may be asked to put in more days of work after privatization. Leave entitlements including annual, causal and sick leaves are higher in the public sector than the private sector.

The employers are obliged to provide various facilities to the workers under law and they do provide most of the services including social security, old-age benefits, workers' profit participation, children's education and accommodation. Proportion of firms providing transport facilities is lower in the private sector. Similarly, the private sector does provide medical facility, but the quality and coverage is inadequate.

Whereas in the public sector both provident and gratuity is provided or pension is provided in most of the cases, in two-third of the cases in the private sector, workers have a right of either provident fund or gratuity.

8. The environment for private sector and medium term projections of investment and employment

Whereas level of employment declines in the short run following privatization, over longer run it may result in higher levels of employment through higher levels of investment and production. As a result of privatization, the public investment starts falling but the private sector may more than compensate and as such total investment may rise. This is because more avenues are opened up for the private sector and it builds up the confidence of the private sector especially of the foreign private investors.

Fiscal incentives, de-regulation, privatization, tariff rationalization, removal of non-tariff barriers, no restriction on investment activity, allowing private sector in all types of economic activities etc. creates a conducive atmosphere for investment. The after-effects of sanctions, inconsistent policies and lack of continuity have been some of the problems in attracting both the indigenous and foreign investors. With announcement of a very clearcut investment policy and the resolve of the government to stick to the policies is expected to result in higher level of investment.

Special efforts have been made to attract foreign private investment. There are no longer any restrictions on entry in any economic activity or on the proportion of the equity held by the foreign firms. The liberalization of the foreign exchange market has removed restrictions on the payment of royalties and technical fees, on raising funds from the local capital markets and the banks and on repatriation of principal, capital gains and profits. The foreign investors have been guaranteed the safety of their capital. The privatization policy, in addition to the measures enumerated above, has also encouraged the foreign investors. While during 1991-97 period foreign private investment did increase and most of these have been in the energy and other infrastructure projects, after the sanctions and row between WAPDA and the IPPs, the investment has fallen. Moreover, foreign investment is not expected to generate significant levels of employment because of their high capital intensity.

8.1   Medium term projections of investment and employment

Soon after initial privatization total investment had started rising with major share accounted for by the private sector. However, since 1992-93 the investment has started declining and after the sanctions it has gone down very sharply and fixed investment has fallen to just 14.5 per cent of GDP. No doubt these rates are rather low, and the privatization and deregulation policies would result in higher level of investments. However, what would be the response of private sector is too early to say. Therefore, three alternative scenarios are presented below (Figure 5.11).

Figure 5.11

Projected level of investment GDP ratio

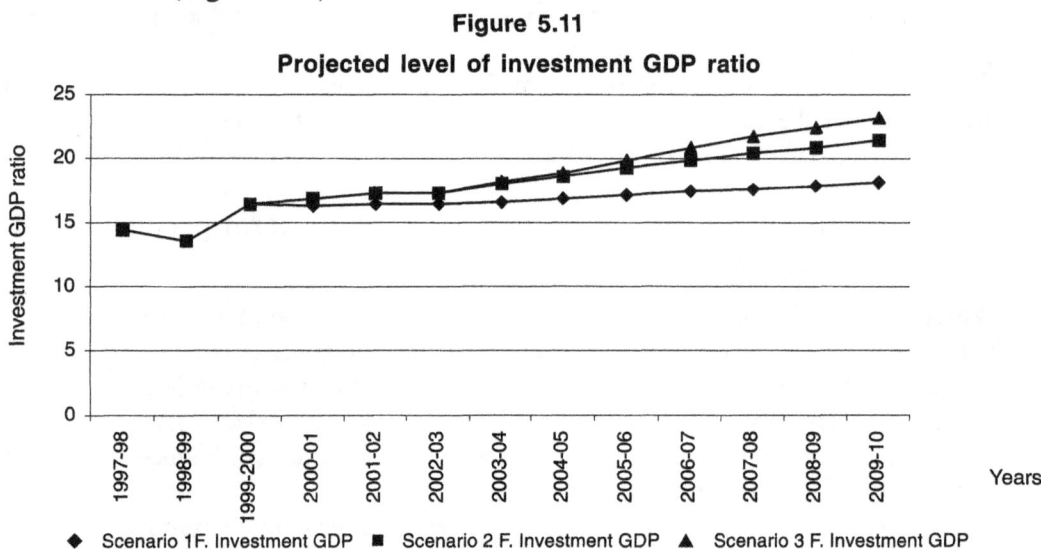

◆   Scenario 1F. Investment GDP   ■   Scenario 2 F. Investment GDP   ▲   Scenario 3 F. Investment GDP

The first scenario essentially assumes that investment would rise slowly to 18.2 per cent of GDP by 2010. Scenarios 2 and 3 are more ambitious where fixed investment would rise to 21.4 and 23.5 per cent respectively by 2010.

A high rate of investment, via a higher growth of the GDP, is expected to stimulate the demand for labour to absorb the increments in the labour force. The increase in the demand for labour is projected on the assumption that employment elasticity would be 0.36. In the modest growth of investment, labour demand does not increase sufficiently and even by the year 2010 the unemployment remains around 6 per cent. Even in other two scenarios where there is a rapid growth of investment, unemployment remains above 6 per cent level. Thus, there is a need to use more labour intensive technologies if unemployment problem is to be resolved.

9.   Regulatory reform

Only an efficient regulatory framework can ensure higher level of productivity in monopolistic framework. Baumol (1996) points out that the six mechanisms of regulation usually employed to regulate firms must be avoided. First strategy could be to break the monopoly injecting more competition by introduction of additional firms into market especially when the scale of economies are significant. Second strategy could be maintaining cross subsidies and thus driving out of line the prices required for economic efficiency. Third strategy could be imposing exclusive territories for different competitors and thus increasing the cost. Fourth, there are inconsistencies in the regulators' policy. Fifth, there could be delays in decisions in accordance with the market conditions by the producers just because the regulators have not been able to make the decision in time. Sixth could be regulation through accounting conventions such as fully distributed cost boils down generally to cost plus formula for prices, eliminates any incentives for reducing the cost.

Let us examine the extent to which Pakistan has been able to follow the suggestions of Professor Baumol. Demand for a large number of industries in Pakistan is not even sufficient for even a single plant of optimum size. But the competition has been encouraged in these industries, thus reducing the levels of efficiency even further. Cross subsidies can play an important role but the international organisations do not allow that. Case in point is the inefficient use of phosphatic and nitrogenous fertilisers. A few years back, sugar mills were not allowed to buy the sugarcane from other than their own zones, thus increasing the cost of production. As regards inconsistencies and delays by the regulatory authorities, the two agencies so far established for power and telecommunications do not hold much of promise. It seems that the regulatory authorities are following a full cost pricing rules and the guaranteed return on equity, which can hardly result in higher levels of efficiency.

Regulation of the industry is to facilitate and encourage effective competition. In the presence of scale of economies, marginal costs pricing are incompatible with solvency of the firms. Baumol outlines the following seven rules of economic regulation.

1.   Where there is evidence of competition, regulators should refrain from intervention.
2.   Where competition can be stimulated, it must be done.
3.   The regulators should make sure that prices in the long run do not exceed the levels, which in a perfectly competitive market would make entry profitable.
4.   Prices should not be permitted to go below those that would be viable for any substantial period in a competitive or contestable market[1], i.e. prices should not fall short of the marginal cost of any product or the per unit incremental cost of the entire output of any homogenous product.

---

[1]   Contestable markets are defined as the state of a market in which there is totally costless and an unimpeded freedom of entry and exit.

5. Because in a contestable market, one may encounter prices close to the stand-alone cost ceiling or the marginal-average cost floor, the firm should be left free to adopt any price within these limits.

6. Price caps may substitute the ceilings on total earnings or rate of return on investment.

7. When inputs are supplied by a regulated firm, both to itself as a component of one of its final product, and to a competitor producer, the regulated firms should charge the rival the same price for that input that the former implicitly charges to itself.

10. Summary and conclusions

Privatization Policy is the cornerstone of economic policy of Pakistan and the paper examines impediments to realising the objectives of privatization, which include higher levels of efficiency, investment, production, employment, and physical and social infrastructures and retirement of the public debt. So far 106 units have been divested and government has received Rs 59.6 billion through the sale of these enterprises. The principal method of divestiture has been through sealed bidding. The floatation of shares on the stock exchange has so far been used to divest ten per cent of the shares of the Pakistan International Airlines (PIA) and 12 per cent shares of Pakistan Telecommunications. Twenty six per cent shares of Kot Addu thermal power station has been divested with handing over of the management to the private sector firm.

Privatization has not been able to reduce the fiscal deficit, which has continued to be in the range of six per cent. The deficit might have fallen further had the interest rates not risen following the financial sector reform. Over the period of privitization in the nineties development expenditure has declined from 8 to 3 per cent of GDP, thus suggesting that privatization probably had no impact on fiscal deficit. Since cumulative receipt from privatization does not exceed Rs 59.6 billion, which compared to a debt of Rs 2,500 billion is rather small and could have only a limited impact on debt servicing. Nevertheless, privatization of large banks and telecommunication can have significant influence on the fiscal deficit.

Privatization can result in higher growth, increased productivity and lower prices but only in a competitive framework. In a monopolistic framework, however, producers restrict the output to maximise their profits. By regulating the monopolies a producer may be forced to reduce price and increase the level of output. While such regulation is relatively easier in tradable goods industries by reducing the imported duties on competitive imports, in case of the non-traded goods it may not even be feasible.

The average growth rate of GDP has gone down from 5.44 per cent to 4.15 per cent and the compound growth rate has fallen from 5.44 to 4.13 per cent during pre and post privatization period. Similarly average growth rate of investment fell from 5.55 per cent to just 1.82 per cent and the compound growth rate from 5.49 to 1.76 per cent. The decline may have been due to the deflationary monetary and fiscal policies pursued under the stabilisation programs but privatization has also been responsible for that.

The analysis of variance does not show any difference in the growth rate of output in the pre-and post-privatization period. Similarly, there is no difference in the return to equity or return to fixed assets in the pre-and post-privatization period. The analysis also shows that the growth rate of privatized industries fell subsequent to their privatization. However, this could be attributed to a general decline in the manufacturing output during 90s. Controlling for the general decline in output, privatization had no impact in 9 out of 14 industries, in two industries growth rate increased and in 3 industries growth rate fell.

Total factor productivity of the manufacturing sector fell by 6 per cent over the 1990-91 to 1995-96 period. However, it increased, on average, by two per cent in the privatized industries over the same period. Nevertheless, improvement in productivity is observed only in vegetable ghee and transport equipment and has fallen in the remaining sector.

The real prices deflated through the wholesale price index of the products of the industries produced by the privatized industries have not fallen. As a matter of fact they have increased.

Restructuring of public enterprises, prior to privatization has also resulted in loss of employment. Almost ten thousand workers lost jobs as Habib Bank and United Bank were restructured. Similarly 2,225 out of 3495 employees of the heavy engineering industries have taken golden handshake or voluntary retirement and 2195 employees in vegetable ghee mills not yet privatized have taken voluntary retirement.

Compared to an annual compound growth rate of 2.0 per cent growth in the overall employment in the pre-privatization period, the growth rate fell to 1.39 per cent in the post-privatization period. Similarly, in the pre-privatization period employment in the manufacturing grew at a rate of 6.5 per cent, but has declined at a rate of 13.5 per cent in the post-privatization period.

The Census of Manufacturing Industries indicates 9.7 per cent decline in employment in the large-scale manufacturing sector over the 1990-91 to 1995-96 period. It shows 12.4 per cent increase in employment in fertilizer industry but a decline of 45 and 75 per cent in vegetable ghee and textile machinery industries. In other sectors the decline in employment has been in the range of 20 to 40 per cent.

With a view to protecting the workers against the loss of job, the government and the representatives of the workers had reached an agreement in 1991. Notwithstanding the agreement, a very large number of persons have opted for the golden handshake scheme; as many as 63.3 per cent of the employees opted for golden handshake. The incidence across the industries however has been different though except for fertilizers in almost every industry at least one-third employees have opted for golden handshake. In privatized units of fertilizer only 10.5 per cent of the employees opted for the scheme. Whereas in the Newspaper industry, almost everyone opted for voluntary retirement scheme, in rice and roti plants it exceeded 90 per cent, in engineering, ghee and chemicals it exceeded 70 percent and in automobiles and cement it exceeded 30 per cent. Event though Habib Bank and United Bank have not yet been privatized they have made payment amounting to Rs 13 billion as golden handshake.

There has been no labour shedding in the two privatized banks. The employment cost has gone up from Rs 677 million in 1990-91 to Rs 2017 million in ABL and from Rs 1048 million to Rs. 4361 million in MCB. The increase comes out to be 197.9 and 316 per cent respectively significantly higher than 104.0 per cent increase in consumer price index. It indicates a sharp increase in wage rates in the banking sector.

Interviews with employers indicate not surprisingly that they welcome privatization. Nevertheless, the manufacturers while welcoming privatization of manufacturing enterprises did not appreciate the privatization of infrastructure enterprises unless prices of utilities are controlled. They are of the view that more transparent privatization is necessary. They also believe that the workers have gained by way of increase in the wage rates. On the other hand the workers do not share this view. They complain of job insecurity, reduction in bonuses and less fringe benefits.

Real wage rates in Pakistan have increased in the pre-privatization period but have fallen since then. The CMI data show that wage rates in the large-scale manufacturing sector have increased by only 2.5 per cent during the five year period. Though the average increase in the privatized industries is 5.1 per cent, in vegetable ghee, compressed gases, and textile machinery the wages declined by 12.3, 22.3 and 30 per cent respectively.

Privatization and other incentives offered are expected to increase the investment levels. As a matter of fact the investment had started rising but political instability, sanctions and the problems with IPPs have resulted in lower levels of investment. What will be the response of the private sector is difficult to predict. Therefore three investment scenarios have been developed. First scenario projects an increase in fixed investment to 18.2 per cent of GDP by 2010. In scenarios 2 and 3, investment is projected to rise to 21.4 and 23.5 per cent by the year 2010. Assuming a relatively high employment elasticity of 0.36, unemployment rate would still exceed six per cent by 2010. The unemployment would still be around six per cent in 2005 even if we assume high investment rates but then start falling at a rapid rate. This shows clearly the need to adopt labour intensive technology and to make sure that monopoly is regulated.

Since monopolist can restrict output and keep capital stock idle, regulatory framework is essential. The regulatory authorities have to make sure that their decisions promote higher level of efficiency.

10.1 Policy suggestions

Privatization policy needs to be pursued with the main objective of improvement in the efficiency in economy. Since competitive framework is absolutely necessary for improvement in welfare, tariff rationalisation, anti-trust laws and control of monopoly, authority coupled with regulatory frameworks must precede privatization. Automatic systems to check the monopoly powers needs to be built into the system

The sale of public assets should bring maximum prices to the government so that the budgetary deficit is reduced and resultant inflationary tendencies may subside. This is possible only if the privatization process is transparent. Transparency requires that reserve price is appropriately estimated, they are made public before the opening of the bids and no sale must be allowed below the reserve price. Since investors bid in view of the value of assets and liabilities, they should be allowed to make the bid on the basis of the information provided by the commission and to slash the bid accordingly in case of deviation.

The public enterprises may be restructured before they are offered for sale to the private sector. This is absolutely essential because of two reasons. Firstly, a losing concern will fetch lower prices. Second, if the government has to bear the cost of golden handshake then the government should restructure prior to privatization. The private sector should not be provided a chance to convert the regular workers into contract workers. At present, the producers encourage workers to get golden handshake and then employ them on contract.

The timing of the privatization should be such that it has minimal impact on the workers. Probably the worst time for privatization is when a country is implementing IMF stabilization programmes. The declining growth rates of investment and output result in very slow employment growth, and privatization would result in an alarming unemployment situation. It would result in falling real wages. The agreements reached with the workers should be fully implemented. Retraining of workers should be given the priority.

The utilities, such as, power, railways and telecommunication should not be privatized unless it is ensured that they can be effectively regulated. Instead of divesting such enterprises, the government may consider leasing and franchising. The rules for regulatory agencies should be so formulated that they can function independently without any coercion. There should be proper checks and balances on these authorities without compromising their autonomy.

Annex 1

Table A-1: Average and compound growth rates of GDP, Investment and Employment

	GDP	Investment	Employment
Average growth rate			
Pre-privatization (1986-87 to 1990-91)	5.44	5.55	2.05
Post-privatization (1992-93 to 1996-97)	4.15	1.82	2.35
Compound growth rate			
Pre-privatization (1985-86 to 1990-91)	5.44	5.49	2.00
Post-privatization (1991-92 to 1996-97)	4.13	1.76	1.39

Source: Based on data obtained from *Economic Survey*, various issues.

Table A-2: Growth rates of GDP, investment and employment in manufacturing (Post and Pre-Privatization)

	GDP	Investment in manufacturing	Investment in Large Scale	Employment
Average growth rate				
Pre-privatization (1986-87 to 1990-91)	3.86	6.06	7.44	6.46
Post-privatization (1992-93 to 1996-97)	3.45	2.19	-2.45	-13.48
Compound growth rate				
Pre-privatization (1985-86 to 1990-91)	6.03	7.44	6.46	0.44
Post-privatization(1991-92 to 1996-97)	2.16	-3.84	-6.64	-3.47

Source: Based on data obtained from *Economic Survey*, various issues.

Table A-3 Bid values and payments on golden handshake of selected industries

S.No.	Particulars	Bid value	Payment on golden handshake	Per centage payment	Total employment	No. of officers	Per centage
1	Automobiles	1032.77	133.085	12.88622	4604	1749	37.98871
2	Cement	6352.27	701.722	11.04679	8289	2992	36.09603
3	Chemicals	5320.53	801.2	15.05865	6342	4493	70.84516
4	Fertilizers	435.39	3.047	0.699832	688	72	10.46512
5	Engineering	193.35	98.696	51.04525	2661	2061	77.45209
6	Ghee Mills	620.05	348.054	56.13322	5057	3759	74.33261
7	Rice	237.35	92.603	39.01538	810	756	93.33333
8	Roti Plant	18.9	4.892	25.8836	676	670	99.11243
9	Newspapers	231.1	441.402	191.0004	1142	1142	100
10	Miscelleneous	175.15	934.774	533.6991	5056	4921	97.32991
	Grand Total	14616.86	3559.48	24.35184	#REF!	#REF!	63.33516

Annex II

Protection of the interest of workers

Government signed an agreement with the All Pakistan State Enterprise Workers Action Committee on 15th October, 1991 prior to launching the privatization program. The package had three components, viz. protection of workers, a scheme of golden handshake and the buy-out by the workers. These packages are give below:

Package A

(i) Workers are accorded all protection available to them under the Labour Laws. As a special measure no retrenchment of the workers is allowed during the first twelve months.

(ii) 10 per cent of the shares of the privatized units is offered to the workers at a mutually agreed rate.

(iii) Workers rendered surplus after the initial period of 12 Months, are entitled to the following benefits:

    (a) Priority in matters relating to the employment abroad.

    (b) Availability of easy credit for facilitating their self-employment.

    (c) A surplus pool of laid off workers was to be maintained by an agency appointed for the purpose and the Privatization Commission is endeavor to find jobs for such workers. Till such time, these workers are placed in employment, they are entitled to unemployment benefit at the rate of Rs. 1000 per month for a maximum period of two years. This benefit would be available to only those workers who have been rendered and remain unemployed involuntarily.

    (d) Suitable arrangements are to be made to provide training to surplus workers in new trades and occupations.

    (e) Grants are to be given for the marriage of their daughters.

    (f) Scholarships are to be provided for education of their children.

Package B

(a) One month's gratuity for each complete year of service is payable to the workers. Wherever this gratuity is non-existent or less than one month, the gratuity is assumed to be of one month.

(b) Four month's last drawn basic salary for each year of service will be paid in addition under the arrangements of the Privatization Commission.

(c) All dues are paid only after the sale of units. However, all possible measures are adopted to settle the dues before handing-over of the units.

(d) List of workers opting for golden hand shake is to be provided by the respective CBAs.

(e) All those including seasonal regular workers, who wish to avail the facility have their option before the sale agreement is signed.

Package C

(1) In case of employee buyout, negotiations is facilitated in consultation with the Supreme Council of All Pakistan State Enterprises Workers' Action Committee.

(2) Workers are provided all opportunities to purchase a unit if they make a bid. They also have a right of negotiations on the highest bid.

(3) All bids made by the workers have to be competitive and in accordance with the bid documents.

(4) Workers are given concessions through negotiations if they are declared successful bidders.

(5) Wherever gratuity fund is maintained as a trust, the funds can be used for investments as per rules.

(6) The savings in the Provident funds can also be utilized for bidding purposes subject to Government rules and Regulations.

(7) A management plan (which should include a financial plan) is submitted by the workers for any bid they make for a unit.

(8) Any unit owned by the Federal Government in FATA will avail the same facilities as available to remaining units of state owned enterprises.

(9) The facility of group insurance for workers who opt for golden hand shake is available for continuation provided he subscribes from his own resources.

Bibliography

Alam, Quamrul, A. M. (1989): "Privatization Policy and the Problem of Industrial Development in Bangladesh", *Journal of South Asian* Studies, December.

Baumol, William J. (1996): "Rules for Beneficial Privatization: Practical Implications of Economics Analysis", *Islamic Economic Studies*, June.

Beesley, M. E. (1997): *"Privatization, Regulation and De-regulation"*. Rouledge. London.

Canadian International Development Agency (CIDA) (1987), *"A Study of Divestment of Industries in Bangladesh"*, Vol. 1, Dhaka.

Candoy-Sekse Rebecca (1989): *Techniques of Privatization of State owned Enterprises, Inventory of Country Experience and Reference*, World Bank Technical Paper 90

Caves, D.W. and Christensen (1980): "The Relative Efficiency of Public and Private Firms in a Competitive Environment: The Case of Canadian Railroads", *Journal of Political Economy*, October.

De Walle, Nicolas van (1989): *"Privatization in developing countries: A review of the issues.* World Bank.

Dotgson, John (1987): "Privatization", in (eds) Howard Vane & Terry Caslin, *Current Controversies in Economics*, Basil Blackwell, Oxford.

Employer's Federation of Pakistan (1996): *"Study on terms and conditions of employment in the manufacturing and services sector of Pakistan"*, FES, Islamabad.

Foreman-Peck, James (1989): *Ownership, Competition and Productivity Growth: The Impact of Liberalization and Privatization on British Telecom,* Warwick Economic Research paper No. 338.

Kemal, A. R. (1993): *Retrenchment Policies and Labour Shedding in Pakistan*, Occasional Paper 17, ILO, Geneva.

Kemal, A. R. (1996): "Why Regulate a Privatized Firm? *The Pakistan Development Review*. Winter.

Kikeri, Sunita, John Nellis and Mary Shirley, *Privatization: The Lessons of Experience.* The World Bank, 1992.

Lawai, Hussain (1991): "Post Privatization Experience: Case Study of M.C.B.", A paper read at Seminar on Privatization organized by *Management Services Division*.

Nankani, Helen (1989): *Techniques of Privatization of State-owned Enterprises - Selected Country Studies,* World Bank Technical Paper 89.

Naqvi, Syed Nawab Haider and A. R. Kemal (1991): The Privatization Experience of Public Industrial Enterprises in Pakistan", *The Pakistan Development Review*, Summer.

Naqvi, Syed Nawab Haider and A. R. Kemal (1994): Structural Adjustment, Privatization and Employment in Pakistan" in Rizwanul Islam *Social Dimensions of Economic Reforms in Asia,* ILO, SAAT, New Delhi, India.

Naqvi, Syed Nawab Haider and A. R. Kemal, (1998): "Privatization, Efficiency, and Employment in Pakistan" in Tony Bennet (Ed). *Privatization - How it works,* Routldge, London.

Pakistan Federal Bureau of Statistics, *Census of Manufacturing Industries*, Islamabad.

Pakistan Federal Bureau of Statistics, *Labor Force survey*, Various Issues. Islamabad.

Pakistan, Finance Division, *Economic Survey,* Islamabad, various issues.

Pakistan, Finance Division, *Government Sponsored Corporations*, Islamabad, various issues.

Pakistan, Privatization commission, *Privatization in Pakistan*, Islamabad.

Pakistan, State Bank of Pakistan, *Banking Statistics of Pakistan*, Karachi.

Punjab, Provincial Bureau of Statistics, *monthly Industrial statistics*, Lahore.

Rothscheld, N.M. et al (1989): "*Privatization and public participation in Pakistan*, Islamabad, International Finance Corporation.

Selim, R. (1988): "*Public and Private Enterprises in Bangladesh: A Case Study of the Jute Manufacturing and Textile Mills*" (Unpublished M.S. Thesis Submitted to the Postgraduate School of Studies in Planning, University of Bradford), England.

Sen, Binayak (1992): "Privatization in Bangladesh: Process, Dynamics and Implications", in *Privatization: Trends and Experiences in South Asia*, Paper presented at an International Seminar organized by CSCD, Colombo, and Sri Lanka.

Sind, Provincial Bureau of Statistics, *monthly Industrial statistics*, Karachi.

Stigler, George (1975): "*The citizen and the state*, Chicago, University of Chicago Press.

Vuylsteke, Charles (1989), *Technique of Privatization of State owned Enterprises - Methods and Implementation*, World Bank Technical Paper No. 88.

Wolf, C (1979): "*A theory of non-market failure. The public interest*".

Yotopolous, Pan A. (1989): "*The (Rip) Tide of Privatization: Lessons from Chile*", World Development.

6

Privatization in Sri Lanka

Rozana Salih*

1. Introduction

Privatization has been pursued aggressively in Sri Lanka since 1989. By mid-1994, 43 enterprises in the industrial sector and 92 bus depots in the public transport sector had been privatised. By 1997, the number rose to 75, with several plantation companies and large utility-oriented industries such as telecommunications and gas being privatised.

The social impacts of the exercise were felt by many, including workers, consumers and the public in general. Worker issues became significant during the process because most state owned enterprises (SOEs) were by and large overstaffed since employment had been given under political patronage and as a last resort by the government. This meant that at the time of privatization a critical question the government faced was how to handle the issue of surplus labour. Should the surplus workers be retrenched? Should they be offered alternative employment? How should retrenched workers be compensated? Even workers who were absorbed into the new firms faced various economic and psychological challenges through variances in wages, working conditions, entitlements and work ethos. Privatization also affected indirect workers of the SOEs. Very often, SOEs were found to have developed their own networks of input suppliers over the years, aiming at realising regional development, establishing backward linkages in industries and creating employment. Hence, privatization implied that workers indirectly linked via input supply networks would be affected when the private owners severe the input-supplier networks as more economical and efficient sources are found.

Apart from the workers, the social effects of privatization were also felt by consumers in general, via price changes, differences in the quality of the product (or service rendered) and distributional consequences.

In this paper, the analysis of 'social effects' of privatization will be limited to a discussion mainly on the impact privatization has had on direct workers of State Owned Enterprises (SOEs). The impact will be analysed in terms of the welfare of workers who remained with the SOE after it had been privatized and those workers who were retrenched during the exercise. The paper also looks at the regulatory mechanisms that were created during privatization to safeguard public interest and to limit potentially monopolistic tendencies of privatized firms.

---

[1] Paper presented by Rozana Salih on behalf of The Institiute of Policy Studies, Colombo.

2.   Brief Background on Privatization

At the time of economic liberalization in 1977, the state sector of Sri Lanka played a dominant role in production, distribution and financing in the economy. Major economic and social activities such as banking, plantations, large scale industries, transport, insurance, telecommunication, postal services, ports, electricity, import and distribution of petroleum, roads, health and education were either under public sector monopoly or largely undertaken by public enterprises. The dominant role the state played in economic activity was a reflection of the sharp increase in state intervention from mid 1950s to late 1970s. During this period new public enterprises were set up, monopolies were created and selected private enterprises were nationalised. Some indications as to the size and performance of the public sector in the early-1950s and mid-1970s are tabled below:

Table 6.1: Size and performance of the Government Sector

	Early 1950s	Mid 1970s
Average size of the Government (share of expenditure as a % of GDP)	23.4	27.1
Average annual rate of growth of government expenditure (%)	15.6	26.1
Share of Public Sector in:		
Tea plantations (%)		51
Industrial production (%)	15	55
Public Sector employment as % of total employment	8	17

Source: Central Bank of Sri Lanka (1998: 211)

The economic performance of the firms was tainted by the fact that non-financial objectives governed the administration and activities of state owned enterprises (SOEs). Amongst these objectives were (a) redistributive justice - that often led to the subsidised provision of goods and services as in the transport sector, (b) regional development – which meant that industries were set up in rural or remote areas, (c) price regulation of essential products - as in the case of the co-operative wholesale establishment (CWE) and Salu Sala (a textile-based organisation), that controlled prices of their goods at a lower rate than in the open market, (d) employment creation - the government employed about 15 -20 per cent of the labour force during the mid-seventies (Kelegama, 1993). Most SOEs were subsidized and ran at a considerable loss. This was a considerable burden on the government budget.

Most state owned firms were by and large over-staffed because employment was offered in the public service under political patronage and the employment creation motive of the government. Labour redundancy, therefore, was a significant problem in the Sri Lankan SOEs. Fiszbein (1992) estimates this to be around 40 - 50 per cent of a workforce of 120, 000 workers (excluding the plantations sector) in 1991.

Despite economic liberalization in 1977, the share of the public sector in the economy remained high in the 1980s. Government involvement in some sectors continued to expand, especially as large-scale infrastructure projects were undertaken with foreign assistance.

The reforms of 1977, however, created an environment conducive to private sector growth and curtailed government expenditure by targeting welfare programmes and non-essential expenditures. Nevertheless, many SOEs proved to be a considerable burden on the budget. Most of them were subsidised and operated for years at a loss. They suffered from operational inefficiency resulting in poor financial performance, poor product quality and supply shortages, and inability to mobilize resources to meet large investment requirements and labour unrest.

The turnaround in the Sri Lankan economy, in terms of the share of government expenditure as a ratio of GDP, came in the 1990s when privatization was pursued rather aggressively.[1]

The key motivations for privatization included improving the efficiency of the enterprises through the infusion of private capital, knowledge and expertise. It was also intended to reduce the burden on the government budget. In some cases, privatization proceeds were often looked upon by the government as a fertile source of finance for the on-going ethnic conflict in the North and East of Sri Lanka.

3.   Preparations for Privatization

Privatization was announced as a state policy in 1987 with a view to reducing the financial burden some SOEs posed on the government as well as to improve efficiency, profitability and productivity. In preparation for privatization, certain steps were taken by the government from the early 1980s. Among these were:

- Improving the commercial orientation of the SOEs
- Allowing the private sector to compete in commercial activities by abolishing public sector monopolies
- Transferring management of some loss making public enterprises to the private sector under a contract system
- Franchising certain parts of public enterprises to the private sector
- Closing down of several non-economical enterprises.

In setting up the legal and institutional framework for privatization, the following was done: two legal enactments were passed in parliament. These were the Public Corporations Act No. 22 of 1987 for the conversion of government owned business units into public corporations and the Public Company Act No. 23 of 1987 for the conversion of public corporations and government owned business units (G.O.B.U) into public companies. The public companies so formed were relatively free to determine their employment levels, pay scales and were only partially subjected to government tender and investment approval procedures.

---

[1] There were, of course, a few sporadic instances of "privatization" during the 1977-87 period. The management of selected companies were privatized, and certain commercial activities were deregulated. There was also the partial (or full-scale) privatization of parts of state-owned enterprises through reorganization into subsidies (see Kelegama 1993 for more details). These early initiatives were not referred to as privatization possibly because it did not involve the transfer of assets to the private sector. Even when they did, their significance in the national economy was so small (compared to some other SOEs) that such transfers were not disputable.

However, this did not mean that substantial deviations from the public sector code of operation was permissible. Act No. 23 also stipulated that the share capital and the workers of the firms were to be transferred to the secretary to the treasury, and that all assets and liabilities of the company were to be rested as an integral step towards privatization. The two enactments mainly facilitated the building up of the share capital base for divestiture. Neither of the acts made any specific mention of how to handle surplus labour during privatization or how to compensate workers retrenched, apart from a brief mention in one of the Acts that said '*those workers not absorbed in the conversion shall be compensated on such terms as determined by the cabinet of ministers*'.

A committee was appointed by the President in 1987 to study and prepare a general framework within which privatization was to be carried out. The committee was initially called the Presidential Committee on privatization only to be renamed as the Presidential Committee of Peoplisation in 1989, to appease trade union and social resentment to privatization by hinting broadly at the "people-friendly" side to the process. Specific recommendations were made by the committee in terms of handling labour issues.

The responsibility of carrying out the privatization programme and handling various issues that emerge during the process have been transferred from institution to institution during the past decade. In 1989, the Public Investment Management Board (PIMB) was established to undertake the privatization programme. The privatization of industrial enterprises, however, was to be handled by a special unit, which was established in 1989 at the Ministry of Industries under the World Bank's Public Manufacturing Enterprise Adjustment Credit Fund.

The PIMB was renamed the Public Investment and Management Company (PIMC) in 1990 and was empowered to prepare public enterprises for privatization and to manage such enterprises until their divestiture. The supervision of the process of privatization of small public enterprises was handed over to the Commercialisation Division of the General Treasury to work with the relevant line ministries in 1990.

The privatization of the plantation sector was handled by a different body, due to the industry-specific complexities that had to be faced. The plantation restructuring unit (PRU) (1989) and the National Transport Commission (NTC) (1990) were set up to co-ordinate the privatization of these enterprises.

In 1990, the main responsibility for the privatization programme was transferred to 37 Cabinet Appointed Divestiture Committees that worked with the Commercialisation Division of the General Treasury and the respective line ministries for the process of divestiture.

In 1995, the Public Enterprise Reform Commission (PERC) was established and became the sole authority to undertake the privatization programme in a more efficient and transparent manner. The PERC was entrusted with the required legal powers under the Public Enterprise Reform Act No. 1 of 1996. Since the inception of the PERC, 35 transactions have been completed as at 31 December 1997. These include 20 plantation companies, nine manufacturing and trading companies, four enterprises in the utility and service sector, and one enterprise in the agricultural sector. The total privatization proceeds that came into the capital account from 1995 to 1997 amounted to US dollars 373 million. The process of privatization has contributed to the development of the Colombo Stock Market, by brining in 12 new companies, there by increasing the number of listed companies to 238 by the end of 1997 from 226 in 1995. It has also led to the creation of a 'Plantation Sector' in the stock exchange.

In 1996, the Rehabilitation of Public Enterprises Act No. 29 was passed in the interest of workers in privatized companies that have failed to perform well. The Act has been passed 'in the interest of the national economy, and for the purpose of securing the recognition of, and respect for the rights of the workers of such companies and upgrading the production of such companies for general welfare'. The powers under the legislation can only be used in a situation where there is a cessation or reduction of the activities of the units comprising these enterprises, on account of an omission or failure that is directly attributable to the board of management of the enterprise in question, and thus it affects workers. By 1997, around six privatised companies had failed, resulting in you retrenchment and non-payment of wages and statutory dues to the workers of such companies. The Act generated much controversy especially because it was seen as a move towards re-nationalisation. However, many consider it rather innocuous, especially because employment considerations are the prime motive for the enactment. Further, the Act specifically states that the provisions therein are operative only for a period of six months since the date of its commencement.

Apart from the above mentioned legal enactments and institutional support structures there have been other policy measures the government took to support the privatization programme. These included tax incentives, measures to develop the capital market, policies for the labour market and certain measures to develop competition policy. These are listed in Appendix 1.

3.1 The Regulatory Framework

With the on set of liberalization and privatization, significance of the role of regulation in the private sector was recognized. Especially in the case of the privatization of public utilities such as telecommunication and gas, and in the privatization of services such as bus transport, the importance of an external regulator became significant. This was for many reasons. The key reason was that the privatization of certain monopolies and natural monopolies meant that the ownership of these industries transferred from the hands of the public sector to the private sector. The monopolistic market environment meant that the private owners could exploit their situation by charging higher prices, reducing the quantity of production and compromising on quality at the expense of the consumer. Even when the market created an oligopolistic situation with a few key players, the role of a regulator was strongly felt to taper the effects of (possible) collusive behaviour. In the case of a Stackleberg situation (where the first entrant to the market enjoys advantages of being the first mover) or in cases where one player was more dominant than the others, there was much room for competitive manoeuvre. The latter was evident in consequence to the privatization of the Ceylon Oils and Fats Corporation (See Dunham and Kelegama, 1996).

In order to face the rise (and the possible rise) of anti-competitive and/or monopolistic behaviour, the government established the Fair Trading Commission (FTC) in 1987. Issues pertaining to consumer protection, however, were handled by the Department of Internal Trade under the Consumer Protection Act No. 1 of 1979. This separation of functions between competition policy and consumer protection was counterproductive and inefficient, given the complementarity of these functions. The Government has recognised this, and is currently working on amalgamating the Consumer Protection Act and the Fair Trading Commission Act.

Even though the FTC has been vested with powers of monopoly control and the control of anti-competitive practice, certain exclusive rights granted to certain companies during the privatization process are contrary to fair play. In order to entice the private buyers and investors, companies such as Shell and Lanka Lubricants have been given exclusive monopoly rights in certain operations in the Sri Lankan market. Even though the contract that the companies have entered into with the government has certain limits with regard to pricing, etc., exclusive rights of the private buyer in the local market for 5 to 10 years easily allows to reap the benefits of being the first-mover in the market.[1] This means that the company may create conditions in the market that may actually deter the entrance of a new player or develop economies of scale (and advantages through learning) that deem a new entrant's costs non-competitive. The actual costs and benefits of the exclusive rights and the impact they will have on the consumers and workers both in the short and long term cannot be analysed immediately.

Even in sectors such as bus transport, the absence of a regulator is felt strongly especially after privatization. Privatization was introduced to the sector in the hope of improving its efficiency. However, the influx of a large number of unregulated private players simply meant that the consumers bore the brunt of a rather 'unjust', inefficient service. Box 1 explains the problem further.

In contrast to the bus transport case, the privatization of the telecommunications industry was accompanied by the presence of a regulator. The Telecom Regulatory Authority was a body established by the government in order to regulate the activities of the industry that was opened up in the mid 1990s. Before 1996, the industry was regulated by a Director General of the Office of Telecom under the Sri Lanka Telecom Authority. But in 1996 an amendment was made to the Sri Lanka Telecom Act that provided for the establishment of a board of five members as the Telecom Regulatory Commission of Sri Lanka. The members include the former Director General, a Secretary to the Ministry of Telecom and counterparts for management, law and finance. The Commission only monitors the licensing part of the industry. Price floors and ceilings are now absent in the industry, and prices are determined purely by the interaction of demand and supply.

The apparent success of the privatization of Sri Lanka Telecom (this will be discussed further in section 5.2.3.) and the usefulness of having a regulatory body for that industry has offered interesting lessons for other utilities that may be privatized in the near future. For instance, the privatization of the power sector is likely to be preceded by the establishment of a Power Regulatory Commission, akin to the Telecom Regulatory Authority. Currently, all

---

[1]   In the case of Lanka Lubricants, the new owners were granted the sole right of importing and distributing lubricants for a given period, and will be given tariff protection by the government (of at least 10 per cent)upon the liberalisation of lubricant import. The Government also agreed that Ceylon Petroleum Product outlets will market only products of the new owner for a period of 10 years. The new company will also have exclusive right to store lubricants and greases at CPC outlets for a period of 10 years.

private sector investment in power has to go through the Ceylon Electricity Board (CEB), since private sector investment is only open for power generation. The CEB still has a monopoly over the transmission and distribution of power. Opening the power industry to the private sector will entail the separation of the three key functions of the industry- production, transmission and distribution. The Power Regulatory Commission will regulate players involved in all three aspects of the industry.

Box 1: Privatizing Bus Transport

In 1978, the Transport Board Law No. 19 dissolved the Central Transport Board and decentralised its functions by creating 9 regional Transport Boards and the Sri Lanka Central Transport Board (SLCTB). In 1979, private bus operators were permitted to participate in the provision of passenger transport services. However, the service provided was inefficient. By early 1990, severe problems emerged in terms of pricing (i.e., bus fares unchanged for too long), increasing competition among operators, organisational weaknesses, etc. As a result, passenger complaints regarding overloading, bad road discipline, poor service, non-existence of time schedules and the non-existence of night service began to increase. During the mid-1990s, private bus operators faced severe financial difficulties. The 'peoplised' bus service, which formed in 1990, attempted to solve some of these problems. Under the peoplised bus service, the depots under SLCTB were converted into independent companies. The programme ended in 1993, when 93 Peoplised Bus Companies (PBCs) were formed.

Much needs to be done to make these companies viable. These include human resource development, modernisation, alternative institution building, co-ordination and other situational and logistical requirements. The Committee appointed to investigate the matter came to the conclusion that the most effective way of inducing modernisation and efficiency, is through creating clusters of peoplised bus depots and bringing in the private bus into a corporative system.

Hence the National Transport Commission (Amendment) Act No. 30 of 1996 was passed. The act now enables the Minister to issue directions to amalgamate peoplised companies and specifies the functions of the Registrar of Companies upon receiving such directions. It also provides for the allotment of shares in the amalgamated peoplised companies. Further, such companies registered under this Act can now be directed by the Commission. The amalgamation is also expected to attract corporate investors into these companies. It is doubtful, however, whether these measures have in fact improved bus service, especially given that there is no proper regulatory authority.

---

4. Approaches to privatization

There are various methods, which may be used to privatize state-owned enterprises (SOE's) either wholly or in part. During the 1983-88 period, the methods adopted were mainly in the form of partial divestiture, liquidation, management contracts and franchising. No serious attempt was made to fully privatize SOEs during this first phase of liberalization. However, after 1988, various other methods of privatizing were adopted, following recommendations in the GOSL (1987) report. The most widely used approach was the sale of a majority of shares (over 50 per cent) to a corporate investor on the basis of open tenders and competitive bidding. Around 87 per cent of the transactions conducted during the 1989-1998 period have adopted this method of privatization. The evaluation of bids in the tender process was on the basis of the investor's ability to introduce capital and technology into the enterprise and to provide access to foreign export markets for its products. Thus the key motive of offering a majority of the shares to corporate investors rather than the public was technological modernisation and further capital inducement into the SOEs. Broad-basing ownership was also a concern, especially to appease public and worker opposition to privatization. Hence, of the balance equity, around 30 per cent were offered to the public, usually at par, on an equitable basis.[1] The shares were re-saleable, and thus it was possible to make capital gains on them. A part or whole of the remaining equity usually around 10 per cent was gifted to the workers of the enterprise on the basis of length of service.

Kelegama (1997a, P. 463) points out various advantages of the above method of privatization: 'First, the share given to the core investor (above 50 per cent) ensured that the investor had sufficient incentive to make the enterprise work. Secondly, the public sale helped in augmenting the much needed supply of shares for sale on the market, thus encouraging the expansion of Sri Lanka's capital market. It also served as a watchdog on the corporate investor by requiring that the company issued annual reports and held public stockholder meetings. Thirdly, the employee share, which was basically a sweetener to win their support, helped to convert a group who would otherwise have opposed privatization to one supporting it'.

Other methods of privatization were also used. They included:

(a) Management contracts: In some cases, as a precursor to full privatization, the management of a company is transferred to a private sector firm with the necessary management and technical expertise required for running the enterprise. There is no transfer of ownership and only transfer of management through a management contract for a stipulated period on the payment of an agreed fee. The quantum of management fee is usually dependent on the profits made by the enterprise during the period covered by the management contract. Management Contracts are treated as an interim step towards full privatization or as a means of making an unprofitable enterprise profitable before privatizing it. It usually culminates in buy-out or sale on the capital market. Box 2, below, offers a brief case study on the privatization of the plantation sector, where management contracts were used. The textile mills in the state sector, for example, were revived by the infusion of foreign management, during the late-1980s. Once the privatization programme started, shares of these enterprises were issued to the public when they became viable.

(b) Sale of assets of public corporations while the state takes over liabilities e.g. Ceylon Plywood Corporation. The method was adopted mainly to finance large debts that the SOEs had incurred, before selling them off as operating entities.

(c) Employee buy-out: Under this method a majority of shares is sold to workers of the firm. This transfer of ownership to the labour force as a method of privatization has

[1] Kelegama (1997a, P. 463) explains this basis as follows: 'All applicants irrespective of the number of shares they have applied for, in the first instance, got 100 shares each. Therefore all applicants for 200 or more shares got another 100, and so on. Usually the authorities did not got beyond the second slab, and all investors got the same number of shares, i.e., between 100 and 200 shares.'

Box 2: Privatization in the Plantation Sector

In 1992, state owned plantation companies were formed into 23 Regional Plantation Companies (RPCs) under the Janatha Estate Development Board (JEDB) and the Sri Lanka State Plantation Corporation (SLSPC). The management of these companies was handed over to private organisations on a profit sharing basis, for a period of five years. By 1995, 13 out of the 23 plantation companies were making profits. However, the main problem with such short-term management contracts was that it was a disincentive for longer-term capital investment, because the management companies did not have a long-term stake in the performance of the plantations.

Therefore, in 1995, shares in the RPCs were sold to the private sector, based on the powers vested in the PERC. Under this arrangement, the full risk and benefit of management was passed on to the private companies. The land was leased to the private sector for a period of 50 years, with the option to renew the lease agreement. Initially, 51 per cent of the total shares in profit making RPCs were sold, with the offer first being made to the company managing the plantation. Later on, 51 percent of total shares in loss making RPCs were sold on the Stock Exchange on an "all or nothing" basis. The public enterprises were sold 39 percent of the total shares (CB 1998: 85). By 1997, majority shares of 18 RPCs had been sold to the private sector. (CB 1998: 86).

---

a very strong positive incentive effect, which leads to increased productivity. This particular method of privatization has not been possible in Sri Lanka except in the case of very small enterprises as neither the management nor the labour force has access to the required amounts of capital. It has been implemented in the case of certain brick and tile factories of Lanka Ceramics Ltd. and in a restaurant called Buhari Hotel, where 80 per cent of shares were sold to the workers, with the balance kept with the treasury.

(d) Negotiated sale of shares: In the negotiated sale of an enterprise the state can sell all or part of the assets of an enterprise; or all or part of the shares in the company into which a public enterprise has been converted, by a negotiated sale, either to a single purchaser or to a group of purchasers. This process is carried out in the following manner.

1. Once the state decides to privatize a certain enterprise a committee is appointed to draw up the specifications under which the privatization is to take place and tenders are called for the given enterprise.

2. Bids are collected and evaluated by the committee on previously agreed criteria.

3. The tender is awarded to the best-evaluated offer.

   This method of sale may be advantageous where a person or a group of persons who takes over the enterprise has special management or technical expertise for the running of the enterprise, or where the purchaser has a particular forms of market access either locally or abroad, or large volumes of capital are needed to make the privatization successful.

   This method was used in instances where the prospective buyer and his suitability in terms of his ability to bring in such benefits as technology, market access and sound management were known in advance. The method was adopted in the case of Pugoda Textile Mills, where an Indian company Lakshmi bought the SOE.

Lakshmi had managed the company before full privatization, and was hence known to the government.

(e) Sale of less than 50 per cent of shares: The Ministry of Industries, for example, decided to divest up to 40 per cent of shares of companies involved in the mineral sector (e.g., Phosphate Lanka Ltd., Bogala Graphite Lanka Ltd., Mineral Sands Corporation and Lanka Ceramics Ltd).

The legislation and the policies that were implemented with regard to privatization did not fully specify the details of the method of privatization. It therefore left a lot of room for flexibility. However as Kelegama (1997 a: 465-466) notes, the main steps involved in the process were: (1) valuation of assets and liabilities, (2) restructuring of debt/capital, (3) conversion of public corporations into companies under the Companies Act, and (4) divestiture of ownership. The valuation of SOEs has been done by the Chief Valuer of the government. Together with this an independent valuation has been done by Ernest & Young, Colombo. This would be followed by advertising the sale of the company. The advertisement runs in local papers as well as the *Financial Times* and the mid-Atlantic edition of the *Wall Street Journal*. Bids were generally received six weeks from the date of the advertisement from both local and international contenders. Investors were told that they could visit the SOE and interview the management before preparing their bids. According to some investors, gaining access to some SOEs had been difficult.

5. Economic and social effects of privatization

5.1 Economic performance after privatization

The divestiture programme during 1989-1998 generated Rs. 47.3 billion (US $ 715 million) to the government. It attracted foreign investments of around US $ 465 million, easing domestic liquidity conditions and strengthening country's external assets. The proceeds also helped reduce government borrowing, reduced interest costs and generated permanent revenue sources by way of lease rent, income tax and dividends while reducing government subsidies to loss making enterprises. Privatization also contributed to the development of the Colombo Stock Exchange. During the two years ending 1997, privatization brought in 12 new companies into the stock exchange, increasing the number of listed companies from 226 to 236. Privatization also led to the creation of the 'plantation sector' in the stock exchange.

Most annual reports of companies indicate that privatization has improved the performance of the companies and has improved worker welfare. Moreover, there are several instances where the companies have benefited from technological upgrading and the further infusion of capital. In the case of the plantation companies that were privatized, profits have boosted. Already, some poor quality tea lands have been put to alternative use, for the cultivation of spices or other crop, or to be converted into golf courses. Such developments and diversification seem to be sustained to a large extent by the buoyant tea prices in the world market during the past couple of years. However, the real test for the companies lie in how they would behave when net sales and prices go down in the future, especially in response to the fall in the Russian tea market.

However, in instances where the privatization process was not as transparent as the public wished it to be or when certain exclusive monopoly rights were granted to the companies, there have been instances of protests and uproars. For instance, the privatization of Ceylon Oil and Fats Corporation in 1991 and the consequent 'competitive manoeuvring' by the privatized company that caused a crisis in the poultry industry of Sri Lanka (See Kelegama and Dunham, 1996) generated a lot of controversy and debate. Similarly, when privatised companies 'failed', the ensuing public outcry was loud. Six companies were very conspicuous in their failure to perform. These were Colombo Commercial Fertilizer Ltd, Kantale Sugar Industries Ltd., Hingurana Sugar Industries Ltd., Kahatagaha Graphite Lanka Ltd., Lanka Loha Hardware Ltd., and Mattegama Textiles Ltd. In the case of the sugar industries, the failure to perform normally was somewhat justified given their physical proximity to the war-torn zones of the country. But overall, does the poor performance of these companies indicate a tendency towards deindustrialisation? This would be an unfair and overly pessimistic view of the privatization process. In terms of proportions only about eight per cent of the privatized companies have failed to deliver and left their workers stranded without compensation or even wage payment. The government, however, "rehabilitated" these companies and in a sense renationalised the companies in the interest of the worker. Some of these companies may have engaged in asset stripping, but this is not to a highly significant level in any macro sense.

5.2 Social effects of privatization

As discussed in the introduction, the social effects of privatization are vast. It covers the impact of privatization on workers (both directly and indirectly employed by the SOEs), on consumers (via changes in prices, quality of products, accessibility, etc) and possible distributional consequences. Especially in instances where exclusive rights are granted to companies, as in the case of Lanka Lubricants, impacts may translate into price rises, quantity restraints or changes in quality. Such effects, however, can only be gauged later on, when the consequences of the exclusive rights are more visible.

In this section we will focus only on the impact of privatization on the direct workers of the SOEs.

5.2.1. Effect on workers who opted to remain with the privatized firm

Overall, the working conditions of workers who remained in the privatized enterprises seem to be at least as favourable as they were when the firms were SOEs. In several instances there have been wage rises and better working conditions. For example, some firms now offer workers transport (Kabool Lanka Ltd), wage rises (Telecom) and better housing and sanitation facilities.

In most transactions, a proportion of the shares were gifted to workers. In several of the early privatization activities, shares were given to remaining workers as well as those who opted to leave the firm. Valuing the worth of shares gave rise to several unusual problems. One problem was that the nominal value of the share, at the time of privatization, was at times largely underestimated, resulting in retrenched workers enjoying wind-fall capital gains on the shares, once they are sold in the market after privatization. This is true of the privatization of Ceylon Oxygen Ltd., Orient Lanka Ltd and Shell Gas Private Ltd. The converse is true for companies with low-yielding shares. Most companies in the plantation sector fell into this category.

The element of uncertainty involved in offering shares as part of the compensation, suggests that it may be best to avoid compensating retrenched workers with shares. Including shares in the compensation formula can also exacerbate the adverse selection problem, especially in better-performing firms. This is because workers in the upper-tiers of management, who often have better knowledge and information on share market proceedings, dealings and trends, tend to opt for the retrenchment package and leave the firm.

There have been certain instances where the privatized enterprises failed, thus jeopardising the interest of workers who opted to stay on with the firm. In response to this the government 'rehabilitated' the companies as stipulated under the Rehabilitation Act, 1996.

5.2.2. Worker Redundancy[1]

5.2.2.1. Handling the problem of surplus labour: Extent, issues and preparation: Worker redundancy has been common in Sri Lankan SOEs. It was caused by two factors. First, and most importantly, SOEs have been largely overstaffed because employment had been given under political patronage and as a last resort to fulfilling the state's objective of reducing unemployment. Recruitment was easiest in the semi-skilled and unskilled tiers and thus, not surprisingly, surplus labour was most common in the grades of labourers, minor staff, clerical and other allied grades rather than at the management and executive grades, and grades requiring skilled labour.[2]

Second, worker redundancy has been common in public enterprises because the work ethos that has prevailed has not been one that generated high worker productivity. Since the profit motive was not the main drive in the public enterprise, implementing efficient corporate management and productivity enhancement techniques were not high on the SOE agenda. On the part of the workers, they have had little incentive to improve productivity levels especially since wages were linked to inflation rather than productivity. Further, workers were entitled to take 42 days leave annually: absenteeism was not heavily penalised; and public holidays were high. They also enjoyed a high sense of security and treated the public sector job as their entitlement rather than a position that had to be secured by efficient performance.[3]

Overstaffing meant that worker redundancy was common in SOEs. (Theoretically, a worker is redundant if his marginal productivity is below the received wage). It also meant that enterprises incurred a loss on the redundant labour, equivalent to the "excess" wage paid to workers (i.e., the difference of wage over productivity). The issue was important in Sri Lanka, for as Fiszbein (1992) estimates, the redundancy level was as high as 40 - 50 per cent

---

[1] The discussion in this section is based entirely on Salih (1998).
[2] See, for example, the management study on the Distilleries Corporation as cited in GOSL (1987:22).
[3] In Sri Lanka, employment in public service assured the worker a life-long income guarantee: a steady job until the time of retirement, and after that a pension programme.

in 1991 in the public sector (excluding plantations), which employed roughly 120, 000 people. Table 6.2. shows Fiszbein's estimates on redundancy rates using aggregate information on output and employment calculated for eight Selected SOEs. The level of redundancy in the Sri Lanka Transport Board was estimated at six employee per bus (the optimal ratio of employee per bus is estimated at 6.5 as compared to Sri Lanka's 13.1; the additional amount is thus considered as redundant labour —Svejnar and Terrell, 1991, P. 18).

Table 6.2: Redundancy rates in selected SOEs

Company	Redundancy %
Ceylon Electricity Board	51
Lanka Electricity	45
Railways	48
Sugar Corporation	86
Ceylon Petroleum	40
Sri Lanka Cement Co.	46
Lanka Cement LTD	63
Ceylon Shipping	43
Average Redundancy	53

Source: Fiszbein (1992).

The government, therefore, faced a difficult problem: What should be done about the surplus labour in the face of privatization? One option was to purge the firm of excess labour (through a retrenchment programme) in order to improve the financial viability of the firm ceteris paribus, and to attract private equity. This option has been pursued in most countries, both developed and developing, as well as the economies in transition in the former Soviet bloc. The other option is to sell the firm with the excess labour and pass on the problem of dealing with surplus labour to the private sector.[1] Both the above options have been pursued in Sri Lanka.

The option of retrenching is fraught with many problems. Some of these problems are intrinsic to any retrenchment programme. These include, firstly, questions pertaining to targeting: Who is redundant, how do you measure redundancy and how many workers are in surplus? Secondly, there are questions arising with regard to timing of the retrenchment programme: should it be before privatization or after privatization? Thirdly, there are a host of questions that accompany the problem of worker compensation for the welfare losses incurred as a result of retrenchment: What is an 'optimal' compensation package and what worker characteristics should be included in designing such a package?, Should compensation be solely monetary or should it include a non-monetary component as well, in the form of skills development or training to assist the worker in finding alternate employment? Should the package be fixed (across the board) or be flexible (defer on a case by case basis, depending

---

[1]   The 'no pre-privatization retrenchment' policy, however, did not apply to privatized enterprises that had to be rehabilitated by the PA government due to their poor performance.

on the company)? It is vital that these questions are addressed explicitly in any retrenchment programme during privatization. A loose framework vastly exacerbates the complexity of retrenchment.

In Sri Lanka, the framework set out for handling labour issues (including labour retrenchment) during privatization was extremely poor. First, the legal provisions made for the privatization programme itself was contained in two acts passed by the parliament in 1987:

(a) Act No. 22 of 1987 which deals with the conversion of public enterprises into public corporations or companies; and

(b) Act no. 23 of 1987 that gives legal backing to the conversion of public corporations into public companies.

Neither of these acts mentions labour issues apart from a brief reference in one of them (Section 3.2 (c), Act. No. 23, 1987), where it is stated that those workers not absorbed in the conversion shall be compensated on such terms as determined by the Cabinet of Ministers.

Second, the main policy recommendations for handling surplus labour were set out briefly in a report prepared by the Presidential Committee for Privatization (PCP) in 1987 (See Box 3).

The report suggested a potential monetary compensation package, advised the pre-mature payment of gratuity (EPF/ETF) payments to those workers who opted to retire and recommended pre-privatization retrenchment. These recommendations, however, were problematic, as the ensuing discussion highlights.

5.2.2.2. Compensating retrenched workers: The package recommended by the PCP was considered by workers to be less than full compensation, and was never used. This gave rise to the eventual adoption of various ad hoc packages whose value rested mainly on the bargaining power of the trade unions. One clear trend in the compensation packages paid since 1989 is that they have gradually increased over time, even after accounting for inflation. Packages have all been monetary, and the basic package (excluding gratuity, share gifting and other add-ons such as encashment of unutilised leave for the year) has increased from roughly 17 months salary to 53 months salary from 1989 to 1997 (for a 40 year old worker with 18 years service). Appendix 2 details the various compensation packages and formulas offered. By the time Lanka Loha (a key player in the steel industry) was privatised in 1997, the package was considered so attractive that all the workers opted to leave the firm, beyond the amount targeted as being in surplus. In an economic sense, this is a clear indication that the package was over-compensating, and hence inefficient. Figure 6.1 and Appendix 2 illustrate the rising trend in packages.

The government's attempt in 1997 to curb the rising value of the packages by recommending a uniform compensation to all SOEs shedding labour (PE circular 114, GOSL 1997) was largely futile. In design, the package was similar to the Bullumulla package but included a generous implicit add-on component. The add-on came from the benefit of being able to import certain types of vehicles duty-free or on a concessionary level of duty (one vehicle per employee). This provision was included with the intention of opening up avenues

---

Box 3: Recommendations made for Handling Labour Issues during Privatization

Retrench workers before privatization. Do not conduct involuntary retrenchment of labour.

Compensation:

• Offer only a monetary compensation package according to a particular formula.

Provident Fund Benefits and Gratuity Rights:

• Enable workers, irrespective of age to withdraw from the Provident Fund on termination of employment due to privatization. (Under normal law a worker has to serve until retirement age to withdraw from the Employees' Provident Fund (EPF) — see Note below). This recommendation was legalized subsequently by the EPF Amendment Act No. 14 of 1992.

• Ensure that an employee does not forfeit his gratuity rights consequent to the change of employer. Thus, past service of the workers in SOEs (Public Corporations) are deemed service rendered to the new company that has taken over the business of the SOE. This recommendation was legalised subsequently, by the Payment of Gratuity (Amendment) Act No 41 of 1990.

Identify surplus workers at each staff level, and offer only these workers the option to retire. If workers not in surplus wish to leave, they will be entitled only to gratuity payment.

Notes: (1) EPF: An institution created by the government which manages the fund. When an employee retires a lump sum could be obtained. This is managed by the Labour Department and the Central Bank of Sri Lanka. (2) Under the Gratuity Act of 1983, workers are entitled for this payment on the termination of services. Employers are expected to make this payment at the time of termination of services. Every year, the minimum contribution to be made by the employer is half month's salary to the Fund and at the time of retirement of the employee, the interest plus principal should be paid to the employee.

Source: GOSL (1987)

---

for self-employment amongst those who opted to retire. But the attempt was received with little enthusiasm. Very few SOEs offered the package (e.g. Paper Corporation). A majority of trade unions vehemently opposed this package, and bargained aggressively for packages of a much higher value.

Figure 6.1
Compensation packages (excluding gratuity) offered: 1989 - 1996

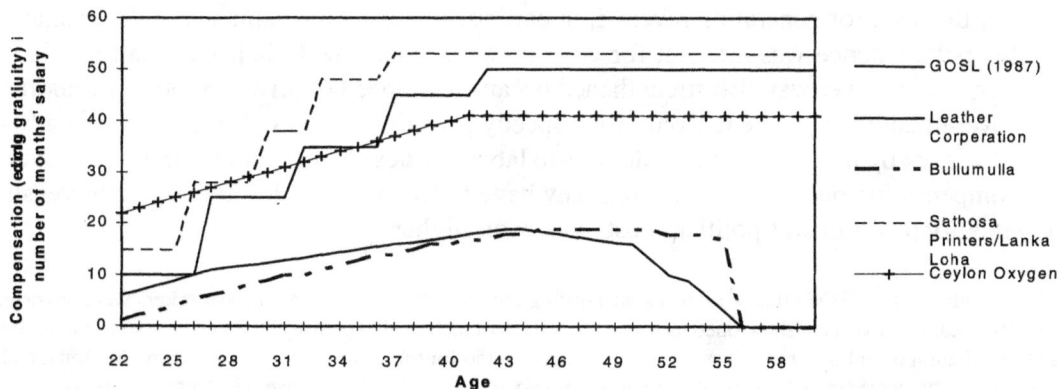

Assumptions: Retirement age is 55, Age at joining the company is 22.
*In working out the compensation for Ceylon Oxygen, monthly wage was assumed to be Rs. 4000.
Source: Salih (1998)

Why did the average value of the compensation packages increase over time as seen in Table 6.3.? Part of it can be attributed to inflationary tendencies. However, even if the packages are weighted for inflation, a rising trend is visible. The other more important factor then, is that the bargaining power of trade unions has increased over time.

Table 6.3: Average compensation (excluding gratuity) from 1987-1997

Year	Average compensation (excluding gratuity) in number of months salary
1987	17.5
1989	16
1991	45
1993	45
1995	53
1997	53

Source: Kelegama and Salih (1998).

Trade union bargaining power may have strengthened over time partly because: (a) the economy was not growing fast enough to rapidly absorb retrenched labour, (b) unionists felt that welfare losses and uncertainty incurred due to retrenchment have increased over time, and (c) because they have become avid rent-seekers, exploiting the labour-friendly attitude of the post-1994 government.

A significant factor, which contributes to the notion that the costs faced by workers are high, is the ad hoc and lackadaisical manner in which labour issues were handled during the early stages of privatization, and the lack of transparency in the privatization process itself (Kelegama, 1993 and 1997a). In particular, the failure of some privatization schemes have increased worker resentment to privatization.[1] The rent seeking powers of trade unions seem to have increased due to a probable rise in the marginal political cost of the new government that took over after 1994.[2]

The new liberalist tendency of a formerly socialist party for privatization was influenced mainly by the need for generating revenue, in particular to meet the demands of the escalating war. This policy stance was difficult for workers to reconcile with their expectations. Trade union bargaining power was also strengthened because the speed of privatization was important to the government for revenue reasons. Such speedy privatization was also important to attract private investors by providing quick solutions to labour issues. Thus, on the part of the provider of the compensation package, the amount they have to finance in order to mitigate increasing trade union opposition and political costs has been higher.

---

[1] For example, in three SOEs that were privatised during the pre-1995 period, over 1000 workers were adversely affected because the owners abandoned the firms due to lack of technical expertise and financial resources. In 1996, a Rehabilitation of Public Enterprises Act, No. 29 was enacted for the government to restructure the firms, make payments to the workers and re-privatize them within six months after the takeover (Kelegama, 1997b).

[2] During the post-1994 period, the ruling party — which was a coalition — had less influence over the dominant trade unions because of its earlier anti-privatisation stance, and thus had little control over determining the compensation packages.

A key result that emerges from the discussion in this section is that even though a customised compensation package negotiated between workers and employers (i.e., varying across firms) may seem "ideal" (World Bank, 1995, P. 90), in Sri Lanka, compensation packages so formulated were downwardly rigid, and led to rent seeking. Moreover, in recent years, the increase in rent seeking activity led to the formulation of packages so attractive that more workers than targeted opted to leave the firm (e.g., Lanka Loha, Ceylon Steel Corporation, etc.).

The high rent seeking and increase in bargaining power of the trade unions meant that the government could not afford to retrench workers during privatization. Therefore, after the Lanka Loha experience, the government changed its stance to one of promising employment security. Still, however, unions resented privatization and the government has had to take several steps to appease workers and assure that their rights and interests are preserved during and after privatization. Remaining workers seek as much rent as possible from the government before an SOE is privatized. They demand for changes in pension rights, gratuities, leave entitlements, etc. In the case of Telecom, for example, unions used their rent seeking abilities to secure extremely advantageous pension deals that are very costly to the government in the long term. The danger of such 'victories' is that they leave a precedence for trade unions to act upon in the future process of privatization - establishing a pattern of downward rigidity in terms of the trends set.

Even the recommendation for the pre-mature withdrawal of the gratuity entitlements had a fundamental problem in that it contradicted the main objective of having provident funds, which is to offer an old-age social security scheme for workers. The change to gratuity laws -rather imprudently- takes away an worker's future consumption entitlement and gives it away for current consumption, for as the SLBDC (1992) study shows, very few workers invest their compensation in any income generating avenue. The danger of the situation is evident when looked at in the context of the changing demographic composition in Sri Lanka (i.e., the rapidly ageing population, where those above 65 will be double the current number within the next two decades) and the increasing likelihood of old-age poverty.

5.2.2.3 Pre versus post privatization retrenchment: The recommendation of retrenching before privatization, where it was followed, leads to another dilemma. Most new owners of enterprises where workers had already been retrenched found that the retrenchment process had concentrated on getting the number of workers down, regardless of their type. Further, when targeting surplus labour, authorities had failed to account for the dynamic environment in which the firms operate and the structural adjustments that take place in a firm in the context of privatization. The optimal number and composition of workers employed depends crucially on the capital structure, technology and production techniques used in a firm. Since capital restructuring, the influx of technology and changes in production plans are likely to ensue privatization, one cannot realistically target who is in surplus, before privatization. It is a decision best left to the new owner. In fact, some new owners have had to rehire workers with skills identical to that of those retrenched before privatization.

In this context, not retrenching workers before privatization seems to make economic sense. But how easy is it for the private sector to retrench workers? The presence of the

Termination of Employment of Workman Act (1971) (TEWA) that applies to the private sector implies that it is not easy at all. The Act stipulates that an employer with 15 or more workers, wishing to terminate services of an employee with one or more years of service on non-disciplinary grounds, should obtain the written consent of the employee or the approval of the Labour Commissioner. If the dismissal is approved by the commissioner, he can then use his discretion with regard to payment of compensation. This is a time consuming, cumbersome and costly procedure. Trade unionists claim that this has at times led employers to circumvent the TEWA and lay off workers on false allegations of insubordination and other violations of discipline. Of course, the worker has the right to appeal to the Labour Tribunal. However, many do not possess the legal resources to go through with an appeal.

5.2.2.4   Incidence of those retrenched[1]

The number of people retrenched as a result of privatization up to July 1994 (before the change of government) is in dispute. There are highly divergent estimates. The Labour Department puts the figure at 18,000-20,000 whilst the Employers' Federation of Ceylon estimates it to be 35,000. On the other hand, the main public sector trade union the Jathika Sevaka Sangamaya claims that 50,000 of their members have been retrenched. The dispute over the number of retrenched workers is indicative of the haphazard way in which the government had conducted the retrenchment exercise, and the fact that involuntary retrenchment has taken place both before and after privatization (under private sector ownership).[2]

Given the unavailability of data, it is very difficult to find accurate information regarding the types of workers who have opted to retire. The majority who took the compensation packages were persons beyond the age of 45 (Weerakoon, 1992). However, the type of workers who opted to retire seems to have followed a bi-modal tendency: one type of workers were those who had a dire need for the money offered by the compensation package because of high indebtedness or some other personal reason such as a wedding in the family. These workers were often semi-skilled or unskilled and felt it was advantageous in the short-run to opt for the package and leave employment.

Several such retrenched workers had claimed later that they have not found sustainable alternative sources of income. A survey done by the Sri Lanka Business Development Centre (SLBDC) in 1992, for instance, showed that most workers used compensation received to pay debts, rather than investing in income generating activity (Kelegama, 1995).

The other set of workers were the more skilled type, such as engineers and mechanics, who could find jobs elsewhere relatively easily. Included in this set, were workers who faced a lesser degree of financial insecurity either because their spouses were employed or because

---

[1]   The Following discussion is taken from Kelegama and Salih (1999).

[2]   There was no specific number of employees targeted as in, for example, India (ILO, 1996). Involuntary retrenchments are executed very discreetly in stages and normally little is spoken about them. The Labour Department and other relevant government departments speak of their financial inability to monitor the process.

they had personal wealth.[1] Thus, for some workers, compensation seemed a 'wind-fall' gain whilst many others were left worse-off with no sustainable source of income, a high psychological sense of dislocation, and high susceptibility to old-age poverty since their provident fund benefits had already been dissipated (Section 3.2). The psychological sense of dislocation came about because the economy was not growing fast enough to create new employment opportunities for the new entrants to the labour market.

When voluntary retirement was used in the pre-privatization scenario, the government gave at least three months notice to workers to decide. In the post-privatization scenario, the workers were given only roughly 2-3 weeks by the new owners to decide whether they wanted to take the compensation package and leave. In some cases the deadline for the decision was extended indefinitely so that the workers could leave the firm whenever they wanted.[2] The firm terminated this provision when the number of workers were brought down to the level deemed optimal by the management.

Even when tiers of surplus labour were identified before putting VRS into operation, some workers maintained that this was discriminatory and that the option of voluntary retirement should be extended to all workers. However, the main opposition to targeting tiers for retrenchment came from workers who were not targeted. Opposition came from the more skilled grade of workers who felt they could obtain windfall gains through the compensation packages, since they could find alternative jobs without much difficulty.

Hence, identifying tiers of redundant labour for voluntary retirement was eventually dropped and across-the-board voluntary retirement was applied. This is why the problem of adverse selection (better workers leaving) was common in Sri Lanka's voluntary retirement process. The problem was exacerbated during pre-privatization retrenchment because SOEs were worried mainly about the number of people that left work, and not the type. For example, during the privatization process of the bus transport system, most of the workers who opted to take the package and left were mechanics, engineers, stenographers and other skilled workers (Kelegama, 1997a).

Even where workers of an identified tier were subject to VRS, the problem of adverse selection could not be altogether avoided because the better workers within the tier opted to leave. It was difficult to screen the high quality workers from the low quality workers. Even where exams were held for this purpose, those workers who wanted to leave the firm performed in the exams very poorly.[3]

---

[1]   For example, one worker informed that both he and his wife opted to be retrenched from Ceylon Oxygen Ltd., in 1992 because the total compensation they jointly received amounted to around Rs. 1,000,000 (rather than the average Rs. 200,000 - 300,000 that most workers obtained during the period). This is because the package included the direct monetary compensation payable to workers in the executive grade, as well as shares of the company which rose in price from Rs. 10 to Rs. 152 per share within months of privatisation, enabling the couple to obtain windfall gains. They invested the money in a house, which now affords a source of regular income since it has been rented out.

[2]   This was the case, for example, in a firm called United Motors.

[3]   This was the case in the Airport Aviation Authority at the secretarial level.

5.2.2.5. Lessons learnt: The Sri Lankan experience in handling labour issues during privatization highlights the importance of explicitly considering labour issues before the transaction commences. Ad hoc formulas and piece meal legislative changes only confuse the parties involved and increases worker hostility towards privatization. This is often reflected in the increasing value of the financial compensation given to retrenched workers over time. It is difficult to gauge accurately the impact of compensation on retrenched worker welfare, due to the unavailability of any form of consistent data. Trade unionists claim however, that workers' costs of being retrenched have increased over time and the packages do little to reduce welfare losses incurred by them. As far as the firms are concerned, the lackadaisical retrenchment procedures by SOEs have often been left them with a non-optimal composition of work force due to problems of inconsistency and adverse selection. Only a few firms have looked into other aspects of handling surplus labour through better corporate management and part-time employment. The root cause of all these problems is the lack of a firm and transparent exit policy for workers in Sri Lanka. Factors to be considered in designing an exit policy as well as other lessons learnt through Sri Lanka's retrenchment experience are given below.

(a) Improving Flexibility in the labour market

Sri Lanka has been moving into a market economy. Liberalization re-inforced itself with a second wave in 1989, and the 'free market' doctrine is being preached and practised in several parts of the economy. The private sector has been branded as the engine of growth. However, the labour market is still inflexible because of the Termination of Employment of Workmen Act (TEWA) that causes asymmetric legal costs adverse to the private sector, and makes retrenching workers a cumbersome and time consuming process. If privatization aims to develop, amongst other things, a market oriented system with "free entry", then correspondingly "free exit" too should prevail. This would make the labour market more flexible and the private sector more responsive to sudden changes in the macroeconomic environment.

Free exit does not mean, however, that uncompensated firing should be made possible. Uncompensated retrenchment is particularly unsuitable for a developing country such as Sri Lanka, where no social security system for the unemployed people prevails. Instead, free exit suggests that the private sector too should be given the option to maintain an optimal amount and composition of workers without having to incur any more legal costs than does the public sector.

Hence, the TEWA has to be modified such that efficiency and flexibility in retrenchment prevails. A good starting point would be to, eliminate the inherent arbitrariness involved in awaiting the labour commissioners' approval on retrenching, by abolishing this requirement.

If the TEWA was modified to equate legal costs of retrenchment in both sectors, then the option of post privatization retrenchment followed, avoiding the problem of inconsistency in the number and type of workers retrenched.[1]

A main constraint to removing the TEWA and imposing the recommendations however are the political costs of doing so. The TEWA has been enacted as a result of long-fought battles of trade unions in this regard. Removing it therefore will be politically very difficult especially at a time when the political situation in the country is not very strong.

(b) A fixed formula for compensation

A clear, fixed formula for compensating retrenched workers should be designed by the government in order to eliminate the lack of transparency, arbitrariness and time consumption of ad hoc compensation schemes, at the very onset of the privatization process. This is especially so because ad hoc compensation packages are downwardly rigid in the context of a political economy.

A fixed formula will also reduce a firm's uncertainty regarding costs to be borne when retrenching workers. Even workers will benefit from knowing exactly how much they will be compensated with, on retrenchment.

A formula being fixed does not imply that it is not based on worker characteristics, employment details, etc. Indeed, the convenors of the privatization programme should design a package that is as reflective of losses faced as possible. But fresh formulas should not be sought on a case by case basis for every transaction especially in a political economy where unions are strong and rent seeking is rampant.

(c) Employee share ownership

One reason for the failure of share issue as an incentive to improve worker productivity was the lack of knowledge and information on the part of the workers about the stock market and about their rights as shareholders. Hence workers should be educated in this regard before being issued shares. The lack of knowledge in this regard causes unnecessary distributional inequities amongst workers. Often workers in the upper tiers of management have better knowledge and information on share market proceedings, trends and dividends. They are able therefore to secure better profits on share sales. When shares are offered as a part of the compensation package, such informational asymmetries can increase the adverse selection problem of more viable firms. This leads to the related query, should

---

[1] Dynamic inconsistency can also be reduced to some extent if privatisation was done through the 'negotiated sale of shares'. Under this methods the prospective buyer is known in advance and therefore prospective changes to production techniques can also be known. The privatisation of Pugoda Textiles was done under this method. It is also advisable to restructure an SOE until a suitable private sector buyer with the most enticing plan comes along, without rushing into immediate privatisation (Bos 1994).

retrenched workers receive shares as compensation at all? If high-yield shares were distributed, then the real value of the package is higher than what is nominally calculated. The converse is true for low yielding shares. The element of uncertainty involved with offering shares as part of the compensation, suggests that it is best avoided.

(d) Pre versus post privatization retrenchment

Post privatization retrenchment seems better for the firm in the long run since the private owner is better at gauging the extent and type of labour in surplus. This recommendation is based on economic arguments. The Sri Lankan government has now implicitly resorted to this path for financial and political reasons.

5.2.3. Effects of Improving Worker-Management Dialogue

Effective dialogue between workers and the management can be vital in assuring a smooth transition during privatization. The discussion in the previous section showed that the lackadaisical and ad hoc handling of surplus labour leads to various inefficiencies in a social, fiscal and economic sense. The privatization process of Sri Lanka Telecom identified the significance of worker co-operation to ensure a smooth transition. Various phased-out strategies were adopted in this case to strengthen worker-management dialogue. Workers were informed and often made aware of restructuring that was happening in the sector and the process of privatization.

Sri Lanka Telecom (SLT) was not an SOE with a significant problem of surplus labour. But even though workers were not retrenched, it was recognised that worker resentment to privatization could cause significant problems given the large work-force SLT had (over 8000 workers in 1992) and its island-wide span. It was also recognised that workers will have to be re-trained and that their skills will have to be improved to work in a modernised environment after privatization. These issues were considered explicitly during the SLT privatization. The overall process itself went through a long period of preparation and sectoral restructuring. Details as to how the labour-management dialogue was developed are discussed in Box 4. As the discussion highlights, the gradualist approach adopted did not mean that problems were not encountered. Direct social costs seemed to have been minimised only at the expense of higher fiscal costs.

Box 4
Handling Worker Issues during the Sri Lanka Telecom (SLT) Privatization[1]

The manner in which labour was handled during the privatization process of Telecom was unique. This is because the issues of redundancy were considered explicitly from the time privatization was envisaged in the sector. The sector was large, employing over 8000 workers in the early 1990s. It was clear from the onset that worker support was essential if privatization was to be done smoothly, even though over-staffing was not a critical issue.

The sector itself was prepared for privatization gradually. The process started in the late 1980s, with the industry opening up to private investors providing wireless and mobile telephone service. Prices were revised and subsidies were reduced. Over a period of five years, from 1992 to 1997, various strategies were adopted to involve and increase worker awareness on preparations for privatization and the process itself.

A National Steering Committee was appointed to make high level decisions and recommendations regarding the transaction while a Telecom Cell was created at the PERC to handle implementation of the transaction. The Cell was meant also to liase with the trade unions. Sri Lanka Telecom had 31 trade unions. However, for the purpose of liasing and closely interacting with the Cell, the unions were represented as a 'joint front' involving nine trade unions. Already, six union leaders had been sent to visit privatized telecommunications companies in Chile and Mexico, to familiarise themselves with the facilities available in those countries.

An independent consultancy group (the National Institute of Business Management) was appointed to study labour issues relating to the reconstruction of SLT. A key finding by the NIBM was that TU leaders do not always voice the opinion of the majority of workers. This suggested that the trade unions had to be contacted individually and the workers had to be addressed directly. Such dialogue was found to be much more productive than dialogues with the union leaders alone. In fact, certain trade unions with skilled workers (accountants, engineers) were well in favour of privatization, recognising the fact that this would lead to enhancing of company worth and career development opportunity. In some instances, the Cell corresponded with the families of the workers directly, addressing letters and articles to them informing about the pros (and cons) of privatization and the significance of worker cooperation, in a bid to quell worker resentment. An in-house magazine Amathuma was launched by a media sub-committee. SLT also conducted regional open house 'awareness' forums at offices throughout the island along with representatives from the Ministry of Posts and Telecom, PERC and NIBM. Several media campaigns were also launched addressing the need for restructuring SLT and the telecommunication sector.

All such careful and tedious preparation led to the well deserved, comparatively smooth transition of Telecom from being a government department to being a privatized enterprise. No workers were retrenched during the process. The government however, had to pay a high price for this relatively non-turbulent transition. This was not just in the form of expenses incurred during the awareness campaigns, or in terms of airfares for the unionists. The staggering expense came in handling the disputes that arose with regard to handling pensions. The handling of pensions in the case of Telecom was a complex issue that will not be dealt in any detail in this case study. Just to get a flavour of the argument though, the conversion of Telecom from a department to a corporation in 1991 and the subsequent change from a corporation to a private company meant that there were various categories of workers claiming pension rights from the government. Extensive bargaining by the unions with the government led to substantial revisions and laxing of various provisions regarding pensions provided so far, leaving the government with a staggering commitment to pay pensions to a several hundred Telecom workers for several decades hence.

---

[1] SLT was privatised in 1997. It involved the divestiture of 35 % of shares and management of SLT to Nippon Telegraph and Telephone Corporation, Japan.

6.   Post privatization actions

The privatization experience of Sri Lanka so far has very much been one of trial and error and one of learning-through-experience. The establishment of PERC in 1994, for instance, was a response to certain criticisms that were made about the process, valuation and methodology of privatization. It was recognised at that time that the complexity of the transactions required a single institutional body or authority that could provide the skills required for the purpose. Therefore, on the recommendation of the Presidential Task Force appointed in 1995 to investigate the matter, the PERC was formed and was vested with the sole powers of formulating an appropriate policy framework for public enterprise reform, identify enterprises to be reformed, recommend the sale of shares, etc.

Another instance where the government responded to a lesson learnt comes from the over-compensating package that was paid during the privatization of Lanka Loha Ltd. As discussed in section 5.2, the over-compensating package paid by Lanka Loha Ltd. led to all workers of the firm opting to take the package and leave the firm, only to rejoin the company once it was privatized. This prompted the government to include a clause in the termination contracts that workers who opt to leave the firm with compensation, cannot rejoin the company. This retrenchment exercise also highlighted the downward rigidity of compensation packages, the rent-seeking nature of trade unions and the rising cost to the government of retrenching workers. The episode, therefore, sealed the government's determination not to retrench workers before privatization-more because it cannot afford to pay the large compensation demanded, rather than through altruistic concern for workers.

A lot of public discussion, controversy and scrutiny ensued almost all major privatization including the plantations, airlines, gas, telecommunication, etc. Some of these discussions stemmed from misinformation and highly opinionised viewpoints while some of the more constructive discussions offered insight as to how to minimize social costs of privatization. For instance, the privatization of Telecom and the way labour issues were handled in this transaction were much discussed topics. Positive lessons learnt included the benefits of involving unions and workers in the privatization process, increasing worker and public awareness as to what was going on, etc. It also highlighted the benefits of planning privatization over a period of time and considering worker issues in the process. On the negative side, the strength of bargaining skills and rent seeking on the part of the workers came to fore. The telecom privatization also highlighted the definite advantages of restructuring the entire industry gradually before privatizing a large monopoly, and of improving corporate governance. Overall, therefore, the Telecom experience has been hailed as a case study that offers guidelines and lessons that can be used in the future to ensure a smooth transition, even though some unfortunate precedences have been created in the handling of pensions, which can be used by trade unions in future privatization, to make demands.

The lessons learnt have been noted and discussed in various internal and public forums. It is possible that they will be taken into account in future privatization. There is no indication, however, that they will be translated into concrete policies or legal action. Much seems to depend on institutional memory, given that research and development is not a point of priority within the PERC.

7. Future privatizations planned

Currently, the environment is being built for other major privatizations in subsectors, such as transport and utilities (water, power). The key reason is to improve efficiency in these sectors. However, the privatization will take place only in the next wave which will probably be a couple of years hence, after the background has been built. Key preparation in this regard is being done in terms of establishing regulatory bodies, especially for the privatization of utilities, such as power. The regulatory framework is also being strengthened with the amalgamation of the Fair Trading Commission Act with the Consumer Protection Act, and bringing the functions of maintaining competition policy and consumer protection under the purview of a single authority.

In the mean time, further privatization of enterprises such as Telecom has been taking place. This has been helpful towards bridging the widening budget deficit. The widening trend in the deficit is likely to continue in 1999.

8. Recommendations for minimizing the social effects

Social effects of privatization can be gauged mainly from the way labour issues were handled during privatization. Labour retrenchment, in particular, is a critical issue in any privatization programme, that can have significant social impacts. For instance, the retrenchment experience in Sri Lanka, as illustrated in Section 5, was a nettle with various complexities that had both positive and negative impacts on the workers. These complexities were exacerbated because the legal and policy framework did not account for labour issues during privatization. The process so far has been so ad hoc that there is no single credible record of how many workers were retrenched or any statistical record as to how much the entire exercise cost the government. Moreover, compensation packages that have been paid have been largely inefficient and subject to avid rentseeking on the part of the unionists.The rent-seeking behaviour of the workers may have been advantageous to the workers of the firms and those retrenched. But the indirect impacts are being felt by the unemployed, the poor and the public at large as fiscal costs rise, probably taking its toll on welfare and capital expenditure.

The retrenchment exercise has been abundant with instances of adverse selection - where the better workers opt to leave the firm. There have also been instances when the number and type of workers who have to leave the firm is miscalculated especially when labour is shed before privatization. Thus the primary recommendation is that careful preparation (that considers labour issues explicitly) has to be made before privatization (see section 8.1 below). Social impacts can also be minimized by improving the labour management dialogue. Further, alternatives to retrenchment such as better corporate management, part time employment or labour hoarding can also reduce social costs to some extent. These issues are discussed in Sections 8.2 and 8.3 below.

8.1 Pre-privatization preparation

The most important preparation has to be done in terms of creating the appropriate institutional and policy environment to facilitate a smooth privatization process. Section 5.3. discussed some issues that were specific to the Sri Lankan labour market. Most of these conclusions can be extended to privatization programmes in general. Amongst these recommendations are: (a) formulate an overall labour market exit policy (b) If political costs permit, retrench workers after privatization since this is better for the firm in the long-term (c) Compensation should be fixed and the package/formula should be decided at the very onset of privatization to reduce uncertainty and rent-seeking tendencies.

A vital aspect of preparation is to increase worker and public awareness on privatization. This can be done via discussions with trade unionits and workers in general, through public seminars, newspaper articles, special union-based journals on the subject, etc. It is critical that workers are well-educated on shares and share markets.

It is also beneficial to restructure the entire sector or industry before privatization per se, if the SOE is a monopoly. Restructuring may include opening the industry up to private sector competition, removing price regulation, subsidies, etc. A good example to illustrate the benefits of such an approach is the telecommunication industry in Sri Lanka, where competition was introduced, management was restructured, and public/worker awareness campaigns were organised well in advance of the actual privatization itself. This gradualistic approach ensured a reasonably smooth (albeit costly) transition.

The other important aspect is the design of an appropriate regulatory framework, especially for public utilities that have been or will be privatized. This encompasses the transport sector, water and power sectors as well. Moreover, to ensure fair play, the role and functions of the Fair Trading Commission should be strengthened. As important a consistent regulatory and clear framework is, so is its strict implementation. The latter aspect has to be given serious attention by the convenors of privatization and policy makers.

8.2 Improving labour-management dialogue

The Telecom privatization experience discussed in Section 5.3 shows that the explicit consideration of labour issues at the onset of restructuring and privatization makes the transition much smoother. Mutual awareness of problems encountered can allay fears, inculcate cooperation and a sense of involvement and ensure public support. It should be noted, however, that such an approach may reduce social and psychological costs, but not necessarily fiscal costs especially in a political economic situation where union bargaining power is strong.

A safety net for workers and an overall exit policy cannot be designed in isolation of the wider macro economic framework. Other complementary policies should add to the effectiveness of a retrenchment policy. These include policy reforms that enhance labour market efficiency, those that consider recessionary trends that may ensue privatization and most importantly policies that ensure transparency and accountability in privatization itself.

The design of an exit policy should look into current trends in the labour market such as the move towards contract labour, and casual employment. A comprehensive policy should analyse these trends and account for them accordingly.

8.3 Offering non-monetary safety nets

The Sri Lankan experience in retrenchment shows no evidence of offering workers non-monetary safety nets. Non-monetary compensation often encompasses the broader social aim of minimizing worker dislocation and offering the worker security in the medium and long term. Such safety nets include retraining, assistance in developing entrepreneurial skills, developing a strategy for the fast reallocation of labour etc.

An important area to develop in this regard, therefore, is worker's entrepreneurial and managerial capabilities. Those workers keen on starting up small and medium term enterprises should be encouraged to do so. This can be done through informing and directing workers to vocational training institutes and training schemes carried out by both the public and private sectors. For example, in Sri Lanka there were nearly 3000 publicly supported training programs in 1992 conducted by 22 different ministries (see Kelly 1992). Workers can also be referred to development banks or merchant banks to gather further information on matters of assistance to such ventures. What is important is that workers are made aware of the options available. Private sector participation is vital in this regard.

Should the government start up a new scheme or fund focusing on reallocating retrenched workers? In India the National Renewal Fund (NRF) was set up by the state to cater specifically to retrain workers for reemployment, to help them set up independent business and to fund monetary compensation. It has been financed by the world bank, the restructured enterprises and the state. The NRF proved to be good at providing compensation, but weak at providing retraining, redeployment and the creation of an employment generation fund. Reasons for the failure lie in the lack of adequate funding, red tape, bureaucratic bungling and the lack of innovativeness on the part of administration. Further, there was no satisfactory fund disbursement and monitoring mechanism. Thus, even though the idea of a fund aiming at providing both monetary and non-monetary safety nets is appealing, it is administratively complex. (see Mishra undated). This means that setting up a similar fund in Sri Lanka is an idea, which needs careful consideration and further investigation.

In any case, even though the provision of retraining, skills enhancement etc. is appealing, such strategies focus more on improving the supply side of the labour market, implicitly assuming that training creates job opportunities. It is not just a skill development strategy that matters but an appropriate skill utilisation framework as well, if one wants to avoid the problem of having a more qualified (and more frustrated) lot of retrenched unemployed workers. In essence, if a skills development strategy is sought, it is necessary to first analyse the Sri Lankan labour market situation carefully and remove some of the impediments it currently contains and focus on the labour demand side as well, not just the labour supply side.

Another caveat regarding the provision of skill development schemes is that they attempt to predict future demand trends for skills and train the participants accordingly. This, however, is not very rewarding due to practical errors in prediction. It is more sensible for the private sector itself to train specific skills as required. This ensures the adaptability and flexibility of workers.

It is also necessary to consider the impact retraining programmes would have on the currently unemployed. Kelly (1992) estimates that in Sri Lanka there is a concentration of

202 PRIVATIZATION IN SOUTH ASIA

unemployment among youthful first-job seekers. The 1990 Labour Force Survey for the first quarter indicated that nearly 60 per cent of those between 15 and 24 were unemployed. Further, the low labour flexibility with respect to turnover in Sri Lanka results in an extremely long duration of unemployment. Nearly half of the unemployed remain without jobs for over 5 years, on average (Kelly, 1992). Thus funding for retraining retrenched workers (just a small segment of the unemployed pool) for reemployment seems inequitable and may well stir social unrest. It may also affect the currently unemployed adversely and increase the long-term unemployment rates.

8.4 Alternatives to retrenching labour

8.4.1 Better corporate management

If the SOE did not fully utilise its capacity (labour, capital etc.) due to budget constraints then there is much scope for restructuring and/or forming an efficient corporate management plan that can reduce labour redundancy. Several SOEs have been bought by the private sector along with the idle or under utilised capacity. Private firms have utilised such resources including land, equipment, labour in different ways. There has been diversification, expansion of activities and computerisation. Excess labour can be successfully redirected and absorbed in such new areas. Further labour can be transferred within the firm, and worker skills can be improved to cater to the expanding activities of the firm. This has been tried in the plantation sector privatization.

A key complaint some workers make regarding transference within the firm, however, is that they have no choice whatsoever, as to where they are transferred. This at times makes workers feel 'punished' or forced to leave the firm. Thus, an important element in effectively implementing this option is to develop more dialogue between workers and management, in order to avoid the occurrence of worker demotivation and underemployment.

8.4.2 Offering part-time employment

Another alternative to laying off workers is offering part-time employment instead of (or in parallel with) the option of retrenching. For instance, part-time work can be offered with the option of being reabsorbed into the full-time work-force once the economy picks up or with the option of leaving the firm at the end of, say, 2 years if the employer cannot afford to finance a compensation package immediately. The employer can also opt to give the worker the choice to retire at any time during the part-time employment period. This will give the worker the added advantage of being able to gauge the performance of the privatized firm before deciding whether to leave or stay on.

Part time working is a rising trend in developing countries. Even the current trend in most private enterprises in Sri Lanka seems to be shifting to contract labour and casual employment. Even though all three types of employment (especially part-time and casual) involves working hours less than full-time employment, and normally a commensurate reduction in wages, a main difference is that part time workers receive more legal protection than do casual or contract workers. Therefore, in the light of worker security and less uncertainty, part-time employment seems to be a better option to settle for, than being retrenched and reemployed by the firm on a contract basis.

Further, part-time employment reduces worker dislocation costs, search costs (because costs incurred in looking for a better job can be negated by the income earned during the search period) and can even be seen as a period of 'training', if the worker benefits through technological and capital influxes ensuing privatization. The part-time option may be more appealing to particular categories of workers such as females, mothers, youth etc. A key draw back with part-time employment, however, is that it will increase visible underemployment. This means that the worker works for less hours than they wish to, thereby transferring the problem of unemployment to one of underemployment.

8.4.3 Hoarding workers

It is also possible to 'hoard' workers by not retrenching until effective demand picks up and the firm can operate in full capacity. This may save the firm costs of retraining. However, hoarding might affect the firm's, short/medium term competitiveness and profitability. It may also cost the firm more in the long run, particularly if skilled labour is available in the labour market and training is not a significant issue (as in organisations where worker skills are not firm specific).

The suggestions above are by no means exhaustive. However, unless an effective retrenchment framework (preferably in the context of an overall exit policy) is designed for the Sri Lankan labour market, alternatives to retrenchment in the face of excess labour, seem to be more appealing.

Bibliography

Bos, D. (1994): 'Safety Net and Social Implications of German Unification', *International Roundtable on Safety Net and Social Implications of Structural Adjustment Programs,* CIER and SCOPE, New Delhi, India, 13-15 December 1994.

Central Bank of Sri Lanka (1998): *Economic Progress of Independent Sri Lanka 1948-1998,* Central Bank of Sri Lanka, Colombo

Central Bank of Sri Lanka, Annual Reports, Various Issues

Cukierman, A. (1992): *Central Bank Strategy, Credibility and Independence: Theory and Evidence,* MIT Press, Cambridge.

De Silva, I. (1997): *Population Projections for Sri Lanka: 1991-2041,* Institute of Policy Studies, Colombo.

Diwan, I. (1992): 'Public Sector Retrenchment and Efficient Severance Pay Schemes', First Draft, World Bank, Washington D.C. (mimeo).

Dunham, D. and Kelegama, S. (1996): *Problems Facing the Poultry Industry in Sri Lanka,* Unpublished report prepared for the President of Sri Lanka, April 1996.

Fiszbein, A. (1992): *Labour Retrenchment and Redundancy Compensation in State Owned Enterprises: The Case of Sri Lanka,* World Bank, Washington D.C.

GOSL (1987): *Report of the Presidential Commission on Privatization* (B. Mahadeva and others), Ministry of Finance, Government of Sri Lanka, Colombo.

GOSL (1989): *Report of the Committee on Payment of Compensation for Redundant Staff in Government Corporations and Statutory Boards* (R. Bullumulla and others), Ministry of Labour, Government of Sri Lanka, Colombo.

GOSL (1995): *Policy Statement* (06 January 1995), Government of Sri Lanka, Colombo.

GOSL (1997): *Payment of Compensation – Public Enterprises,* PE Circular 114 (03 December 1996), Ministry of Finance and Planning, Government of Sri Lanka, Colombo.

ILO (1996): *India: Economic Reforms and Labour Policies,* ILO, South Asia Multidisciplinary Advisory Team (SAAT), New Delhi.

Kelegama, S. (1993): *Privatization in Sri Lanka: The Experience During the Early Years of Implementation,* Sri Lanka Economic Association.

Kelegama, S. (1995): 'The Impact of Privatization in Distributional Equity: The Case of Sri Lanka' in Ramanadham V. V. (ed.) *Distributional Aspects of Privatization in Developing Countries,* Routledge, London.

Kelegama, S. (1997a): 'Privatization in Sri Lanka: An Overview' in A. Bennett (ed.), *How does Privatization Work? Essays on Privatization in Honour of Professor V.V. Ramanadham,* Routledge, London.

Kelegama, S. (1997b): 'Privatization and the Public Exchequer: Some Observations from the Sri Lankan Experience', *Asia Pacific Development Journal,* Vol. 4, No. 1.

Kelegama, S. and Salih, R. (1999): *Labour Retrenchment in a Privatization Programme: Policy Issues from the Sri Lankan Experience, Journal of Social Sciences,* Sri Lanka, Volume 21.

Kelly, T. F. (1992): *A Strategy for Skills Development and Employment Policy in Sri Lanka,* Research Studies, Employment Series No. 11, Institute of Policy Studies, Colombo.

Mishra R. K. (undated), *Safety Net, National Renewal Fund and States Level Public Enterprises in India: A Case Study of Hyderabad Allwyn Limited,* Institute of Public Enterprise, Osmania University, Hyderabad.

Salih, R. (1998): Privatization and the Problem of Surplus Labour, *Achievers*, National Development Bank of Sri Lanka, Volume 4 No. 4, October 1998.

SLDBC (1992): 'Survey of Retrenched Persons of Public Sector Institutions", Sri Lanka Business Development Centre, Paper No. 25, Colombo (mimeo).

Svejnar, J. and K. Terrell (1991): 'Reducing Labour Redundancy in State-Owned Enterprises', Infrastructure and Urban Development Department, The World Bank, Washington D.C., WPS-792 (mimeo).

Weerakoon, G. (1992): 'Economic Liberalization and Workers Rights', Paper presented at the workshop on Labour and Economic Liberalization, Sri Lanka Business Development Centre, 8 December (mimeo).

World Bank (1995): *World Development Report, 1995* (Workers in an Integrating World), The World Bank, Washington, D.C.

Policies carried out by the government to build an environment conducive to privatization

Tax and investment incentives

The government has made various attempts since 1989 to mobilise funds for the privatised companies by stimulate the capital markets. Incentives offered have been tax-oriented and investment-oriented. In the early 1990s, several measures were taken to make share issue more attractive. Some such measures were:

1. Abolition of the 100% transfer of property tax on share transfers between foreign persons.
2. Approved country and regional funds and individuals resident outside Sri Lanka were permitted to invest in up to 100% of the issued equity of listed companies.
3. In 1991 the abolition of taxes which inhibited the development of the share market.
4. In 1992 total abolition of the capital gains tax.
5. The withholding tax on dividends paid on listed shares was abolished
6. The wealth tax on listed shares was abolished.

Since 1994, the government has placed special emphasis on boosting export-oriented private sector led growth. Policies in this area include:

1. Various incentives granted over the years to Board of Investment companies to attract foreign and local investment
2. Tax holidays, tax and duty exemptions granted to industries using advanced technology

Measures to develop the capital market

Various measures were taken to stimulate, develop and deepen the capital market, in order to support the privatisation programme. Some of the measures implemented during the early stages of privatisation were:

1. The establishment of equity funds and unit trusts.
2. Exemption from income tax (up to Rs. 50 000 or $1/3^{rd}$ of assessable income whichever is lower) on investment in venture capital companies and unit/mutual trust funds.
3. A five-year tax holiday for unit trusts, while a ten-year tax holiday was granted to approved venture capital companies
4. Corporate income taxes have been reduced to 35% since April 1994 from its former 40% rate.

The government has also been keen on implementing financial sector reforms in order to improve efficiency of financial intermediation and to promote private savings. The reform measures that have been taken are:

a) Developing a viable bond market – Since 1997, a new medium term debt instrument –the treasury bond—has been introduced. The central bank also plans on moving towards issuing long-term debt instruments in the year 2000.
b) Developing a treasury bill market mainly through extensions to the maturity structure of government treasury bills.
c) Banking Sector Reforms – performance contracts linked to specific annual performance targets (e.g., loan recovery, cost reduction) were established in the state-owned banks.
d) Mobilizing Domestic Savings—attempting to reduce fiscal deficits, accepting obligations under Article VIII of the IMF Articles Agreement, etc.

Measures to Develop Competition Policy

For nearly a decade following the liberalization, competition policy in Sri Lanka was governed by the National Prices Commission (NPC) Law No 42 of 1975. The NCP had the limited function of undertaking price-surveillance. In 1987, a new law was passed — The Fair Trading Commission (FTC) Act No 1 of 1987—to set up a stronger body than the NPC to control monopolies, mergers and restrictive business practices and continue with price surveillance.

Currently the FTC deals with issues regarding competition policy i.e., monopolies, mergers and anti competitive practices(FTC Act No.1 1987). Issues pertaining to consumer protection are handled by the Department of Internal Trade under the Consumer Protection Act No.1 of 1979. It has been realized that both competition policy and consumer protection are best handled by a common authority and hence there is an Act to amalgamate the Consumer Protection Act and the Fair Trading Commission Act being drafted currently. BOI companies are excluded from FTC control.

Trade Policy : The main aim of the government with regards to trade policy is to increase competition and eliminate distortions through tax and tariff simplification. The tariff structure has moved from a 4-band to a 3-band structure in 1995 and there is a possibility of a move to a 2 band structure.

The 35% import duty and the 20% BTT on OFCs have been reduced or wavered completely since July 1996. Quantitative restrictions were removed on several agricultural products in October 1996.

Duties have been removed on yarn, fabrics and all intermediate and capital goods for the textile and garments industry in 1998.

Annex 2

Types of Compensation Packages Offered in Sri Lanka

Company	Date of approval	Number of months salary					Other Additions	Maximum payable Rs.
		less than 5 year	5<10 years	10<15 years	15<20 years	more than 20 yrs		
Bullumulla Package*	1989-1991	Compensation = 1 months salary * (55-age) * (age/55) * (years of service/30)						
Leather Products	1991 July	10	25	35	45	50	-Gratuity/provident fund benefits 250,000	200,000
Ceylon Oxygen	1991 July	Compensation = Rs. 85,000 + (monthly wage* number of years of service less than 20 years)					-Gratuity/provident fund benefits	
		less than 5	5<10 years	10<15 years	15<20 years	more than 20 yrs		
B.C.C	1991 September	12	25	35	45	50	-Gratuity/provident fund benefits	200,000
Consolidated Exports and Trading Ceylon Oils and Fats	1992 March	12	25	35	45	50	-Gratuity/provident fund benefits	200,000
Lanka Fertiliser	1993 Feb.	12	25	35	45	50		min [250,000; (55-age)*monthly wage]
Kantale Sugar	1994 March	12	25	35	45	50	- Gratuity/provident fund benefits - payment for unutilised leave for the year. - interest-free recovery of all loans obtained from the company.	Managerial grade: 250,000 Others: 200,000
		less than 4 years	4<8 years	8<12 years	12<16 years	16> years		
Sathosa Printers	1995 May	15	28	38	48	53	- Gratuity/provident fund benefits - Base wage used in the formula was	Managerial grade: 355,000 Others: 290,000

Lanka Loha Hardware GOSL (1997)	1997 May 1997 January	15 28 38 48 53	30% higher than the final wage paid.
		Compensation = (1 months salary * years of service) + 1.5 months salary* (55 – age) * (age/55) * (years of service/30)	350,000
			- Gratuity/provident fund benefits - Duty free import of buses/bus chassis of not less than 40 passenger capacity. - Agricultural tractors/trailers for transport of goods at the concessionary duty free rate of 25% (as opposed to 35%).	Executives 130,000 Non-executives 100,000

Source: Kelegama and Salih (1998)

7

Report of the Sub-Regional Workshop on Privatization in South Asia

Kathmandu, 24-26 November 1999

A three-day high level tripartite meeting on Privatization in South Asia was held in Kathmandu from 24-26 November 1999. The meeting was organized by International Labour Organization (ILO).

A total of 32 participants representing five nations - Bangladesh, India, Nepal, Pakistan and Sri Lanka attended the meeting. The participants from each country comprised of representatives of employers' and workers' organizations and the governments. The three-day programme included an inaugural session, nine working sessions and a concluding session. The detailed programme of the meeting is attached as Annex 1 and the list of participants as Annex 2.

OBJECTIVES

The meeting brought together the participants to discuss the privatization activities in South Asia and ways to mitigate their social effects. Specifically, the workshop had following objectives:

- share experiences or lessons learned from privatization activities in the South Asian countries;
- focus on social effects of privatization and restructuring of the public enterprises in South Asia;
- examine how adverse social effects can be mitigated through restructuring of public enterprises; and
- seek ways to find better ways to promote and strengthen social dialogue between workers and employers to resolve the issues arising from privatization.

DAY 1: Wednesday, 24 November 1999

Opening Ceremony

Welcoming the guests and participants to the meeting, Mr. A.S. Oberai, Director, ILO-South Asia Multidisciplinary Advisory Team (SAAT) stated that privatization of public sector enterprises has been gaining momentum in most South Asian countries with the increasing pace of economic and trade liberalization and growing budgetary deficits. However, some countries have rushed through the programmes without providing adequate measures for workers' protection. A more worrisome feature is that surplus labour in the public sector carried over from the past is threatening to become open unemployment adding to the already difficult employment situation. This has therefore caused serious concerns among policy makers, workers' organisations and the society in general.

Mr. Oberai noted that some countries have attempted to deal with the problems of retrenched workers by establishing social safety nets largely consisting of severance payments. For example, in India, National Renewal Fund (NRF) was established in 1992 but the experiment has not been very successful. When set up in 1992, it had three major objectives: (i) to provide a package of compensation to retrenched workers; (ii) to provide funds for retraining/ redeployment of displaced workers; and (iii) to provide funds for employment generation schemes. Although these were laudable objectives, there have been serious problems in operationalizing the concept of NRF. The coverage has been small, and very little training has been provided to the displaced workers. In Pakistan also, some enterprises have paid generous compensation to affected workers. However, it has not helped many workers to get reabsorbed in the labour market. Besides severance payment, what is needed is an unemployment insurance benefit system which could provide more effective safety nets to laid off workers by allowing them reasonable time to look for alternative work. Also required are strong labour market institutions such as active employment exchanges, labour market information and training systems to assist retrenched workers in reskilling and searching for jobs.

He pointed out that although the present spate of privatization is heavily influenced by the economic compulsions, the experience of privatization itself is not new. In the nineteenth century even the public utilities such as gas, power and water were initially privately owned, operated and funded in most countries, which were over a period of time regulated or nationalised although in varying pattern across and within countries and sectors. Some of the motives behind this nationalization, such as promoting social interests, maintaining national security and reducing foreign domination, may have been reasonable but others such as using nationalisation as a means of providing subsidies to industry, controlling prices and extending patronage were perhaps misguided. Over time, however, there was disenchantment with the performance of these nationalised firms, particularly in terms of poor quality and dismal services besides being a burden on the state exchequer. The result was the start of deregulation and privatization in many countries. The wave of infrastructure privatization that swept Chile, New Zealand and the United Kingdom in the 1980s is now sweeping the globe. The momentum is driven by dissatisfaction with state provision, precarious government finances and new technology.

Mr. Oberai affirmed the need for privatization and continued that while private firms do not always outperform public enterprises, the evidence shows that they usually do. Many studies around the world have noted that rates of return on equity invested in industrial or commercial public enterprises often are almost a third of those invested in the country's industrial private sector. One may argue that rate of return in public enterprises is low because public sector may be pursuing certain social objectives. Even if this is true the issue still remains: can these objectives be not achieved through other means rather than reducing the overall efficiency of the economy? One could also argue that differences in the rates of return between public and private enterprises may also be due to the differences in technology, pricing, market, level of competition, tariff structure, etc. rather than due to the differences in management efficiency. But several studies controlling for these factors have convincingly demonstrated that private firms are generally more efficient than public enterprises.

Then, Mr. Oberai raised the issue as to why privatized firms perform better. Neoclassical economic theory suggests that the relationship between ownership and performance is tenuous. Efficiency is seen mainly as a function of market and incentives structures. In theory, therefore, it should make little difference whether a firm is privately or publicly owned as long as: (i) it operates in a competitive market: (ii) owner instructs management to follow signals provided by the market; and (iii) management is rewarded or sanctioned on the basis of performance. The problem, of course, is that these conditions are almost never met in the case of nationalised companies. Public sector enterprises are supervised by disinterested bureaucrats who often have more than profit on their minds. Political interference is also a major cause of efficiency reducing conditions in public enterprises.

The issue is not only whether or not to privatize but also when, what and how to privatize. The speed of privatization itself is an important factor determining the success or failure of a particular programme. Britain took 8 years to privatize 14 enterprises. Malaysia took 3 years to privatize container terminal. Mexico took 2 years to privatize one large coffee company. There is also the issue of developing effective regulatory mechanisms to safeguard the interests of consumers against formation of private monopolies following privatization.

He further noted that there are no standard models for privatization. While developing the preferred mode of privatization, it is important that different options are explored and the preferred privatization solutions are tailored to suit the local political and social environment. It is equally important that the privatization programmes are transparent, and there is a demonstrated political commitment to provide credible guarantee to the investor. Implementing the privatization successfully in the real world then would require support of institutional mechanisms that address stakeholder concerns in a creative manner. The process of privatization has been difficult and lessons have been learned along the way - in relation to the structuring of transactions and sale process, and in relation to balancing the interests of investors and consumers, as well as those of government, workers and regulators. He also cautioned that no country can claim to have delivered privatization without some failures and some highly criticized deals. So, each country needs to evolve its own approach to privatization, keeping in view the lessons learnt from others.

He further stated that the view that the government sector should concern itself only with the delevery of public goods and services is generally held among western economists and policymakers. In their economies, governments do not play a direct role of productionn through investment. Their private enterprises are large, efficient and multinational in scope. However, this is not the case in South Asian countries. Therefore, it could be legitimately argued here that in some important areas public enterprises should continue to exist at least till the private enterprises come of age. Thus for South Asian countries, instead of debating the question as regards whether there should be wholesale privatization, one could agree on certain specific steps to increase the efficiency and reduce the financial burden on the governments. Governments may for example, consider: (a) selling or closing down loss-making public enterprises producing all non-strategic goods in a phased manner; and (b) bringing private share-holding into profit-making public enterprises in all areas except railways, atomic energy and most defence related industries.

Lastly, Mr. Oberai raised certain issues for discussion during the workshop. Some of these issues were: Is the privatization process raising high expectations?; Is privatization conceived mainly as a means of reducing fiscal deficit?; Is adequate pool of funds available in the private sector to assume ownership of public sector enterprises without adversely affecting the pace of investment in new industries? How do we ensure that monopolies are not formed after privatization?; What kind of regulatory mechanisms do we need to protect the interests of consumers?; Can the private sector take over certain social functions which are currently being performed by the public sector such as those promoting employment among backward classes or other disadvantaged groups in society? How do we evolve social dialogue and social consensus on the need, extent and form of privatization?

Mr. Indra Deo Mishra, Vice-president of Nepal Trade Union Congress (NTUC), representing the workers' organization, stated that privatization, economic liberalization and globalization are creating problems for the workers. He said it was not clear whether the concept of privatization is expected to benefit the workers. He also pointed out that both the private and public industries in Nepal have been operating at a loss. He said the impact of privatization on workers should be studied and a solution should be sought.

Representing the employers' side, Mr Pradeep Shrestha, President of Federation of Nepalese Chamber of Commerce and Industries (FNCCI), stated that if an economic function can be better performed by the private sector, it should be left for the private sector. However, he pointed out that privatization alone may be insufficient condition for desired changes in the economy. Mr. Shrestha cautioned that privatization may bring worse results if it is used primarily to shed the administrative and financial burden of loss-making enterprises.

Inaugurating the workshop, the Finance Minister of Nepal, Mr. Mahesah Acharya, stated that inward-looking and protection-oriented policies in the past restricted the prospects of realizing decent rate of economic growth and employment. The last two decades of this millennium has, however, witnessed significant transformation with respect to the roles and responsibilities of the government and the private sector. Economic liberalization and privatization process have been initiated for improving the investment climate and optimizing the resource allocation pattern through competitive market and catalytic role of the government in the economy.

Mr. Acharya observed that the need for political support and the social justification for the private sector-led growth strategy always requires that the issues relating to the welfare and involvement of the labour be given utmost importance. While the economic compulsions would warrant expedited privatization, successful privatization rests on the enlistment of social support to the program. Appropriate compensation packages for those opting for early retirement and a guarantee for continuation of the existing compensation package for the remaining workforce in the privatized sector would be essential. Alternative arrangements could be made to ensure that the discontinuation of the services provided by the public enterprise to the economically deprived and geographically remote sections of the society are not unnecessarily affected on account of the privatization.

The privatization process could give rise to contentious issues in the context of job tenure and security, which are more secure in public enterprises by legal provisions than in the case of the private sector. Similarly, the perceptions with respect to terms and conditions like the job status, new skill requirements, working hours, wage differentials, benefits, bargaining power, and tougher employee performance and work discipline in the privatized enterprise may not reconcile with the needs and expectations of the work force. So, the effects on employment conditions and labour-management relations due to privatization should be recognized as a matter of utmost importance. Particularly, privatization programs which incorporate and enforce specific measures safeguarding workers' rights and protection along with the support measures for retrenched work-force, promotion of skill enhancement and self-employment programs, and use of privatization proceeds for socially-related measures are bound to be more socially successful.

The Finance Minister noted that privatization in Nepal, which began as an important strategy after the restoration of democracy in 1990, has so far witnessed privatization of 16 enterprises. The Privatization Act, which came into force in January 1994, has made various provisions with respect to promoting the social welfare and employee interests in the privatization process. The Privatization Committee of the Government includes Secretary in the Ministry of Labour as its member; and, if required, labour representatives would also be invited in its meetings. The Act provides that the Government may require the continuity of service of the existing work force, or they can be retired by arranging for reasonable compensation or benefits. The Government would also make available a certain percentage of shares of the privatized enterprise free of cost or at discounted price to the workers.

The Finance Minister pointed out that a recent study conducted in Singapore, a country where public enterprises are faring well, shows that the private sector is, at least, 15% more efficient than the government sector. Similarly in some of the public utilities in the USA, performance-based contracting out of the activities to the employees has raised the productivity and saved tremendous amounts of money to the city authorities. It may be noted that providing the employees in the public enterprises with a certain level of social and economic protection as well as a reasonable incentive and reward for good work is quite essential. However, if such facilities have to be made available in the form of privileges at the cost of public at large, then such facilities would be hard to be justified, particularly in the context of the economic situation that the South Asian region faces. Likewise, if the social restructuring and reform process are to be sustainable and successful, then a culture of work value system irrespective of the nature of the job has to be established, the link so far missing both in the public and private sectors of this region.

The Finance Minister concluded by stating that in the process of privatization "what is privatized is business, not the responsibility". At a time when the concepts of slimmer government and good governance are becoming the hallmarks of the day, it is but quite natural for the government to withdraw from the business of doing business and instead effectively discharge its function of governance. He expressed his belief that the deliberations of the workshop would contribute towards formulating a strategy for privatization that would take into account the social effects and the restructuring requirements.

Mr. H.S.S. Fonseka, Officer-in Charge of the Senior ILO Advisor's Office, thanked the speakers and the participants in the opening ceremony.

Overview Presentation

Mr. Gopal Joshi, Senior Specialist on Enterprise and Management Development, and Professor G.S. Bhalla, Jawaharlal Nehru University, presented an overview of *Privatization in South Asia*. Mr. Joshi stated that there are three general reasons why privatization is being pursued: greater economic democracy through increased private initiatives in economic activities; higher levels of economic growth and employment; and reduction in budgetary deficits.

He pointed out that when the public sector undertakings are privatized largely to reduce the budgetary deficit, there is bound to be a tendency to focus on off-loading a heavily loss-making enterprises as quickly as possible without much regard to long-term consequences to such privatized units. As a result, the social effects of privatization have been presumably much greater than what would be the case, had the privatized public enterprises not been loss making.

Therefore, the PE's need to be first restructured to minimize the social costs. He presented the dilemma of the need for restructuring and the inability of the PE's to improve their management. Restructuring should take place in the manner that the enterprises are turned around with professionalization of management. This could be achieved by creation of a transparent, accountable and representative system of regulating the enterprises and involvement of employers and workers even before the turnaround and privatization begins.

Prof. G. S. Bhalla pointed out that efficiency was the rationale behind privatization. According to him, several factors have been responsible for the new economic thinking that stresses on efficiency and market. He further stated that the efficiency in management can be achieved regardless of whether the enterprises are privatized or not.

Mr. Michael Henriques, Director, Job Creation and Enterprise Department, ILO, shared international experiences on the privatization programme implemented some years back and social impact of privatization can be minimized by learning from such experiences.

He said privatization is widespread in many countries, with over 100 countries having significant programmes. Some 75,000 large and medium sized, and hundreds of thousands of small firms and shops have been privatized all over the world to date. It is an ongoing process and the total proceeds of this global privatization programme are estimated at over US$ 735 billion.

Strong and growing economies with visible private sectors, well functioning legal and administrative institutions; adequate infrastructure; broadbased support for objectives; understanding of long term benefits and social measures contribute to successful privatization. Other contributing factors are effective system of corporate governance; social safety net to protect redundant workers and participation and involvement of all stakeholders in the process.

Privatization requires changes at several levels. It needs to consider wide range of adjustment requirement of the privatized enterprise; appropriate measures for retrenched workers; and national economic and institutional environment. As a key alternative to job creation, he outlined possibility of creating new activities leveraging on unique internal skills, diversification into a new activity and identifying and fostering the development projects in the region.

The discussion that followed stressed that it is important to reduce the financial losses made by the public enterprises. Professor Goyal from India pointed out that South Asian experience shows that the privatization has not necessarily delivered the goods. It could be due to the lack of well-defined objectives and regulatory mechanism.

Dr. L. Mishra of India pointed out that Professor Bhalla did not elaborate on the lessons learnt from failures. He also raised a question regarding whether the presenters have an answer to minimize financial volatility resulting from large-scale scams. It was also pointed out that when privatization was pursued as a philosophy to get rid of mismanagement, especially in the social sector, desirable results have not been achieved.

Trade unions stressed that the policy makers should have a clear guideline for privatization. It is pursued in an extreme haste leading the workers to question the very motive behind the privatization.

A representative from the employers' organization stated that private enterprises may not operate in the backward areas where employment is needed.

The chairperson, Mr. I.P. Anand, concluded the session with remarks that it has become clear that even the state is incapable of delivering as a guarantor of social, political and common rights in all aspects of public life. Therefore, the role of the individual and economic entity has to be recognized. Privatization is an effort towards such a direction.

Country Presentation I - Bangladesh

Prof. Momtaz Uddin Ahmed, University of Dhaka presented the paper on *Privatization in Bangladesh*. He pointed out that both internal policy dynamics and external stimuli have encouraged privatization in Bangladesh. Internally, privatization has become an inescapable necessity to remove the huge fiscal and financial burden imposed by the loss making state owned enterprises (SOEs) by improving efficiency and facilitating higher economic growth for social transformation. The external stimuli were the result of donor pressure to introduce economic reforms designed to ensure macro-economic stability, liberalization of trade and increased external competitiveness of the economy.

Privatization in Bangladesh began in mid-1970s and evolved gradually through different phases marked by many ups and downs. A host of policies were formulated and implemented to encourage privatization under an overall private sector-led industrial growth regime. Direct sale of SOEs through international tenders has been the dominant method, followed by off-loading of publicly owned shares.

Economic and financial performance of the privatized SOEs has been mixed. However, a more systematic research needs to be carried out to reach any conclusive judgement.

Contrary to the prior optimism, privatization has led to a considerable loss in employment from labour retrenchment and closure of many enterprises. The total retrenchment has been estimated at 90,000 by the end of 1997. Currently, the government offers a "golden handshake" as a monetary compensation measure and arranges retraining for the retrenched workers. The government has formed a sizable Special Workers Fund for retraining. Although the training facilities are available, retrenched workers have to wait for about three years to get trained; and the prospects of redeployment are still not very good.

Representing the workers, Mr. Md. Asharaf Hossain of Bangladesh pointed out that workers in private sector are now getting less wages/benefits than in the state owned industries. In most cases, no compensation has been paid to the retrenched workers, and the idea of golden handshake has been a big failure. Hardly any compensation has reached the workers. Workers in privatized units are getting fewer wages than SOEs. When the workers leave their jobs, they are not paid their provident funds and gratuities. There are no provisions for retraining or alternative employment for retrenched workers He pointed out that public sector monopoly is being replaced by private sector monopoly and added that privatization has created more problems in the country. He also added that the paper failed to fully discuss the social effects of privatization on retrenched workers.

From the employers' side, Mr. M. Aniz Ud Dowla of Bangladesh said that the progress in privatization has been slow and limited; and the privatization process has been fraught with ups and downs mainly due to political instability. He blamed absence of political support for the poor performance of the privatized companies. He also drew attention to the fact that the workers have failed to realize that privatization comes with some price and further added that the trade union's viewpoint is prejudiced. He pointed out that private ownership now allowed in the energy sector has led to a huge flow of foreign investments. The energy sector in the next two years is expected to witness 3.5 billion-dollar investment. He said jute and textile industries, which consist of 50 per cent of the SOEs, have lost their viability due to antiquated technology in use. He also underscored the need for privatization of jute, textile, telecommunication, railways and power. Since PSEs have drained the economy, privatization ranks high as an agenda for high economic growth.

From the government side, Mr. Md. Abu Wahid of Bangladesh, suggested the integration of the Board of Investment and the Privatization Board.

The general discussion that followed focussed on the difference between golden handshake and Voluntary Retirement Scheme (VRS), causes for nationalization of privatized companies and the difference between privatization and re-privatization. A participant pointed out that a survey of 205 privatized units concluded that many of such units were performing very well. Private sector should be allowed into infrastructure, which still has had dismal performance. Another participant stated that political parties are inconsistent in their stance on privatization, and the results of privatization are mixed. More research needs to be done to ascertain the impact of privatization.

The Chairperson, Dr. L. Mishra, commented that the paper should have provided the evidence on the efficiency of the privatized units. Successive governments did not seem to have pursued privatization with equal vigour. High population adding to the already high level of unemployment requires careful examination of the strategies for maintaining jobs in the face of privatization.

Country Presentation I - India

On behalf of The Institute for Studies in Industrial Development, Professor S K Goyal presented the paper on *Privatization in India*. Two objectives appear to have been effectively pursued by government initiatives concerning privatization. One is resource mobilization by the government through transfer of public sector undertakings (PSU) equity to public sector financial institutions and mutual funds. Second is to honour the assurances that government had given during the Fund-Bank negotiations that India would take effective steps to reduce the role of the state in internal management of the economy.

Privatization has been strongly opposed by labour. There is bound to be conflict between the management and the trade unions if the two sides did not have regular communications. It has to be accepted by the government, workers and the public at large that privatization needs to be accompanied by restructuring of the existing regulatory mechanism. The new system must have well defined objectives and should allow total transparency and adequate powers to effectively administer the regulatory provisions of law and least possible discretion.

It has been accepted in principle by the government to pay cash compensation to workers under the Voluntary Retirement Scheme (VRS). The emphasis should be in seeking alternatives which provide an effective safety net that can ensure regular incomes to the retirees.

Representing the workers, Mr. Veereshwar Tiagi from India stated that the awareness about privatization is lacking in the country. He pointed out that privatization in India has been purely for commercial purpose. Private entrepreneurs are not able to meet all the requirements of the society. He noted that Trade Unions too are to be blamed as they have failed in educating workers on the necessity to work hard and honestly. He blamed the poor monitoring mechanism and political interference for the sad state of SOEs requiring privatization.

From the employers' side, Mr. B.P. Pant from India cautioned that the paper stokes fears of privatization. Creation of public sector came as a part of the development strategy when private sector was at its nascent state. Privatization was in response to the problems plaguing the public sector like overstaffing, bureaucratic red-tapism and political interference. He noted that pension scheme will be preferable to VRS while privatizing SOEs. He also pointed out that abolition of contractual labour has diminished employment opportunities for unskilled labour.

Representing the Indian government, Ms. C.L. Malviya mentioned the two government sponsored schemes for minimizing the social consequences - one is the Voluntary Retirement Scheme (VRS) and the other retraining scheme. A scheme called the National Renewal Fund is currently being implemented by the Department of Industrial Development, Ministry of Commerce and Industry as a safety net for the displaced workers. As a solution to the adverse effect, she suggested promoting self-employment by giving easy access to credit for workers.

The general discussion that followed focussed on the impact of privatization on labour in terms of retrenchment and accompanying confusion generated in implementing voluntary retirement scheme and golden handshake. It was observed that retraining and redeployment have not been taken up in a big way. If the social costs of privatization are not well assessed, it could result in social upheavals. A participant commented that people were paying for the monopoly cost of the public enterprises. He said all the costs should be brought into account.

The chairperson, Dr. L. Mishra, concluded the session by pointing out the need for regulation of privatized enterprises so that the public interests are not sacrificed. He suggested drawing a line between the state and market force and assign a role to each which they can discharge within their respective areas. On the issue of ideology versus quality, he said one need not be bothered about the ideology at this stage. He said concentration should be on quality. He also added that privatization is no recipe for fiscal deficit.

DAY 2: Thursday, 25 November 1999

Country Presentation II - Nepal

Dr. Narayan Manandhar from Industrial Relations Forum and Dr. Pushkar Bajracharya from Tribhuvan University, Nepal presented the paper on *Privatization in Nepal*. There is a sort of political consensus in Nepal on privatization amongst the major political parties though they differ considerably on the degree of emphasis and the mode of privatization. Nepali Congress, for instance, has taken privatization as a matter of "(internal) necessity" while the second largest party UML has taken it as "(an external) compulsion", pushed mainly by donors.

As provisioned in Article 14 of the Privatization Act, three policy measures have been opted for mitigating privatization related labour problems.

1. No redundancy clause: The workers have been guaranteed continuity of their services in privatized enterprises. Where the continuity of the services cannot be guaranteed, the government is to provide necessary retrenchment compensation.

2. Guarantee of accrued salary and benefits: The workers willing to continue their services will be guaranteed salaries and benefits "no less favourable" than what they earned under government ownership.

3. Availability of shares at a discounted price. In all privatized units, the government has allocated five percent of the total shares to workers at a discount of 25 percent payable on an installment basis.

4. Apart from these three provisions, the government has reduced the deposit money to Rs. 10,000 if the workers wish to participate in the bidding process.

It is very difficult to pinpoint the exact effect of privatization on total employment because both positive and negative factors are simultaneously at work. Some of the privatized units have been closed. If one includes employment figures in these closed units, then the total effect is substantial. Jobs of about 3,200 people have been directly affected by the closures of four units. However, if one excludes the closed units and seeks to analyze the total employment figure, the total effect is marginal. Interestingly, the total employment declined sharply in 1995 and, then after, there has been a gradual rise. This confirms the fact that, in the short run, privatization may heavily shed job but it need not be so in the long run.

Irrespective of the "no redundancy clause" job losses have occurred in almost all privatized units. However, the categories of people whose jobs were affected are not the ones at the top level or at the bottom. Basically, it is the people at the middle level, like the administrators, accountants and supervisors. There is a growing tendency among the new managers to go for contractual, temporary, daily wage, and piece rate wage hiring in the privatized units. This is a way to avoid long-term risk and commitment of carrying a permanent labour force. The rigidity of the Nepal's labour law is partly responsible for this type of managerial behavior.

Representatives from the government side in the meeting commented that privatization has been relatively successful. They pointed out that the employment situation had improved after the initial decline in the privatized units. It was confirmed that the justification for privatization was to reduce the fiscal deficit and lessened liabilities and risk for government. They claimed that privatization has been carried out in the most transparent manner in Nepal. The basic foundation of privatization in Nepal is to create an environment for efficient allocation of resources and not to drain resources on inefficient enterprises. Any subsequent deficiencies noticed in the operation of privatized enterprises may be due to the situation of competitive market rather than privatization per se. They also clarified the procedures followed in the privatization process.

Representative from the employers' organization commented that political intervention and low morale of the staff have led to stagnant public sector. Successive political changes and governments have caused delays in privatization thus affecting the morale of the workers in the SOEs.

The workers' representative stated that there is a need to introduce the privatization process carefully for safeguarding the interests of the workers and people. The monopolistic character of private sector and the unemployment situation in Nepal do not allow a fast process of privatization. Rather than the policy as such, its implementation has become very controversial because of several reasons. 1) Public enterprises were sold below the market price. 2) Promises concerning voluntary retirement and job security have not been kept. 3) There was no increase in competition in the economy but rather an increase in monopolistic tendency among the privatized units. 4) There has been a lack of social dialogue. The government should aim at an environment of consensus and not continue with any controversial programme. For that reason, a high level committee that includes the representatives of the Nepal Trade Unions was requested. Such a committee needs to ensure that the government assumes responsibility for the workers' welfare and create a safety net before handing over the enterprise.

At the end of the session, the Chairperson, Mr. Majyd Aziz from Pakistan, observed that although privatization in Nepal has appeared to be successful, the process of privatization itself needs substantial improvement. It was also stressed that unless the market does not become more competitive the results of privatization may not be satisfactory. The private sector has not had adequate experience in the subsectors being privatized. Therefore, the sector needs to strengthen through professional management. He also observed that there is a need to strengthen the privatization cell. For successful privatization, involvement of the workers and employers in the privatization process through social dialogue is crucial. He also stressed the importance of greater transparency and accountability.

Country Presentation II - Pakistan

The session was chaired by Mr. Majyd Aziz from Employers' Federation of Pakistan. On behalf of the author of the country paper from Pakistan (Dr. A.R. Kemal), Dr. Gopal Joshi, Senior Specialist on Enterprise and Management Development, ILO-SAAT presented the paper on *Privatisation in Pakistan*. Since the appointment of the Privatization Commission in 1991, as many as 106 public enterprises have been divested mainly through sealed bidding. The purpose for privatization was stated to be reduction of the debt burden and fiscal deficit. During the post-privatization period, investments, average growth rates of output, and employment have generally fallen. Thus, economic effects of privatization have been mixed. The objective of reduction in fiscal deficit has so far not been realized as it is still in the range of 6 percent. Because of monopolistic market structure the benefits in terms of productivity gains have not been realized either.

The social effects of privatization on employment have shown similar features. Since the manufacturing sector was the most affected one in terms of output decline, the decline in employment was also most serious in this sector. Whereas pre-privatization period employment in the manufacturing grew at the rate of 6.5%, its share declined by 13.5% after privatization. Small-scale industries were affected even more negatively than the larger units.

During the meeting, there was no representation from the side of the government, although it was invited. Workers' representative stated that prior to privatization, the government tried to give the impression that all the problems of SOEs would end once privatization is carried out. It was claimed that privatization would create more jobs and prices would come down and productivity will rise. All these promises have not yet been fulfilled. The process of privatization has been influenced by nepotism and corruption. No assessment was made about the competence of the buyers in operating the enterprise being privatized. The worst feature of bad policy making has been the complete neglect of the economic well-being of the workers. It was agreed between Privatization Commission and All Pakistan State Enterprise Workers Action Committee in 1992 that the existing benefits to the workers would be continued. Those leaving the job will be given a golden handshake. Not in a single case in Pakistan has this formula been applied, nor did the workers get paid the last salary. Benefits to the workers have been drastically reduced. The industrial relations climate has been anti-labour and against trade unions. There is a clear need for a transparency in the privatization process. The privatization cell needs to provide socially responsible solutions.

Speaking on behalf of the employers, the chairperson stated that the privatization process has turned into a charade due to the absence of transparency. The negative consequences of the process were magnified and the adverse social effects were highlighted as failure of the private sector in bringing forth prosperity that privatization was touted to bring. There has been a lack of coherent, sustained policies in privatization. In addition, the legal framework is imperfect as it allows corruption, nepotism, cronyism and blatant abuse of discretionary powers.

Privatization requires a new approach, which is more transparent, and where the government's funds received from privatization would be invested for social purpose (education, health, welfare). The privatization cell needs to be independent from government control. Economic advisors should be appointed by the government so that the process of privatization of specific units are effectively monitored for a specific period. There is a strong need for regular audits by independent bodies. The safety net being provided by the government for retrenched workers need to improve for ensuring retraining or redeployment.

During the follow-up discussion, representatives from the trade unions mentioned that social dialogue is severely restricted in Pakistan where the government has refused the presence of any trade union in several sectors. One of the government representatives emphasized that the report on privatization has not sufficiently analyzed the context of Pakistan's economic development.

Country Presentation III - Sri Lanka

This session was chaired by Mr. P Devraj, vice-president, Ceylon Workers' Congress, Sri Lanka. Ms Rozana Salih, Institute of Policy Research, Sri Lanka presented the paper on *Privatization in Sri Lanka*. Privatization has been pursued aggressively in Sri Lanka since 1989. Key preparations for privatization began from the early 1980s. They included improving the commercial orientation of the SOEs, abolishing public sector monopolies, transferring the management of loss-making firms to the private sector on a contract basis, etc. The president appointed a committee in 1987 to prepare a general framework within which privatization was to be conducted. The guidelines were broad and by and large failed in practice when it came to the handling of surplus labour. No defined regulatory and coherent framework was set up during this process, the planning of privatization therefore was rather contradictory. The dominant form of privatization was divestment of shares.

The social effects of privatization are numerous, such as, on workers (both directly and indirectly employed by the SOEs), and consumers (via changes in prices, quality of products, accessibility, etc). At the time of privatization, a critical question the government faced was how to handle the issue of mainly unskilled surplus labour. The compensation package was considered by workers to be insufficient. This gave rise to the eventual adoption of various ad hoc packages whose value rested mainly on the bargaining power of the trade unions. One clear trend in the mainly monetary compensation packages paid since 1989 has been that it has gradually increased over time. The basic package has increased from roughly 17 months salary to 53 months from 1989 to 1997.

Retrenchment of the workers, where it was followed, has led to another sort of dilemma. Most new owners of enterprises where workers had already been retrenched found that the retrenchment process had concentrated on getting the number of workers down, regardless of their type. Some new owners have had to rehire workers with skills identical to that of those retrenched before privatization.

The Sri Lankan experience in handling labour issues during privatization highlights the importance of carefully considering labour issues before and during the transaction process. Ad hoc formulas and piecemeal legislative changes only confuse the parties involved and increase worker hostility towards privatization. Lessons learnt through involving unions and workers in the privatization process need to be applied for increasing worker and public awareness regarding the privatization process in the future.

Employers' representative stated that restructuring should be accompanied by complimentary changes in legislation, previously set up in the context of nationalization. Present legislation forbids employing people on a part-time basis. A new exit policy, with possibilities to employ workers on contractual basis will reduce costs of uncertainty for the employers. It was also emphasized that retrenchment should not affect society negatively. The absence of a mode of calculating compensation to be paid still remains a major 'lacunae', and the government's authority to decide upon the quantum of compensation is by far not efficient. In order to minimize social effects of privatization, the establishment of a 'safety net' is crucial. Several schemes have been recommended for implementation. One such scheme is the establishment of the 'Skills Development Fund' that aims at supporting job entry and enterprise based training as well as linkages between training institutions and private enterprises. Additionally, joint activities with the private sector and international funding agencies are planned; such as, the Skills Development Fund Ltd. In this initiative it is hoped that trade unions too will be involved. Another good example where joint efforts have been made for a socially responsible privatization policy is the plantation sector. Finally, there is a clear need for reforms in civil service and governance, which are vital for credible policy initiatives.

Government representative pointed out that the rehabilitated companies have been performing badly. Statutory wages and provident fund benefits for the workers alone will cost the government around Rs. 8 billion. Besides, these companies have no defined local market due to import influxes (especially textile companies). Therefore, the government has now decided to close down these firms and pay workers the compensations. This is a decision that comes too late. The government has already incurred considerable costs and must now incur retrenchment compensation. Those workers, who have received stocks as compensation, need to be educated on shares and the share market. The dialogue between union and PERC (Public Enterprise Reform Commission) is essential. TEWA (Termination of Employment of Workmen Act) needs to be modified, not repealed. Authorities have to be appointed who carry out the monitoring of privatization.

Social impact should be seen in a wider context, not just in terms of job losses. The wider effect of privatization has to be borne in mind, such as, consumer rights, their access to quality products, quality of life of workers etc. All of these have been deteriorating. The need to liberalize does not automatically mean privatization of public enterprises. Competition with the public sector companies could be another possibility.

Workers' representative stated that corruption should be eliminated, and transparency needs to be maintained. Social dialogue has been lacking in pre-privatization period as well as during privatization. He pointed out that despite the absence of a social dialogue, earlier government policy was much more in favour of labour than the present one. There is a clear need for more transparency as well as proper planning for privatization. Large amounts of money have been lost due to hasty privatization. Civil service and governance should improve. Political interference needs to be minimized. Plantation worker welfare, as a result of privatization, has not improved but rather worsened. When the private sector is given the responsibility of managing funds meant for workers' welfare (sponsored by government or NGOs), they tend to delay spending and instead use it for easing their own liquidity constraints. Monitoring/regulations are important, and careless privatization increases worker resentment and social tension.

During the subsequent discussion, it was mentioned that it is crucial to plan when, what and how public sector enterprises are privatized. Careful planning includes also launching schemes on skill development and HRD, directly linked to market needs. A question was raised as regards the factors behind the pace of privatization. It was also mentioned that the net effect of privatization in terms of enterprise performance, on deficit or on workers has not been discussed enough.

The author clarified that the net result of the process of privatization is not clear. To draw conclusions at an aggregated level is methodologically not adequate as statistics are limited not only at an aggregated level but at enterprise level as well.

Panel Discussion I : Restructuring of Public Enterprises

This session was chaired by Professor G.S. Bhalla, Jawaharlal Nehru University, India. Mr. Raphael Crowe, Senior Specialist on Employers' Activities, ILO-SAAT gave an introduction to the issue of restructuring private enterprises. Mr. Crowe stated that privatization is at the heart of plans for the economic regeneration of a number of countries which are trying to establish a place in the global economy. The relevance of privatization to employers is well reflected in a number of conclusions from key employers' workshops in the South Asian subregion and at international employers' meeting. A key resource document for the International Symposium on the future of employers' organization held in April 1999 in Geneva was a "global survey of employers' organizations." It listed privatization as one of the important market issues of the future.

It is, however, surprising that employers continue to be excluded from the process of retrenchment and privatization in spite of the positive role employers and their organizations could play as one of the three social partners of the ILO. Admittedly, many of the ILO studies, with the exception of those specifically commissioned by the Bureau of Employers' Activities, have tended to highlight the importance of including the trade unions and the management of the public sector enterprises involved in the process, but have tended to ignore the importance of specifically involving employers' organizations who represent private employers.

It is the ILO belief that any process of change in society is better conceived and implemented if the parties affected most by the change are involved and consulted during the process. The ILO believes that through social dialogue, socio-economic policy will be more soundly based and have a better chance of sustainability in the long run. As a consequence, employers' organizations should therefore be fully involved from the start in the privatization process. This is particularly so in South Asia where the governments, theoretically at least have national, state and local tripartite consultative mechanisms in place and have accepted the merit of tripartite dialogue. In the region, the market may have forced for a quick privatization process hindering the social dialogue.

Almost universally, there is a demand for more transparency about the process of privatization not only for efficiency reasons, but also on the basis that society and representative groups in society are entitled to adequate information when public assets are involved. With notable exceptions, employers' organizations have been generally disappointed by governments' attitude towards the involvement of employers in drafting privatization regulations.

Regarding the issues of redundant workers, preparation and training of managers to cope with new forms of industry and with the new competitive environment, employers' organization can play a useful role. It would therefore seem logical that employers and their organizations should be consulted and their advice and assistance sought by those undertaking privatization.

During the panel discussion, Ms. C.L. Malvia, representing the Indian government, stated that the whole idea behind restructuring public enterprises is to do something about loss-making units since there are no takers of those units as they stand. Therefore, if we make them at least commercially viable, they have better prospects of ownership transfer. With restructuring, units are modernized, made more competitive and there is an increase of more operational autonomy like in appointing a management that is accountable for its performance.

But there are public sectors where privatization should not be undertaken. For India, drinking water management or public transport or sanitation, which are unlikely to be commercially profitable ventures, will be such sectors. The investments are huge and the rate of returns low in such sectors.

Mr. Veereshwar Tiagi from India, representing the workers, stated that public sector undertakings have been since long suffering from poor management. The PSEs are state-owned, but they should not be state-controlled; and they should be allowed a certain degree of autonomy. Scientific staffing pattern should be enforced, instead of overstaffing these state enterprises. Due to frequent changes of governments, political interference in the management of the PSEs have caused abuse of PSE resources. If no remedial measures are taken in the initial stage, the sickness becomes deep-seated and later cannot be cured. Participation of labour in management should be allowed in all industries. Intensive industrial training that includes also vocational training should be provided to the labourers before retrenchment.

Mr. M.A. Ud Dowla from Bangladesh, representing the employers, stated that privatization should not be understood as only one strategy. Restructuring is another strategy that has been utilized in South Asia. The rationale behind restructuring and privatization is to avoid pains after the transfer of ownership, fetch good price during divestiture and ensure a long-term success and better chance of survival of the enterprise. The technical restructuring will require balancing and modernization, and improvement in productivity. Human resources may need to be redeployed, and in some cases reduced. Training and skills development of the workers are essential. Leasing and franchising could be possible ways of restructuring before the unit is divested. A slow process of divestment would be ownership transfer through gradual sales of shares and simultaneously restructuring of the board of directors.

During the subsequent discussion, a participant cautioned that in South Asia the western model of privatization cannot succeed. For the time being the countries have to live with both the public and private sectors.

It was also emphasized that restructuring should not happen at the cost of consumers or employment. However, socially responsible solutions for restructuring seem difficult to be implemented. There are no mechanisms for social security so far. Plan of restructuring should be linked to social security schemes, and resources have to be allocated.

Day 3: Friday, November 26,1999
Panel Discussion II: Regulatory Reform

The session was chaired by Mr. Anis Ud Dowla, representative of Bangladesh Employer's Federation. Dr Gopal Joshi, Senior Specialist on Enterprise and Management Development, ILO-SAAT introduced the session by presenting his paper on regulatory reform. Mr. Joshi stated that regulatory reform is like a traffic rule for privatized enterprises, remaining public enterprises and the government, whereby the market forces are strengthened and the government's role is limited. The reforms may take two forms 1) Reforms of existing regulations to facilitate entry of private enterprises in previously restricted subsectors. 2) Government intervention in running economic enterprises is reduced and an entirely new set of policies with an independent regulatory mechanism is created.

Regulatory reforms also provide a sort of guidance for governments, workers and employers in the privatization process. The regulatory reform should clarify the rules of entering the subsector and carrying out the economic activities rather than leaving them under the discretion of bureaucracy or political leaders. Pricing of products and services, particularly in the sub-sectors where natural monopolies are existent, would be determined in a fair way. This would provide reasonable returns on investment without excessive profiteering. Finally, workers' and consumers' interests are safeguarded from sudden excessive burden of privatization, possibly through safety net measures.

Although there are many common features in most of the reforms, the requirements of reform across various subsectors are never the same. Various subsectors may require various specific policy measures due to the issues relating to the natural monopoly, public investment or public interest. Therefore, careful subsectoral analysis is useful for the reforms to be undertaken before privatization. Reforms may be viewed as the process of privatization themselves since liberalization takes place. However, successful privatization without reform is difficult to visualize. If carried out in a transparent and accountable manner, reforms can also hasten privatization.

Regulatory reform should constitute three levels of actions:

- Formulation of a policy for the subsector
- Setting up of a Regulatory Body with its statutory mandate
- Representation of all social partners in the regulatory Body

It is very essential to have transparency, accountability and representation in the reform process. Transparency cannot be guaranteed fully without the workers and employers being integrated in a functioning social dialogue. A regulatory body should be set up outside the influence of politicians and bureaucracy. It should have an independent status similar to a court so that its actions are not challenged in the court or are not overturned by bureaucrats or politicians. Regulatory reform, however, is an ongoing process with constant need for fine tuning and adjusting.

During the discussion, workers' representative emphasized the need for an independent regulatory body which is not controlled and regulated by the government. The set up of such a body which is accountable, efficient and transparent needs to be carefully planned for successful implementation. He also mentioned that a total withdrawal of government control also involves risks. There is a need for a regulatory framework as it provides internal stability. The government representative from India pointed out that the question of practicability of a regulatory body is very important. Workers' representative from Sri Lanka pointed out that there is actually a need for more regulation when reforms of public enterprises are introduced. He mentioned that labour laws are not otherwise followed by the entrepreneurs. There is also a need for a set up of a functioning monitoring mechanism on a sector wise basis.

Panel Discussion III - Social Effects of Privatization

This session was chaired by Mr. S. K. Goyal of India. Mr. D.P. Naidu, Workers' Specialist, and Mr. Saarthi Acharya, Labour Market Specialist, both at ILO-SAAT New Delhi, introduced the subject for discussion. Mr. Naidu emphasized the need for examining the alternatives to outright privatization. Privatization should have been much smoother than it has been since social dialogue has not been pursued in all cases. Unions and workers would be able to suggest alternatives to outright closing down the units or large-scale retrenchment. For socially responsible solutions while restructuring, it is essential to rebuild a social dialogue, which includes trade unions. Issues like effectiveness of compensation packages provided to workers could be the basis for a dialogue, such as, in India. VRS or compensation packages should be designed in a way that social problems would have been minimized. The complexity of retirement and compensation schemes has not been sufficiently examined. Past and current privatizations have not paid close attention to the issues like the right for housing, insurance, and health care, which are lost as soon as workers are retrenched. There is no social safety net in place to protect the workers from the adverse effect of privatization. Training and counseling facilities have been largely inaccessible for most of the workers affected by privatization. There has been less clarity as regards how the costs involved in retraining and redeployment would be covered.

Making introductory presentation on the topic, Mr. Saarthi Acharya pointed out that no-redundancy clause is required for minimizing the social consequences. The issue of labour retrenchment has been found all over the region, but there are variations in how the problem has been addressed so far. A very useful way of avoiding mass retrenchment would be in-house training as it has been practiced in Japan and East Asia.

The whole rationale of inflexibility and high labour costs however is by far overweighed for the South Asian region as soon as the cost-structure of firms is taken into account. Labour costs account for not more than 15-20 percent. Cost cutting through retrenchment, as several studies showed, would not be more than 3 percent. Thus, it raises the question as to whether labour retrenchment is the effective way of cost cutting. Some more analysis in this field would clearly be necessary.

Actual rehabilitation is needed in case retrenchment takes place. A functioning and independent commission which monitors the process of privatization is required which is in-built in a regulatory framework that covers needs of workers being retrenched. The solution of self-employment has to be considered in a realistic manner, as after a certain age, former public sector workers may have difficulties in securing self-employment. Distinct possibilities are therefore needed. Retraining within the firm is needed. They should be able to develop a wide range of skills so that their qualification matches the demand. This is a very crucial and sensitive issue. Retraining facilities should be linked to a market information system so that efficiency of labour exchange improves. It is also absolutely central to rethink the concept of social protection as retrenched workers fall out of existing social facilities (insurance, health care, education, etc.) which are provided by the PSEs when they lose their jobs. Those social facilities should be improved so that livelihood of the whole family would be less severely affected by the retrenchment of the specific worker.

In order to finance such facilities, a central pool could be set up which is financed by tax incomes as well as partly by the employers and workers. The question of financing retraining facilities also needs to be worked out.

During the discussion, workers' representative (Mr. Md. Ashraf Hossain from Bangladesh) mentioned that privatized units were increasingly making profits since privatization. The profit gained was, however, not shared at all with the workers.

Mr. W.M.K.L. Weerasinghe from Sri Lanka, representing the employers, stated that solution for workers' retraining and redeployment can not be worked out without the private sector. In Sri Lanka for instance, a skills development fund has been established which was set up by the government and co-funded by employers. He also pointed out that trade unions should be involved. Private sector should not be considered as only financial resources to cover social costs. Trust funds or pension schemes for unemployed could be set up.

Mr. Mahmood Ahmed Qureshi from Pakistan, representing workers' organization, expressed his agreement that a macro-perspective is needed to be added in the discussion.

Annex 1

PROGRAMME

Subregional Meeting on Privatization in South Asia
Social Effects and Restructuring
Kathmandu (Hotel Blue Star) 24-26 November 1999

24 November 1999

0745-0845 hrs. Closed meetings of the representatives of governments, employers and workers for selecting their respective representatives for panel discussions and closing statements

0845-0915 hrs. Registration

0915-1100 hrs. **Opening Ceremony**

Welcome/Introductory Address by Mr. A. S. Oberai, Director ILO-SAAT

Remarks by Workers' Representative Mr. I. D. Mishra,

Vice President, Nepal Trade Union Congress (NTUC)

Remarks by Employers' Representative Mr. P. K. Shrestha

President, FNCCI

Inauguration of the Sub-regional Meeting and Keynote Address by the Chairperson – Hounarable Finance Minister of Nepal Mr. Mahesh Acharya

Vote of Thanks by the officer-in- Charge of the Office of the Senior ILO Adviser in Kathmandu – Mr. H. S.S. Fonseka.

1100-1130 hrs. **Tea Break**

1130-1230 hrs. **Overview Presentations**

Chairperson: Mr. I. P. Anand, ILO GB Member

Presentation of the overview paper (Privatization in South Asia) by Mr. Gopal Joshi, Senior Specialist on Enterprise and Management Development together with Prof. G. S. Bhalla, Jawaharlal Nehru University (15 minutes)

Presentation on global perspective and lessons learned on privatization by

Mr. Michael Henriques, Director, Job Creation and Enterprise Department, ILO Geneva (15 minutes)

Discussion (20 minutes)

Concluding Remarks by the Chairperson (10 minutes)

1230-1330 hrs. **Lunch**

1330-1500 hrs. **Country Presentations I**

> **Chairperson: Dr. L. Mishra,** Secretary, Ministry of Labour, India
>
> *A . Privatization in Bangladesh*
>
> Paper presentation by Prof. Momtaz Uddin Ahmed, University of Dhaka (20 minutes)
>
> Remarks by Representatives of Government, Employers and Workers from Bangladesh (30 minutes total)
>
> Open Discussion (30 minutes)

1500-1530 hrs. **Tea Break**

1530-1700 hrs. **Country Presentations I (contd.)**

> *B . Privatization in India*
>
> Paper presentation by Prof. S.K. Goyal, The Institute for Studies in Industrial Development (20 minutes)
>
> Remarks by Representatives of Government, Employers and Workers from India
>
> (30 minutes total)
>
> Open Discussion (30 minutes)
>
> **Concluding Remarks by the Chairperson** (10 minutes)

25 November 1999

0900-1230 hrs. **Country Presentations II**

> **Chairperson: Mr. Majyd   Aziz,** MHG Group of Companies , Pakistan
>
> *C. Privatization in Nepal*
>
> Paper presentation by Drs. Narayan Manandhar and Pushkar Bajracharya (20 minutes)
>
> Remarks by Representatives of Government, Employers and Workers from Nepal (30 minutes total)
>
> Open Discussion (30 minutes)
>
> *D . Privatization in Pakistan*
>
> Paper presentation by Dr. A.R. Kemal, Planning Commission, Pakistan (Presented by Mr. Gopal Joshi, ILO/SAAT on behalf of Dr. Kemal) (20 minutes)
>
> Remarks by Representatives of Government, Employers and Workers from Pakistan (30 minutes total)
>
> Open Discussion (30 minutes)
>
> **Concluding Remarks by the Chairperson** (10 minutes)

1230-1330 hrs. **Lunch**

1330-1500 hrs. **Country Presentation III**

Chairperson: Mr. P. Devaraj, Vice President, Ceylon Workers' Congress, Sri Lanka

E . Privatization in Sri Lanka

Paper presentation by Ms. Rozana Salih, Institute of Policy Studies, Sri Lanka (20 minutes)

Remarks by Representatives of Government, Employers and Workers from Sri Lanka (30 minutes total)

Open Discussion (30 minutes)

Concluding Remarks by the Chairperson (10 minutes)

1500-1530 hrs. **Tea Break**

1530-1700 hrs. **Panel Discussion I - Restructuring of Public Enterprises**

Chairperson: Prof. G.S. Bhalla, Jawaharlal Nehru University, India

Introduction to Issues by SAAT Specialist (Mr. Raphael Crowe, Employers' Specialist) (15 minutes)

Panel Discussion by - (30 minutes total)

Government Representative – Ms. C. L. Malvia, India

Workers Representative - Mr V. Tiagi, India

Employers' Representative – Mr. M.A. Ud Dowla, Bangladesh

(30 minutes total)

Concluding Remarks by the Chairperson (15 minutes)

26 November 1999

0900-1030 hrs. **Panel Discussion II - Regulatory Reform**

Chairperson: Mr. M.A. Ud Dowla, Bangladesh Employers' Federation, Bangladesh

Introduction to Issues by SAAT Specialist (Mr. Gopal Joshi, Enterprise and Management Development Specialist) (15 minutes)

Panel Discussion - (30 minutes total)

Government Representative – Ms. N. De Silva, Sri Lanka

Workers Representative - Mr. M. A. Qureshi, Pakistan

Employers' Representative – Mr. M. Aziz, Pakistan

Open Discussion (30 minutes)

Concluding Remarks by the Chairperson (15 minutes)

1030-1230 hrs. **Panel Discussion III - Social Effects of Privatization**

Chairperson: Prof. S.K. Goyal, The Institute for Studies in Industrial Development

Introduction to Issues by SAAT Specialist (Mr. D.P.A. Naidu, Workers' Specialist) (15 minutes)

Panel Discussion by - (30 minutes total)

Government Representative – Mr. M. A. Waheed, Bangladesh

Workers Representative - Mr. Md. A. Hossain, Bangladesh

Employers' Representative – Mr. W.M. K.L. Weerasinghe, Sri Lanka

Open Discussion (30 minutes)

Concluding Remarks by the Chairperson (15 minutes)

1230-1330 hrs. **Lunch**

1330-1500 hrs. **Panel Discussion IV - Social Dialogue**

Chairperson: Ms. Rozana Salih, Institute of Policy Studies, Sri Lanka

Introduction to Issues by SAAT Specialist (Mr. A. Sivananthiram, Industrial Relations Specialist) (15 minutes)

Panel Discussion by - (30 minutes total)

Government Representative – Ms. M. Madihahewa, Sri Lanka

Workers Representative - Mr P. Devaraj, Sri Lanka

Employers' Representative – Mr. B. P. Pant, India

(Open Discussion (30 minutes)

Concluding Remarks by the Chairperson (15 minutes)

1500-1530 hrs. **Tea Break**

1530-1700 hrs. **Closing Session**

Chairperson: Mr. R. B. Gurung, Honourable State Minister for Labour HMG/Nepal

Statements by Representatives of (10 minutes each):
* Government Representative - Mr. T. R. Basyal, Nepal
* Employers Representative – Mr. A. Aziz, Pakistan
* Worker Representative – Mr. V. Tiagi, India
  Remarks by Chairperson

Closing Remarks by Mr. A.S. Oberai, Director ILO-SAAT

1700-1730 hrs. **Tea**

List of Participants

Bangladesh

1. Mr. Md. Abu Waheed
    Deputy Secretary
    Ministry of Labour and Employment
    Government of Bangladesh, Dhaka,
    Bangladesh
    Tel: 880-2-9352504 (R) 8618605 (O),
    Fax: 880-2-8618660
    Email: waheed@spaninn.com

2. Mr. M. Anis Ud Dowla
    Chairman and Managing Director
    Advanced Chemical Industries Limited
    BRAC Centre (10th and 11th floors),
    75 Mahakhali, Dhaka, Bangladesh
    Tel: 880-2-9885694

3. Mr. Md. Asharaf Hossain
    Member
    BJSD, Bangladesh

India

4. Dr. L. Mishra
    Secretary
    Government of India, Ministry of Labour
    Shram Shakti Bhawan, Rafi Marg
    New Delhi - 110 001 INDIA

5. Ms. C. L Malviya
    Director
    Department of Industrial Policy & Promotion
    Ministry of Industry & Commerce
    Government of India, New Delhi INDIA
    Tel: 91-11-3014147 (O) 7253401(R)
    Fax: 3014564 : Email: cmalviya@ub.delhi.nic.in

6. Mr. B.P. Pant
    Deputy Secretary
    All India Organization of Employers
    Federation House Tansen Marg
    New Delhi – 110 001, INDIA
    Tel: 91-11-3316121, 3738760
    Fax: 3320714 , 3321504

7. Mr. Veereshwar Tiagi
    Hind Mazdoor Sabha
    120 Babar Road, New Delhi - 110 001 INDIA

Nepal

8. Mr. Deep Basnyat
    Joint Secretary
    His Majesty's Government
    Ministry of Labour
    Kathmandu, NEPAL
    Tel: 977-1-246845(O) 474013 (R) Fax: 256877

9. Mr. Tula Raj Basyal
    Senior Economic Advisor
    His Majesty's Government
    Ministry of Finance
    Kathmandu, NEPAL
    Tel: 977-1-259753(o) 483062 (R) Fax: 259891

10. Mr. Ravi Bhattarai
    Section Officer
    His Majesty's Government
    Ministry of Finance
    Government of Nepal, Kathmandu, NEPAL
    Tel: 977-1- 259820, 257854 (O), 410612 (R)

11. Mr. Megh Nath Neupane
    Deputy Secretary General
    Federation of Nepalese Chambers of
    Commerce & Industry, P.O. Box 269
    Shahid Shukra Milun Marg, Teku,
    Kathmandu, NEPAL
    Tel: 977-1- 244758, 262061, 262218 (O)
                                351510 (R)
    Fax: 261022: Email: fncci@mos.com.np

12. Mr. Sishir Kumar Jha
    President
    Nepal Inter-Corporation Workers
    Union (NICEU)
    Kathmandu, NEPAL
    Tel: 977-1-250401 (union), 248883, 255094
    Fax: 262498

Pakistan

13. Mr. Majyd Aziz
President
MHG Group of Companies
D/49, SITE, Karachi, 75700 Pakistan
Tel: (9221) 256-2316, 256-3461
Fax: 256-1091 Cell: (92303) 733-1969
Email: hustler@digicom.net.pk
Web: geocities.com/capitolhill/Embassy/1950

14. Mr. Mahmood Ahmed Qureshi
Vice President
Pakistan National Federation of Trade Unions
406, Qamar House, M.A. Jinnah Road
Karachi – 74000, Pakistan
Tel: 92-21-5081428

Sri Lanka

15. Mr. Mahinda Madihahewa
Additional Commissioner General of Labour
Department of Labour
Labour Secretariat
Colombo - 05, Sri Lanka
Tel: 583889(O), 853372 ® Fax: 581147

16. Ms. Nilakshi De Silva
Senior Manager
Public Enterprises Reform Commission of
Sri Lanka (PERC.) 11th Floor 11-01
West Tower
World Trade Centre, Echelon Square
Colombo 1 Sri Lanka
Tel: 94-1-338756 Fax: 94-1-326116
Email: nilakshi@perc.gov.lk

17. Mr. W. M. K. L. Weerasinghe
Industrial Relations Advisor, Employers'
Federation of Ceylon
385 J3., Old Kotte Road
Rajagiriya, Sri Lanka
Tel: 867966/8 Fax: 867942

18. Mr. P. Devaraj
Vice President
Ceylon Workers Congress (CWC)
15/11 10th Lane Colombo 3, Sri Lanka
Tel: 595291, 500858

Resource persons

19. Prof. Momtaz Uddin Ahmed **(Bangladesh)**
Department of Economics
University of Dhaka
Dhaka 1000, Bangladesh

20. Prof. S.K. Goyal **(India)**
The Institute for Studies in Industrial
Development
Narendra Niketan
I. P. Estate, New Delhi - 110 002, India
Tel:91-11- 371-6514 Fax: 371-9112
Email: skg@isid@delhi.nic.in

21. Prof. G. S. Bhalla **(India)**
Jawaharlal Nehru University
New Delhi 110067, India

22. Dr. Narayan Manandhar **(Nepal)**
G.P.O. 8975
EPC 787, Kathmandu, Nepal
Tel: 977-1-537967

23. Dr. Pushkar Bajracharya **(Nepal)**
Tribhuvan University
P. O. Box 1725
Kathmandu, Nepal

24. Ms. Rozana Salih **(Sri Lanka)**
Institute of Policy Studies (IPS)
99, St. Michaels Road, Colombo 3, Sri Lanka
Tel: 94-1-431368 Fax: 431395
Email:ips@sri.lanka.net

25. Mr. I. P. Anand
New Delhi, India

ILO officials

26. Mr. Michael Henriques
Director
Job Creation and Enterprise Department
ILO-Geneva

27. Mr. A. S. Oberai
Director
ILO – SAAT
New Delhi
Tel: 0091-11- 4602101 Fax: 0091-11- 4647973
Email:oberai@ilodel.org.in

28. Mr. A. Sivananthiran
    Senior Specialist – Industrial Relations
    ILO – SAAT
    New Delhi
    Tel: 0091-11- 4602101
    Fax: 0091-11- 4647973
    Email: sivananthiran@ilodel.org.in

29. Mr. D. P. A. Naidu
    Senior Specialist – Workers' Activities
    ILO – SAAT
    New Delhi
    Tel: 0091-11- 4602101 Fax: 0091-11- 4647973
    Email: naidu@ilodel.org.in

30. Mr. G. Joshi
    Senior Specialist-SEMD
    ILO-SAAT
    Tel: 0091-11- 4602101 Fax: 0091-11- 4647973
    Email: joshi@ilodel.org.in

31. Mr. R. Crowe
    Senior Specialist – Employers' Activities
    ILO – SAAT
    New Delhi
    Tel: 0091-11- 4602101 Fax: 0091-11- 4647973
    Email: raphel@ilodel.org.in

32. Mr. S. Acharya
    Senior Specialist- Labour Market
    ILO – SAAT
    New Delhi
    Tel: 0091-11- 4602101 Fax: 0091-11- 4647973
    Email: acharya@ilodel.org.in

33. Ms. Sandra Rothboeck
    Associate Expert
    ILO-SAAT
    New Delhi
    Tel: 0091-11- 4602101 Fax: 0091-11- 4647973
    Email: rothboeck@ilodel.org.in